HALF-HEARTED REFORM

HALF-HEARTED REFORM

Electoral Institutions and the Struggle for Democracy in Indonesia

Dwight Y. King

Westport, Connecticut
London

Library of Congress Cataloging-in-Publication Data

King, Dwight Y.
    Half-hearted reform : electoral institutions and the struggle for democracy in Indonesia
/ Dwight Y. King.
        p.   cm.
    Includes bibliographical references and index.
    ISBN 0–275–97942–3 (alk. paper)
    1. Elections—Indonesia.   2. Democracy—Indonesia.   3. Indonesia—Politics and
government—1998–   I. Title.
    JQ778.K46   2003
    324.6′3′09598—dc21   2002033390

British Library Cataloguing in Publication Data is available.

Library of Congress Catalog Card Number: 2002033390
ISBN: 0–275–97942–3

First published in 2003

Praeger Publishers, 88 Post Road West, Westport, CT 06881
An imprint of Greenwood Publishing Group, Inc.
www.praeger.com

Printed in the United States of America

The paper used in this book complies with the
Permanent Paper Standard issued by the National
Information Standards Organization (Z39.48–1984).

10   9   8   7   6   5   4   3   2   1

Copyright Acknowledgments

The author and publisher gratefully acknowledge permission for use of the following
material:

A slightly modified version of Chapter 3 was previously published as "The 1999
Electoral Reforms in Indonesia: Debate, Design and Implementation," *Southeast Asian
Journal of Social Science* 28, 2 (2000): 89–110, copyright Times Academic Press,
copublished by Brill Academic Publishers and Times Academic Press.

A longer version of Chapter 5 appeared as "The Conduct of the 1999 Election in Sleman,
D. I. Yogyakarta: A Caste Study (with Voting Results)," *Asian Studies Review* 25, 4
(2001): 479–497, copyright Asian Studies Association of Australia, published by
Blackwell Publishers Limited.

For Kathy,
who made it possible

Contents

Tables

Preface

This book had a particularly long gestation period that can be traced back to my first field research in Indonesia about thirty years ago. Haryono Suyono, then chief of the Social Division of Indonesia's Central Bureau of Statistics, his successor Susilo, and Peter D. Weldon of the Ford Foundation invited me to assist in their pioneering efforts to develop social indicators. With their administrative and financial support and technical assistance from Sam Suharto, we began the construction of a computerized data bank containing information that characterized every district, including votes for parties in the first general election conducted in 1971 by Suharto's New Order government. After returning home, I added the returns from every subsequent general election, aided by Ryaas Rasyid, who collected and sent them to me, and by a coterie of capable graduate students, some of whom utilized the data bank in their dissertations. They include Riswandha Imawan, Andi Alfian Mallarangeng, and I Ketut Erawan.

This data bank is an important source of depth and originality in several chapters of this work. To my knowledge, no one else has utilized a comparable data set in analysis of Indonesian politics. Consisting of comprehensive (not a sample), disaggregated (large N that varies from 160 to over 300, depending on the election) data and an interrupted time series spanning eight elections over forty-four years (1955 to 1999), these data lend themselves to fairly powerful techniques of statistical analysis. However, care has been taken to keep the analysis accessible to even statistically challenged readers in all but perhaps Chapters 6 and 7. Much of the scholarly literature on Indonesian politics is mainly descriptive or has a tendency to draw large inferences from little or weak bases. Use of statistical analysis here reflects my interest in testing some of these inferences against more persuasive evidence and in empirically grounded explanations.

The data for Chapters 3 through 8 were collected during several trips to Indonesia, beginning in August 1998, to attend the international conference, "Toward Structural Reforms for Democratization in Indonesia: Problems and Prospects," which was sponsored by the Ford Foundation. I am grateful to Bill Liddle and Rizal Mallarangeng for the invitation. The Carter Center at Emory University sponsored three trips in the first half of 1999 related to election monitoring. On those trips I benefited from the access and diplomatic skills of Gordon Streeb and Charles Costello. Eleven months of field work beginning in September 1999 was made possible by the Fulbright Program, Northern Illinois University (NIU), and an affiliation with the Faculty of Social and Political Sciences at Gadjah Mada University. Upon my return, a sabbatical leave from NIU greatly facilitated the completion of the manuscript.

During the eleven-month sojourn in Indonesia, my wife and I received innumerable acts of assistance. For kindnesses of a personal kind that contributed enormously to our adjustment, maintenance, enjoyment, and well-being, we thank Duane and Reti Gingerich, the Baswedan family (Pak Rasjid, Ibu Aliyah, Anies, Ridwan, and Abdillah), S. Purwaningsih and her late husband, Afan, Sofian Effendi and En, Riswandha Imawan and Mien, Gerry and Helene van Klinken, Jim and Molly Gingerich, Duane and Clare Anne Ruth-Heffelbower, and Cornelia (Nelly) Paliama of the America–Indonesia Educational Foundation. As this book was going to press, word came of the untimely death of Afan Gaffar, my "brother" and colleague of more than twnety-five years. He contributed to many projects, not the least this book, and he lives on in the memories of all who knew him.

My intellectual debts are even broader. Kevin Evans facilitated access to the disaggregated 1999 election returns, suggested lines of analysis, and commented on a couple of draft chapters. Afan Gaffar, Andi Mallarangeng, and Ramlan Surbakti generously shared their "insider" perspectives. Saptopo Bambang Ilkodar collaborated in the research and writing of Chapter 5. In writing Chapter 6, I need to single out Lance Castles for assistance on electoral geography and his persistent questioning of my initial findings and persuasive use of corroborating results from the 1957 election for regional representative assemblies. For their interest and the time they took to give me constructive criticism on earlier drafts of various chapters, I am indebted to Andrew Ellis, Don Emmerson, Byron Good, Blair King, Kathy King, Gerry van Klinken, Bill Liddle, Andrew MacIntyre, and Roger Paget. The late Herbert Feith was an inspiration and constant source of encouragement.

No one could ask for a more supportive home environment than I have enjoyed amidst colleagues and graduate students at Northern Illinois University. With this project, special acknowledgment is due Imat Amidjaja, Andrea Bonnicksen, Charlie Cappell, Paul Culhane, Linda Lucek, Greg Schmidt, Ladd Thomas, Danny Unger, Mikel Wyckoff, and, especially, Clark Neher, who incessantly inquired about my progress and constantly prodded me to "be clearer about the main points." Anies Baswedan located errors and cleaned the 1955 data file with great care and dispatch. Ketut Erawan assisted in the quantitative analysis and in the construction of indicators and tables. Adi Abidin shared useful documents and Srie Ramli drafted the bibliography. Paul Chambers and Noel Morada were indispensable resources on Thailand and the Philippines, respectively (Chapter 9). Without Ernita Joaquin's technical and editorial skills, given tirelessly and always in good humor, the publication process would have been considerably delayed.

CHAPTER 1

The Leading Role of Electoral Institutions in Democratization

In May 1998 Indonesia began a transition from autocratic rule toward becoming the world's third-largest democracy and the only country with a Muslim majority to initiate democratic governance. Asia's longest-serving strongman, Suharto, was compelled to resign suddenly and unexpectedly, only two months after having been reelected to the presidency for a seventh consecutive term. A package of reforms governing the institutions of democratic representation and governance (political parties, general elections, and legislatures) led in 1999 to Indonesia's most democratic general election in forty-four years and culminated several months later in the election of President Abdurrahman Wahid and Vice-President Megawati Soekarnoputri. This marked the first peaceful transfer of executive power in Indonesia's fifty-year history of independence and raised questions about how extensive the reforms were and why the installation of electoral democracy succeeded.

The events of the following three years (i.e., through the end of 2001) raised additional questions about Indonesia's democratization. We are confronted with a paradox. On the one hand there is undeniable evidence of heightened social conflict, persistent economic depression, and continued political instability, bringing some observers to conclude that Indonesian democracy is a mirage. They argue that Indonesia is still in the throes of a protracted political transition, a long labor with high risk of stillborn birth. On the other hand, executive power was peacefully (and constitutionally) transferred again when the Assembly dismissed Wahid and elevated Megawati to the presidency in August 2001. Second, the military refused to intervene, despite Wahid's provocations. Third, the (mostly) democratically elected Assembly has made steady progress since it was seated in 1999 on major issues of constitutional reform. These developments suggest that the conflict and instability that have marked Indonesia under the new regime are less manifestations of democratic backsliding than of a second struggle to consolidate and deepen democracy while simultaneously identifying and removing the nondemocratic elements from the previous regime. This study addresses these issues. It provides a comprehensive and in-depth description and analysis of Indonesia's political reforms through 2001.

The successful installation of democracy in Indonesia depended heavily on three factors in the context of severe economic crisis and international pressure. First, the mode of transition, which began as an exclusive pact among a small group of elites, rapidly evolved into a reform movement that included the moderate opposition elites. It had several noteworthy characteristics. The policy process was inclusive of most segments of the elite, virtually all of whom committed themselves to the reigning Pancasila ideology and to peaceful, constitutional procedures. As a result, supporters of the *ancien regime* were less fearful about negotiating and agreeing to free and fair elections, most of the incumbents remained in place, and the policy process involved intense bargaining and resulted in compromises and half-hearted reforms. Second, extensive mass mobilization drove the transition, but it was disunited on political agenda, so that only small segments of society opposed the new rules and institutions that were inaugurated in early 1999. Last and important, a moderate faction in the military (led by Wiranto) was successful in neutralizing and controlling a hard-line faction (led by Prabowo).

Among the three types of political institutions in democratizing countries, changes in the institutions of democratic representation and governance have led the way in Indonesia's transition to democracy. They have been deeper and more institutionalized than changes either in the bureaucracy or the judiciary and oversight agencies. Electoral reform and the conduct of a free and fair election spearheaded the transition to democracy. The continuing struggle over the design of political institutions (constitutional reforms) in the postelection period reflects a struggle to consolidate and deepen democracy. Analysis of that struggle holds the key to understanding a related issue, the effects of the redesigned institutions on political practice and outcomes.

A number of previous studies have appeared on the multidimensional crisis that erupted in Indonesia beginning in 1997.[1] They include analyses of the unprecedented economic contraction, the forces and constituencies that emerged in the transition, the factors explaining Suharto's downfall, assessment of Habibie's interim presidency, the 1999 election results, and the downfall of democratically elected Abdurrahman Wahid. Surprising little attention has been accorded the sea changes that have occurred in the institutions—the laws governing political parties, the general election, and the legislative bodies—changes that not only reflect underlying currents but have driven the transition and consolidation processes as well.[2]

I argue that in order to understand these processes, we need to get beyond the stress on personalities—Suharto, Habibie, Wiranto, Megawati Soekarnoputri, Abdurrahman Wahid—as the key to political outcomes and shift the focus more toward policies and institutions. Perhaps because they are usually more obscure and inherently less interesting, structures tend to get overwhelmed by agency. What is needed is not a substitution, but a redress of the imbalance. By distinguishing among types of institutions combined with a "developmental" view of democracy, I contend that a type of democracy emerged in a multistage process and that it varies across institutional arenas.[3] Successful democratic installation, signified by free and fair elections; by new, mostly elected, legislative bodies; and by the (indirect) election of a new civilian president who assumed power in October 1999, marked the beginning of a second struggle to consolidate and deepen democracy while simultaneously continuing to identify and remove the nondemocratic residue from Suharto's regime.

It is important to take a historical view of electoral change in any particular country. "Because it will not soon escape his legacy, Indonesia after Suharto cannot be understood without knowing what the country was like during his rule."[4] For example, the conduct of earlier elections in a prolonged series establishes the ground rules for the conduct of subsequent elections. Comparing the results of several elections can reveal important characteristics in the electorate and trends over time. While the post-1998 electoral reforms are the focus of this study, I take a long view by devoting attention to the backdrop of all previous elections. Chapter 2 consists of an analysis of the electoral institutions and election results across six elections from 1971 to 1997. In theoretical terms, it deepens our understanding of how the electoral system contributed to the maintenance of a pseudodemocracy for over thirty-two years. In Chapter 6 I go back further to the first general election in 1955, searching for continuities in both election administration and election results. One important overall finding of several chapters is that the effects of traditional social divisions such as religion and regionalism on voting choices have remained stronger than expected in light of regime sociopolitical engineering and comparative theory that contends those effects will tend to weaken over time.

THE IMPORTANCE OF ELECTIONS

Elections Serve Universal Purposes

In 1999 Indonesia held the eighth general election since it became an independent republic to select most of the members for the national and regional legislative bodies. Except for the first election in 1955 and the most recent one in 1999, these elections were conducted by the pseudodemocratic "New Order" regime under General (ret.) Suharto. His utilization of elections reminds us that elections have universal purposes in the modern world; they are not unique to democratic governance.

But Suharto was not alone. Elections have been a regular feature of Southeast Asian politics since the 1940s. With a few exceptions, they have not directly caused a change in government. Nor has any incumbent party lost a referendum or plebiscite.[5] Similar experiences abound throughout the developing world. If Suharto and other autocrats worldwide have found elections to be indispensable, what purposes have they served?

Some scholars argue that elections are simply means for strengthening state domination. Anderson, for example, writes, "There is no need here to spend any time on the series of elections held regularly since 1971 by Suharto's New Order military regime. They are carefully managed to produce externally plausible two-thirds majorities for Golkar, the government's electoral machine, and a passive parliament without any genuine representative character."[6]

But this viewpoint rests on problematic assumptions and begs the question of why Suharto went to all the trouble and expense involved in elections and did so six times, as regular as clockwork.

Assuming that state domination is complete anywhere is a mistake. The repressive machinery does not always operate efficiently, the degree of domination varies from time to time, the weight of domination varies among groups and classes in society, and it depends heavily on the degree of unity and cohesion in the governing elite. Institutions and organizations set up to facilitate state control, such as elections and a government-backed political party, sometimes acquire a degree of autonomy so that they represent as well as control.[7]

In addition, the study of elections provides a window on social change:

Studied systematically in their specific and their universal circumstances, elections in Southeast Asia clarify important aspects of political, economic, and social change in the region. . . . Ruling elites have found they must concede the importance of elections. New social groups and classes, new and old interests, can then attempt to use the opportunities for organization and discussion, even if greatly constrained by law and practice, to pry open further opportunities and rights for themselves.[8]

Thus far I have mentioned general, theoretical issues about the nature and role of elections in the maintenance of authoritarian and pseudodemocratic regimes that are not specific to Indonesia and the Southeast Asian region. At the same time, the contingent nature of electoral politics in any society must be recognized, as mentioned. In order to understand adequately the meaning and role of elections in any particular society, we need contextual knowledge about the electoral institutions and behavior of that society.

Elections Provided a Secondary Source of Legitimacy for Suharto's New Order

With the swelling of the "Third Wave" of democratization beginning in the 1970s and the collapse of many communist governments, authoritarian leaders worldwide felt the need to cultivate multiple bases of legitimacy in order to stabilize and perpetuate their rule. These bases often included adherence to some democratic norms, such as constitutionalism, elections at regular intervals, and the honest counting of ballots. In the case of Suharto, his adherence to such norms can be viewed as "a useful facade" constituting a "second-line" claim to legitimacy behind economic development and political stability.[9] His New Order closely approximated the concepts of "semidemocracy" or "pseudodemocracy," defined as a regime having multiple parties, elections, and other constitutional features of electoral democracy, but lacking at least one key requirement, "an arena of contestation sufficiently fair that the ruling party can be turned out of power."[10]

But why have Indonesians complied? Why have they followed campaigns with apparent interest and turned out in large numbers to cast their ballots? Possible answers include "being involved in the process of governance, even if vicariously, . . . the prospects of reward for backing the winner, . . . patron–client relationships, administrative pressures, corporatist-like desires for organizational solidarity and control."[11] To this list of reasons should be added the risks and often high costs of noncompliance with the government's election ritual.

Elections Are the Central Institution of Democratic Governance

After thirty-two years under Suharto's pseudodemocratic rule, Indonesia is undergoing fundamental political change. The 1999 election, widely viewed as free and fair by international standards, was the first one in Indonesia's history to bring about a change in government. Support for the New Order–backed Golkar Party plummeted 70 percent from the previous election two years earlier. Golkar's defeat and Abdurrahman Wahid's and Megawati Soekarnoputri's assent to the presidency and vice presidency, respectively, indicated that Indonesia had changed politically from a "pseudodemocracy" into an "electoral democracy."[12]

Electoral democracy is a minimalist definition that descends from Joseph Schumpeter, who defined democracy as a system "for arriving at political decisions in which individuals acquire the power to decide by means of a competitive struggle for the people's vote."[13] In this notion, competitive elections for effective power are the essence of democracy. Later, Robert Dahl elaborated the meanings implicit in Schumpeter's definition with the concept of polyarchy, which has three dimensions. First is opposition or organized contestation through regular, free, and fair elections. Second is participation or the right of virtually all adults to vote and contest for office. Third, without which the first and second cannot be truly meaningful, is freedom to speak and publish dissenting views, freedom to form and join organizations, and access to alternative sources of information.[14] This study will show that political practice in Indonesia since the fall of Suharto has, by in large, reflected these dimensions.

More elaborate conceptions of democracy extending beyond this minimalist definition encounter formidable obstacles when applied to Indonesia. Liberal democracy, according to Diamond, requires "the absence of reserved domains of power for the military or other actors not accountable to the electorate, directly or indirectly."[15] Similarly, Terry Karl's inclusion of civilian control of the military sets her definition apart from Dahl's "procedural minimum."[16] While Indonesian reformers have succeeded in shrinking the quota of legislative seats reserved for military appointees, they have not yet gotten rid of them entirely. Liberal democracy also "encompasses extensive provisions for political and civic pluralism as well as for individual and group freedoms. Freedom and pluralism, in turn can be secured only through a 'rule of law,' in which legal rules are applied fairly, consistently, and predictably across equivalent cases, irrespective of the class, status, or power of those subject to the rules."[17] Law enforcement and legal reform are areas of great weakness in Indonesia, as attested to by corruption in the judiciary, inability to resolve high-level financial scandals, and the lack of prosecutions for human-rights abuses.

However democracy is conceived, the study of democracy requires attention to the electoral system. Competitive elections are a central, if not the central, institution in all definitions. "The future of democracy in both established and emerging systems depends to a large extent on events related to the electoral process, because elections are the one political institution that both leads and reflects many of the social, political, and economic trends."[18] For this reason, any analysis of the trajectory of democracy in Indonesia must consider the electoral system carefully and thoroughly. At the same time, we need to beware the "fallacy of electoralism," which "privileges elections over other dimensions of democracy and ignores the degree to which multiparty elections (even if they are competitive and uncertain in outcome) may exclude significant portions of the population from contesting for power or advancing and defending their interests, or may leave significant arenas of decision making beyond the control of elected officials."[19]

THE IMPORTANCE OF ELECTORAL INSTITUTIONS

The set of institutions a nation adopts is critical to the long-term success of any new regime because they structure the rules of the game of political competition. As institutions become entrenched, they become actors in their own right, affecting and structuring the behavior of participants within the political arena. In other words, institutions not only help to set the rules of the political game, they also impact public policy through their structuring of political choice. Hence, "the study of political institutions is integral to the study of democratization because institutions constitute and sustain democracies."[20]

Among the institutions of democracy, there is no more important choice than which electoral system is to be used. It largely determines what parties look like, who is represented in parliament, and ultimately who governs.[21] "If one wants to change the nature of a particular democracy, the electoral system is likely to be the most suitable and effective instrument for doing so."[22] In this study the electoral system refers to the rules and norms governing the general election, the procedures for translating the votes cast in the election into seats in the legislative body and selecting which candidates will fill them, the mechanism for electing the chief executive (president and vice president), the procedures through which the people hold their elected representatives accountable, and the ways in which the system structures the boundaries of acceptable political discourse or provides incentives for political parties competing for power to couch their appeals to the electorate in distinct ways.

The recent struggle for political reform in Indonesia in large part took the form of a struggle over how to redesign a set of representative institutions so as to make them more democratic. Chapter 3 describes the debate over the three political laws and the choices that were made with regard to certain key issues. This was a struggle over the rules of the game. In Chapter 4 and 5 I analyze the conduct of the 1999 election and the implementation of the rules of the game (laws). Key questions that are addressed include to what extent actual behaviors and choices, especially those of political elites, were structured by the rules of the political game, and how elements of constitutional design impacted democratic performance.

THE UNDERLYING BASES OF ELECTORAL CHOICE

This study also seeks to explain the direction of the vote or the underlying bases of voters' choices. Previous studies have argued that party competition and voting decisions were structured around the broad social divisions in Indonesian society. "After the 1955 election, the majority of analysts concluded that most Indonesians voted on the basis of religious, ethnic/regional, or class/economic interest allegiances."[23] Subsequently, during the New Order elections, these bases were muted or repressed by prohibitions on some parties and tight controls on others, including forced fusion. When most of these were lifted in 1998, the question arose whether the traditional social cleavages would reappear, or whether they had been permanently transformed and weakened as predictors of electoral choice.

This issue is not unique to Indonesia and can be related to a broader, comparative literature on Western democracies. According to Lipset and Rokkan, class and religion historically structured partisan alignments and voting choices. They argued that differences between competing social groups provided the potential for political conflict, furnishing both a possible base of voting support and a set of political interests that parties vied to represent. Such cleavages could be expected to persist over long periods of time: "The party systems of the 1960s reflect, with but few significant exceptions, the cleavage structures of the 1920s."[24] However, studies subsequently have shown that both class and religious cleavages are declining: "The decline of social-based voting is most apparent for the class and religious cleavages, but a similar erosion of influence has occurred for most other sociological characteristics."[25]

In the next chapter most of the existing studies of New Order elections are reviewed, with special attention to factors structuring voting choice. Chapter 6 provides a comparison of the two most democratic elections, 1955 and 1999, which suggests that the effects of traditional social divisions such as religion and regionalism on electoral choice have remained stronger than expected in light of the New Order's sociopolitical engineering and the theory that holds those effects will tend to weaken over time. Chapter 7 presents a sociological model of voting choice for each of the top five parties in the 1999 election, which pose a further challenge to the theory.

This study is unique in its careful utilization of quantitative election results at the local (district) level. If they attempt to measure at all, previous studies utilize highly aggregated election data in which much of the variation within the country gets averaged out and on which only rudimentary statistical techniques (e.g., percentages) can be applied. But here, the utilization of hundreds of units of observation (N = 160 to over 300, depending on the particular election) allows more accurate analysis and use of more powerful statistical techniques.

INDONESIA'S DEMOCRATIZATION IN COMPARATIVE PERSPECTIVE

Recent scholarship arising from the comparative study of democratization has moved away from a once-dominant search for prerequisites of democracy, followed by a more process-oriented emphasis on contingent choice, to arrive at something of a synthesis or a "structured contingency" approach. This approach is based on the recognition that

Even in the midst of the tremendous uncertainty provoked by a regime transition, where constraints appear to be most relaxed and where a wide range of outcomes appears to be possible, the decisions made by various actors respond to and are conditioned by the types of socioeconomic structures and political institutions already present. These can be decisive in that they may either restrict or enhance the options available to different political actors attempting to construct democracy.[26]

Utilizing a structured contingency method involves the identification of the different types of democracy that emerge from distinctive modes of transition, as well as analysis of their consequences. That is, the type of democracy that emerges will depend significantly (but not exclusively) on the mode of transition from nondemocratic rule.

The very uncertain transitional period sets the context within which actors choose the arrangements that are going to govern their future cooperation and competition and influences the identity and power relations of actors. According to Schmitter,

Depending on the mode, they may be compelled to make choices in a great hurry, with imperfect information about the available alternatives and without much reflexion [*sic*] about longer-term consequences. Their fleeting arrangements, temporary pacts and improvised accommodations to crises tend to accumulate and to set precedents. Some may find their way into more formal, even constitutional, norms. It is, therefore, useful to consider the possibility of "birth defects" in the democratization process that are due, not just to the structural features long present in the society, but also to conjunctural circumstances that surround the moment of regime change itself.[27]

Four modes of transition to democracy have been delineated, depending on whether democracy is the outcome of a strategy based primarily on compromise (A1) or on overt force (A2), and on relative actor strength; that is, whether incumbent ruling groups, no matter how weakened, are still ascendant in relation to mass actors (B1) or whether mass actors have gained the upper hand (B2). The cross-tabulation of these distinctions produces four ideal types of democratic transition: "pact" (A1 and B1), "imposition" (A2 and B1), "reform" (A1 and B2), and "revolution" (A2 and B2).[28] Karl acknowledges that transitions in the real world are often a mixture of types, complicating attempts to assess the effects of a particular mode on the character of the resulting democracy.

Fundamental to this approach is the notion of unfolding processes and sequences, from regime breakdown to transition to consolidation, and that one type of democracy can be transformed into another. It suggests that "the dynamics of consolidation must differ in important ways from the transition if 'freezing' is to be avoided."[29] In other words, the installation of a new democracy is only an intermediate point in the democratization process and marks the beginning of a second struggle.[30] A related point is that consolidation of democracy is much more tenuous for democratic regimes that have been installed after a period of authoritarian rule because they must succeed at two tasks: (1) strengthening the democratic elements of the new regime, and (2) identifying and removing the authoritarian elements of the previous one.

With these concepts and frameworks in mind, let us consider the case of Indonesia. Suharto's regime ruptured quite suddenly and unexpectedly in May 1998 when he resigned less than a year after his party claimed its largest electoral victory ever and just a few months after being reelected without opposition to a seventh five-year term as president. A "pact" was instrumental to Suharto's resignation, yet "even if Suharto eventually stepped down of his own accord . . . he was clearly forced to do so by a combination of societal mobilization and fracturing of the ruling elite."[31] The installation of electoral democracy began largely "from above," with a series of initiatives by interim President Habibie that were subsequently ratified by the sovereign Assembly (MPR) meeting in special session in late 1998. The transition continued with the holding of a largely free and fair general election in mid-1999 and culminated later that year in the seating of a new House (DPR) and Assembly.[32] Now under the control of opposition politicians, the Assembly produced more policies to undergird democracy, rejected Habibie's stewardship of the presidency (thereby repudiating an aspect of the initial pact), and elected Abdurrahman Wahid to the presidency and Megawati Soekarnoputri to the vice presidency. In terms of Karl's ideal types, the transition began largely as a pact but evolved toward reform as opposition politicians representing masses became ascendant. The other two modes, imposition and revolution, are not applicable to Indonesia's experience.

How did the pact and reform modes of transition affect the type of democracy that was installed in 1999? This is a major question to be addressed throughout the following chapters, but some of the later arguments can be briefly foreshadowed here. The adherence to constitutional provisions regarding succession and the retention of a presidential pseudodemocracy left power centralized in the presidency, enabling President Habibie to launch within weeks an ambitious reform agenda, including lifting most restrictions on the press and on the right to organize politically, and to appoint the Team of Seven to draft three new political bills. A transition marked by elements of reform (due to pressure from below) brought about a highly competitive (multiparty) democracy, whose political fragility could pave the way to a return to authoritarianism. The agreement to hold new elections three years early placed pressure on the government to adopt an accommodative political style in order to reach a series of subsequent agreements (e.g., passage of the [modified] political bills by the House). The retention of the 1945 Constitution, which was elevated to sacrosanct status under Suharto's regime, enhanced the initial survivability of the new electoral democracy, but became an obstacle to future self-transformation of the polity and deepening of democracy until major revisions (called "four amendments") were crafted.

Chapter 9 places Indonesia in regional context with the Philippines and Thailand. All three countries have been undergoing democratization, which creates interest in comparing their experiences. I focus on electoral reform and the institutions of democratic representation and governance. The comparison illuminates some of the alternatives in the design of electoral institutions that are likely to be perceived and considered by Indonesians as they attempt to consolidate their democracy.

NOTES

1. They include Hal Hill, *The Indonesian Economy since 1966*, rev. ed. (Cambridge: Cambridge University Press, 2000), ch. 13; Geoff Forrester and R. J. May, eds., *The Fall of Soeharto* (Singapore: Select Books, 1999); Adam Schwarz and Jonathan Paris, eds., *The Politics of Post-Suharto Indonesia* (New York: Council on Foreign Relations, 1999); Chris Manning and Peter Van Diermen, eds., *Indonesia in Transition* (Singapore: Institute of Southeast Asian Studies, 2000); Donald K. Emmerson, "Part IV: The Fall of Suharto and After," in *Indonesia beyond Suharto*, ed. Donald K. Emmerson (Armonk, N.Y.: M. E. Sharpe, 1999); R. William Liddle, "Indonesia's Democratic Opening," *Government and Opposition* 34, 1 (1999): 94–116; and R. William Liddle, "Indonesia's Democratic Transition: Playing by the Rules," in *The Architecture of Democracy*, ed. Andrew Reynolds (Oxford: Oxford University Press, 2001).

2. Brief treatments of electoral reform and the 1999 election are Emmerson, "Voting and Violence: Indonesia and East Timor in 1999," ch. 11 in *Indonesia beyond Suharto*, ed. Donald K. Emmerson; David Bourchier, "Habibie's Interregnum: *Reformasi*, Elections, Regionalism and the Struggle for Power, ch. 2 in *Indonesia in Transition*, Manning and Van Diermen, eds.; Marcus Mietzner, "The 1999 General Session: Wahid, Megawati and the Fight for the Presidency," ibid., ch. 3; Donald Weatherbee, "Indonesia," in *How Asia Votes*, John Fuhsheng Hsien and David Newman, eds. (New York: Seven Bridges Press, 2001).

3. My view of democracy has been influenced by Larry Diamond, *Developing Democracy* (Baltimore: Johns Hopkins University Press, 1999), and Philippe C. Schmitter, "Recent Developments in the Academic Study of Democratization," paper presented at the Inauguration and Colloquium of the Habibie Center, Jakarta, May 1999. According to Schmitter, "There is no single democracy; there are only democracies. Many different rules and organizational forms can ensure the accountability of rulers to citizens, as well as satisfy the criteria of contingent consent among politicians and gain the eventual assent of the people."

4. Emmerson, *Indonesia beyond Suharto*, x.

5. R. H. Taylor, ed., *The Politics of Elections in Southeast Asia* (New York: Woodrow Wilson Center Press, 1996), 3. Taylor's exceptions (i.e., elections followed by change of government) were the Philippines prior to Marcos's declaration of martial law in 1972 and the 1975 and 1995 parlia-

mentary elections in Thailand. To update his list, we would need to add the 1998 election in the Philippines, the 1998, 2000, and 2001 elections in Thailand, and the 1999 Indonesian election. Also, the result of the 1999 referendum in East Timor could be considered a defeat for Golkar, Indonesia's ruling party at the time.

6. Benedict R. Anderson, "Elections and Participation in Three Southeast Asian Countries," in Taylor, *The Politics of Elections*, 30–31.

7. Harold Crouch, "Introduction," in *State and Civil Society in Indonesia*, ed. Arief Budiman (Clayton, Victoria, Australia: Monash University, Centre of Southeast Asian Studies, Monash Papers on Southeast Asia No. 22, 1990), 116–117.

8. R. H. Taylor, "Delusion and Necessity: Elections and Politics in Southeast Asia," *Items* (Social Science Research Council) 48, 4 (1994): 85.

9. R. William Liddle, "A Useful Fiction: Democratic Legitimation in New Order Indonesia," in Taylor, *The Politics of Elections*, 34–60.

10. Diamond, *Developing Democracy*, 15. Diamond now prefers the concept of pseudodemocracy. In an earlier writing he defined semidemocracy as a political system that allows competitive elections yet limits the effective power of elected officials or political-party competition and constrains freedom and fairness during elections in a society uncertain of civil and political liberties. See Larry Diamond, Juan J. Linz, and Seymour Martin Lipset, eds., *Politics in Developing Countries: Comparing Experiences with Democracy* (Boulder, Colo.: Lynne Rienner, 1995), 6–9.

11. Taylor, *The Politics of Elections*, 5.

12. Diamond, *Developing Democracy*, 8–10; David Collier and Steven Levitsky, "Democracy with Adjectives," *World Politics* 49 (1997): 430–451.

13. Quoted by Diamond, *Developing Democracy*, 8.

14. Robert A. Dahl, *Polyarchy: Participation and Opposition* (New Haven: Yale University Press, 1971).

15. Diamond, *Developing Democracy*, 10.

16. Terry Lynn Karl, "Dilemmas of Democratization in Latin America," *Comparative Politics* 23, 1 (1990): 2.

17. Diamond, *Developing Democracy*, 10–11.

18. Lawrence LeDuc, Richard G. Niemi, and Pippa Norris, eds., *Comparing Democracies* (Thousand Oaks, Calif.: Sage, 1996), 4.

19. Terry Lynn Karl, cited in Diamond, *Developing Democracy*, 9.

20. Andrew Reynolds, *Electoral Systems and Democratization in Southern Africa* (Oxford: Oxford University Press, 1999), 9.

21. Ibid., 89.

22. Arend Lijphart, "Electoral Systems," in *The Encyclopedia of Democracy*, ed. Seymour Martin Lipset (Washington, D.C.: Congressional Quarterly Press, 1995), 412–422.

23. R. William Liddle and Saiful Mujani, "The Triumph of Leadership: Explaining the 1999 Indonesian Vote," 2000.

24. Seymour Martin Lipset and Stein Rokkan, eds., *Party Systems and Voter Alignments* (New York: Free Press, 1967), 50.

25. Russell J. Dalton, "Political Cleavages, Issues, and Electoral Change," in LeDuc, Niemi, and Norris, *Comparing Democracies*, 328.

26. Karl, "Dilemmas of Democratization," 6.

27. Schmitter, "Recent Developments in the Academic Study of Democratization."

28. Karl, "Dilemmas of Democratization," 8.

29. Ibid., 16.

30. Adam Przeworski, "Some Problems in the Study of the Transition to Democracy," in *Transitions from Authoritarian Rule: Comparative Perspectives*, ed. Guillermo O'Donnell, Philippe Schmitter, and Laurence Whitehead (Baltimore: Johns Hopkins University Press, 1986).

31. The pact was concluded among Suharto, members of his family, the cabinet, and military leaders and was quite limited in scope, providing for Suharto's resignation, handing over executive power "constitutionally" to his long-time protege and chosen successor, B. J. Habibie, and assurance by General Wiranto in public that the military would guarantee the security of Suharto and his family. Aspinall argues that, compared to other "third-wave" democratizations, "relatively few involved an element of 'rupture' as sudden and great as that which occurred in Indonesia." Ed Aspinall, "Opposition and Elite Conflict in the Fall of Soeharto," in Forester and May, *The Fall of Soeharto*, 30.

32. The case for successful transition to democracy is well argued in Liddle, "Indonesia's Democratic Transition."

CHAPTER 2

Historical Background

The primary objective of this chapter is to construct a backdrop against which the magnitude of the 1999 electoral changes described in the next chapter can be understood and assessed. A second objective is to increase our theoretical understanding of how pseudodemocratic regimes, such as Indonesia's New Order, utilize and carefully manage elections in ways that remove most of the uncertainty yet contribute to their legitimacy. Third, this chapter summarizes the findings of most scholarly studies about the factors that influenced voting choice in each of seven elections (1955 to 1997), giving special attention to sociological factors and how their influence appears to have changed over time.

ELECTORAL INSTITUTIONS AND ADMINISTRATION

Colonial and Early Republican
Representational Institutions

A national-level parliament of sorts for what was then known as the Netherlands Indies was first established by the colonial regime in the early twentieth century. Called the Volksraad (People's Council), it had a skimpy electoral basis: "It included substantial representation of Dutch officials and planters; many of its members were appointees; and it had no real power at all."[1] During the Japanese occupation, the Volksraad had even less power and was entirely appointed. With the collapse of the Japanese empire, Indonesian nationalists declared independence in 1945 and the final political settlement with the Dutch occurred in 1949, yet the first country-wide election was postponed until 1955. However, during the revolutionary years from 1945 to 1949, President Soekarno and Vice President Hatta appointed to a revolutionary parliament (KNIP) representatives of all the major political and paramilitary groups, "not least because of the absence of a single powerful party, a united military, and a cohesive, authoritative bureaucracy" needed to carry out elections.[2] Important points in this early history were the genesis of the idea of group representation and the precedent of appointment rather than election.

Parliamentary Democracy and the 1955 Election

For about the first eight years, the political system of the new republic was structured as a parliamentary democracy. Amidst rising dissatisfaction, political instability, and armed rebellion in some regions, the first nationwide election for a constituent assembly was finally held in 1955 for the purpose of channeling the dissatisfactions and resolving questions about the strength of the various political forces. In Anderson's view, "They ended up being the most open and participatory elections held anywhere in Southeast Asia since World War II: full adult suffrage, a competitive press, very little violence or gerrymandering, remarkably little emphasis on money."[3] Due to the highly decentralized character of the revolution and strong participatory tradition that had taken root, there was little debate on the type of electoral system. Proportional representation (PR) using an open list was adopted.[4] Moreover, through travel to the Netherlands or interaction with Dutch politicians, a number of nationalist leaders had been exposed to the practice of PR. But unlike the Netherlands' choice of a single national constituency (single electoral district), they created fifteen electoral districts, most corresponding to administrative subdivisions, in order to accommodate the greater size and diversity of Indonesia. Since the number and identity of election contestants varied among districts, ranging from forty-eight (Central Java and North Sumatra) to twelve (South Kalimantan), each district had its own ballot.[5] At least 172 parties or individuals competed in the election, with 28 of them winning seats.[6] The election revealed a major cleavage in the electorate, reflected in secular and non-Muslim parties obtaining 285 seats and Islamic parties with 230 seats. This was the only national election held during the period, although elections for provincial representative councils were held in 1957.

Parliamentary democracy came to an end in 1957, when President Soekarno, backed by the army, declared martial law, marking the end of parliamentary democracy and the beginning of authoritarian rule. Nevertheless, the parliamentary period has remained a subject of controversy and debate. When General Suharto and the army assumed power in 1966, his "New Order" government promoted a highly negative view of the parliamentary period in their effort to justify and legitimate continued authoritarian rule. Scholarly interest in the parliamentary period was rekindled in the early 1990s by a lively debate on the causes of its demise. One position in the debate, used by the New Order to justify its authoritarian and centralized character, was that the system of parliamentary democracy encouraged intense social conflict and unstable, fractured government. An opposing view held that the cabinets of the period were destabilized by the military, military factions, and to a lesser extent by President Soekarno.[7]

Most recently, many commentaries on the 1999 election have drawn comparisons with the 1955 election. Although separated by forty-four years, the most recent election is widely believed to have had more in common with the first election than with any of the intervening six elections conducted during Suharto's pseudodemocracy. The similarities in political context and election administration are discussed in Chapter 6, as well as the continuities in the bases of party support.

Suharto's "New Order"

Under the leadership of Suharto, the government ordered a simplification of the party system in 1973. Nine of the organizations that had contested the 1971 election were forced to fuse into two: four Muslim parties became the Development Unity Party (Partai Persatuan Pembangunan or PPP), and the Indonesian Democratic Party (Partai Demokrasi Indonesia or PDI) was comprised of three nationalist and two Christian parties. In 1975 the Election Law was amended to recognize only three specific election contestants: Golkar, PPP, and PDI.

New Order authorities, in their effort to create a pseudodemocracy, held a series of carefully controlled and manipulated elections beginning in 1971. They produced two-thirds majorities for Golkar, the government's electoral machine (see Table 2.1). However, if the national totals are disaggregated to the provincial level, we can see considerable interprovincial variation as well as provincial variation across elections (Table 2.2). This finding illustrates the point made in Chapter 1 that the degree of domination varied from place

Table 2.1

General Election Results for House of Representatives, 1971–1997 (%)

Party	1971	1977	1982	1987	1992	1997
Golkar	62.8	62.1	64.1	73.0	68.1	74.5
PPP	27.2[a]	29.3	28.0	16.0	17.0	22.4
PDI	10.0[b]	8.6	7.9	11.0	14.9	3.1

Source: General Election Institute (LPU).

[a]Combined votes won by a group of four Muslim parties (Nadhatul Ulama or NU, Partai Muslimin Indonesia or Parmusi, Partai Syarikat Islam Indonesia or PSII, and Pergerakan Tarbiyah Islam or Perti).

[b]Combined votes won by a group of five nationalist and Christian parties (Partai National Indonesia or PNI, Partai Katolik, Partai Kristen Indonesia or Parkindo, Partai Ikatan Pendukung Kemerdekaan Indonesia or IPKI, and Partai Murba).

to place and from time to time. Elections were an effective means through which, over time, the consensus, inclusionary aspects of governance were overwhelmed by the majoritarian, exclusionary aspects. To understand how this was achieved, we need to examine the electoral institutions and election administration of the New Order. The scholarly literature on New Order elections gives short shrift to these aspects, typically concentrating on explaining the direction of the vote.

As in other states, Indonesian political life was structured formally by a hierarchy of policy decisions and legal authority. The 1945 constitution and the decisions of the People's Consultative Assembly had highest authority and provided general rules and policy direction. Elections were not mentioned in the constitution; rather, they were governed by laws or statutes (*undang-undang*) at the next (lower) level of legal authority. An election law was passed by the House of Representatives in 1969 and amended in 1975, 1980, and 1985.[8] This law was subsequently interpreted in a series of government regulations (*peraturan pemerintah*).[9] These regulations promulgated by the central bureaucracy were open to further specification and interpretation by the semiautonomous heads of regional governments (*gubernur, bupati, walikota*). Not surprising, there were important conflicts and inconsistencies in the legal corpus governing the electoral system. Also, numerous instances have been described where local practice, sometimes guided by formal decisions of local authorities, deviated from statutes and (central) government regulations.[10] Although the Supreme Court had the power after 1985 to review ministerial decrees and regulations, the court never used this power to arbitrate apparent conflicts or inconsistencies among the laws and regulations at various levels.

Central Executive Control

Perhaps the most salient characteristic of the New Order electoral system was that it was highly partisan, under the complete control of the New Order executive who supported Golkar, rather than being directed by some more neutral authority. At the central level, the General Election Institute (LPU) was established in Jakarta as a permanent (executive) agency, headed by the minister of home affairs and a leadership council composed of seven other ministers and the commander in chief of the armed forces, and staffed by civil servants from the Department of Home Affairs. As a symbolic nod toward neutrality, the institute included a fourteen-member advisory council (Dewan Pertimbangan) headed by a minister and containing three representatives from each of the four official political

Table 2.2
General Election Results for House of Representatives, by Province, 1971–1997 (%)

Province	Golkar						PPP						PDI					
	71	77	82	87	92	97	71	77	82	87	92	97	71	77	82	87	92	97
D.I. Aceh	49.7	37.7	40.0	52.0	58.4	64.8	48.9	52.5	59.1	43.0	34.5	31.9	1.4	9.8	1.0	5.1	7.1	3.3
North Sumatra	70.1	60.1	72.5	72.8	71.3	80.3	15.8	20.1	20.4	13.5	10.9	12.8	14.1	19.8	7.0	13.8	17.8	6.8
West Sumatra	63.2	59.1	60.4	78.7	82.1	91.1	34.5	28.8	38.8	19.6	14.4	7.7	2.3	12.1	0.8	1.7	3.5	1.1
Riau	76.7	63.3	71.7	79.7	76.6	82.7	20.6	30.0	25.8	15.0	14.3	13.8	2.7	6.7	2.5	5.2	9.1	3.5
South Sumatra	62.6	49.8	65.1	69.3	70.2	85.0	30.1	36.3	28.1	18.8	11.9	11.3	7.3	13.8	6.8	11.9	17.8	3.7
Jambi	88.2	83.5	84.8	88.9	90.7	92.6	10.4	14.7	13.8	8.2	4.9	5.9	1.4	1.8	1.4	2.9	4.4	1.5
Bengkulu	82.7	76.4	70.6	84.8	86.1	94.8	15.4	19.7	26.1	10.3	5.8	3.8	1.9	3.9	3.3	4.9	8.2	1.4
Lampung	71.8	61.8	59.4	87.0	90.5	93.9	22.1	28.6	30.0	7.3	3.7	4.9	6.1	9.6	10.6	5.6	5.8	2.0
West Java	76.1	66.3	63.3	71.3	70.5	72.3	20.2	27.0	27.2	13.8	14.9	26.0	3.7	6.7	9.5	14.9	14.6	1.7
D.K.I. Jakarta	46.7	34.6	45.0	50.2	54.4	65.3	37.1	38.3	39.2	21.4	23.8	32.9	16.2	10.9	15.8	28.4	21.8	1.8
Central Java	50.3	52.6	60.5	68.2	55.5	68.3	28.7	24.2	27.7	18.2	22.9	29.0	21.0	23.2	11.8	13.6	21.6	2.7
D.I. Yogyakarta	71.6	56.6	60.6	70.2	58.6	62.6	21.7	21.0	23.3	14.5	20.4	34.2	6.7	22.5	16.1	15.3	21.0	3.2

East Java	54.9	58.8	56.8	71.2	58.8	63.0	39.4	33.4	36.6	20.8	25.2	33.9	5.7	7.8	6.6	8.0	16.0	3.1
West Kalimantan	66.7	68.9	71.0	68.7	63.9	69.7	18.7	20.1	20.7	15.2	14.6	15.1	14.6	11.0	8.3	16.1	21.5	15.1
Central Kalimantan	81.8	69.9	84.2	89.2	86.3	86.6	16.4	24.6	14.6	8.5	7.8	9.8	2.2	5.6	1.2	2.4	6.0	3.6
South Kalimantan	64.8	49.4	59.3	71.8	69.7	72.0	33.9	42.5	40.0	24.8	21.1	25.1	1.2	8.1	1.1	3.4	9.3	2.9
East Kalimantan	54.8	57.0	61.3	67.8	62.5	70.0	30.1	30.4	31.9	21.1	17.9	23.7	15.1	12.6	6.9	11.1	20.7	6.3
North Sulawesi	60.7	72.9	87.1	87.5	88.2	95.9	22.9	16.7	6.8	5.4	4.5	2.4	16.4	10.4	6.1	7.1	7.3	1.7
Central Sulawesi	76.8	79.3	81.3	83.1	80.8	84.9	19.0	18.0	15.5	12.0	11.0	10.4	4.2	2.7	3.2	4.9	8.3	4.7
SE Sulawesi	92.4	96.1	96.9	97.2	94.4	97.2	5.8	3.1	2.6	2.0	1.8	2.1	1.9	0.8	0.5	0.9	3.8	0.7
South Sulawesi	78.4	85.2	89.2	90.0	89.8	91.6	18.8	13.4	10.2	8.9	7.7	7.3	2.9	1.4	0.6	1.1	2.5	1.0
Bali	82.8	85.4	88.4	87.7	78.5	93.2	2.3	1.5	1.9	1.7	2.0	3.3	14.9	12.7	9.7	10.6	19.5	3.5
W. Nusa Tenggara	69.8	57.5	68.6	82.6	78.5	80.7	24.7	30.7	28.2	11.9	11.1	14.6	5.4	11.8	3.2	5.6	10.5	3.7
E. Nusa Tenggara	61.5	90.3	96.4	94.7	91.2	94.9	3.1	1.9	1.3	1.3	1.8	1.5	35.4	7.8	2.4	4.0	7.0	3.6
Maluku	47.7	71.9	75.2	81.5	73.9	82.1	24.8	18.0	19.0	13.3	16.0	13.0	27.3	10.1	5.8	5.2	10.1	5.0
Irian Jaya	--	86.9	92.5	93.0	86.6	88.9	--	4.0	3.2	2.7	2.4	3.6	--	9.2	4.4	4.3	10.5	7.5
East Timor	--	--	99.5	93.7	82.6	84.7	--	--	0.2	0.7	1.4	1.8	--	--	0.3	5.6	16.0	13.5

Source: General Election Institute (LPU).

factions: Golkar, PDI, PPP, and ABRI.[11] Among the institute's major duties were planning and preparation for elections (specified to encompass twelve functions), leading (*memimpin*) and supervising (*mengawasi*) committees at all levels, and the collection, processing, and announcement of election results.

To assist the LPU with the administration of an election, temporary committees were established at five levels, paralleling and utilizing the vertical lines of Indonesia's local government organization under the Department of Home Affairs. In each administrative unit within every level of government—central, 27 provinces, approximately 300 districts, approximately 3,600 subdistricts, approximately 67,000 villages—two committees were appointed, one for implementation (PPI, PPD-I, PPD-II, PPS, KPPS) and one for supervision and oversight (Pawaslakpus, Panwaslak-I, Panwaslak-II, Panwaslakcam). Also, a voter registration committee (Pantarlih) was established at the village level, composed entirely of local government employees, and began work a year in advance of the election.

The implementation committees were highly centralized under the New Order executive authorities. Representatives of the "opposition" political factions (i.e., PPP and PDI) were easily outnumbered on every committee. "While it ensured administrative efficiency, this structure no less certainly guaranteed effective governmental intervention and control. . . . In effect, the General Elections Institute assumed the character of a military command with local chief executives as local commanders and election committees as their staffs."[12]

The supervisory committees were no more independent. At the central level, the committee was led by the attorney general, and at each of the two regional levels by the chief public prosecutor—all members of the executive branch—who served at the pleasure of the president or the minister of home affairs. In sum, the New Order executive and its supporting political factions were predominant on every committee at every level, and the rules governing the work and procedures of the committees were stipulated in decisions of the minister of home affairs.

Tilted Playing Field

According to the law, the three contestants (Golkar, PPP, and PDI) had the same status, rights, and duties.[13] But in fact, the playing field was not level, but tilted sharply in favor of Golkar. The PPP and PDI sustained much heavier losses of their legislative nominees in the mandatory screening process. Government officials campaigned for Golkar under the guise of official duties, and Golkar had much greater access to government facilities, including the local government bureaucracy (territorial administration), whose personnel were supporters or functionaries of Golkar. In contrast, PPP and PDI had to create their own organizations and were prohibited from organizing at the grassroots (village) level. Also, there was disproportionately more media coverage of Golkar's campaign activities.[14]

The Village Election Committees (KPPS) had the critical roles of overseeing each polling place and counting the votes, yet the composition of these committees was the least specified. These committees frequently violated regulations in the treatment of witnesses, and fraud often occurred in the vote counting. If a witness did not show up on election day, or the chairperson felt that a witness was improperly certified, the chairperson could draft a regular voter to serve as a (nonpartisan) substitute for the (partisan) witness. The requirements for certification of witnesses were complex and presupposed a considerable degree of party organization and planning. Witnesses had to be resident in the village or neighborhood in which the polling place was located. Witnesses represented a particular party, so they had to be party members and nominated by a party at least twenty days prior to the election. They had to have been approved and certified in writing prior to election day by the district chief or mayor. In the event a party was unable to find a resident witness, another witness could substitute, provided he or she lived in another, contiguous village or neighborhood in the same regency or municipality. There were frequent instances where one of the minority parties was unable to obtain a witness, often due to partisan homogeneity at the village level, and where a party-designated witness was disallowed because one or more of these requirements had not been met. Moreover, the legal basis for all regulations pertaining to the village committees was found, not in the election law (*undang-undang*) enacted by the House, but in less authoritative regulations issued by the executive branch (*peraturan pemerintah*).[15]

According to the regulations, once the polls closed on election day the village committees were immediately to tally the ballots. Witnesses had the responsibility of calling irregularities to the attention of the committee chairperson, who had full authority to handle and decide them. However, the regulations explicitly specified that the absence of witnesses "does not influence the implementation and validity of the vote counting." Once the tally had been completed, the results announced and certified with the signatures of the committee members, and the witnesses given a written recapitulation of the compilation, the ballots were to be returned to sealed boxes and sent to the subdistrict office. Violations of these procedures were often reported, such as ballots being taken away to

the subdistrict office for counting out of sight by witnesses, and witnesses not being given a recap of the compilations.[16]

A study of violations of election regulations in 1992 found that 61
percent were committed by the subdistrict and village election implementation committees and 29 percent by the regular government
administrators (village chief, subdistrict chief). More than half of
the violations were classified as "violations against political party
witnesses," and 25 percent as "violations in the casting and counting of ballots."[17]

Trends in New Order Election Administration

As mentioned, the laws and regulations were amended four times.
The 1975 amendments to the Election Law extended the broad discretionary powers of New Order authorities over the conduct of elections. For example, the amendments specified that the village
implementation committees consist entirely of government functionaries. Having entered into some compromises with the PPP and the
PDI in the law regulating political parties, apparently the authorities decided to hold the line against the parties' attempts to put more
guarantees of fair treatment into the amendments.[18]

The 1980 amendments sought to involve the parties in the administration of elections, to formalize campaign restrictions, to give the
government more than usual discretion in conducting elections in
East Timor, which had been formally annexed in 1976, and to modify
the organization of elections. Representatives of political parties were
added as regular members to the committees at all levels, including
newly mandated supervisory committees. However, as mentioned,
every committee was led by government personnel, who together
with committee members from Golkar and the armed forces composed a commanding majority on every committee. The establishment of the supervisory committees was a response to the accusations
by PPP and PDI of widespread deviations and fraud during the 1977
election. The fact that the subdistrict supervisory committees (*panwaslakcam*) were specifically assigned to oversee voter registration
and the distribution of summons to vote (*surat panggilan*) suggests
that another impetus for the supervisory committees was the
government's concern over rising apathy and election boycotting
(*golput*).[19] Another important provision was that "civil servants who
are members of parties or Golkar and who have been nominated . . .
can engage in campaigning."

The new regulations extended even to the substance of party platforms on which the election contestants were allowed to campaign.
The mandatory required theme was the party's respective program for

national development. Raising questions about the official *Pancasila* ideology or the 1945 constitution were expressly prohibited.

In 1985, the most important amendment to the election law was the requirement of ideological monism or that all social and political groups adhere to the *Pancasila* as their "one and only principle."[20] Having thus required the election contestants to be philosophically indistinguishable, the amendment decreed that Golkar, PPP, and PDI have the same "position, rights and duties."

Following the 1987 election, several noteworthy changes were made in the implementing regulations. In order to increase community involvement in elections and turn out the vote, the official list of registered voters was to be announced publicly by being posted in the village office for twenty days. More restrictions were placed on campaign activity.

The last round of modifications in the election regulations was decreed in advance of the 1997 election. Most of the changes concerned the village-level voter registration committees (*pantarlih*), strengthening their legal basis and specifying and expanding their responsibilities. These changes reflected the governments concern for more accurate and higher rates of voter registration as well as more standardization of procedures at the polling places. Also, the residency requirement for party witnesses dating from 1985 was lifted, removing a obstacle faced especially by small parties.

From this review of major changes in the Election Law and regulations from 1969 to 1997 several conclusions can be drawn. First, the administration of general elections remained highly centralized under the control of New Order executive authorities, despite the fact that concurrent ballots were cast to elect representatives for regional assemblies at two subnational levels (DPRD-I, DPRD-II). The particular conditions and problems encountered in conducting elections in two provinces, Irian Jaya and East Timor, were handled by exemptions and the issuance of regulations specific to each province.

Second, all phases in the administration of an election were increasingly regulated, especially with the promulgation of implementing regulations in 1985 (P.P. 35/1985). In other words, whereas authorities always exercised broad discretionary powers in the matter of elections, beginning in the mid-1980s they made a concerted effort to codify and institutionalize these powers. But such an effort was a two-edged sword. If it ensured a controlled and orderly election process, it has also specified and clarified the rules of the game by which actual practice was measured and often found in violation of the rules.

Third, as the political landscape underwent restructuring through such methods as enforced simplification of political organizations and ideological monism, the political parties were granted an increasing role in the administration of elections. Helping to expand their role as well was the perpetual struggle of the PPP and PDI for equal treatment, since the election administrators tended to be partisans for Golkar.

One of the most repugnant tasks assumed by the New Order authorities was the screening and endorsement of candidates nominated by the three electoral contenders. Elimination of candidates by the security apparatus was antirepresentative and antiinclusionary because it deprived the parties and ultimately the people of the right to choose their representatives and there was no way to appeal the results. Available evidence suggests that this screening became more comprehensive and stringent over time. About 20 percent of the nominated candidates were eliminated through the screening process in 1971.[21] A report in 1977 indicated that the PDI lost 19 percent of its candidates for the House, the PPP 16 percent, and Golkar 5 percent.[22] As a result of a Presidential Decision in 1990 (KEPPRES 16/1990), a much more comprehensive special investigation process (*litsus*) was applied to candidates nominated for the 1992 election. Whereas the screening process for previous elections—as required by the Election Law and regulations—had involved submission of written answers to specific questions of fact and verification by the police, in order to prove that the nominated candidate had no previous involvement in leftist organizations banned after 1965 the *litsus* process required, in addition, written answers to open-ended and subjective (political) questions and an interview with security personnel. In late 1991 the *litsus* process triggered nationwide political controversy.[23] According to the Indonesian poll-watching group, KIPP, in the 1997 election the PPP and the PDI combined lost 236 nominees in the screening process, compared to only 21 lost by Golkar.[24]

Restrictions on campaigning tightened and increased over time. The 1985 implementing regulations required advance permits and gave local security authorities wide discretion over virtually all campaign activities. The official campaign period was shortened from sixty days in 1971 and 1977 to forty-five days in 1982 and finally and permanently to twenty-five days in 1987 and 1997. Beginning in 1982, the campaign period was divided into rounds, with each of the three contestants taking their turn for one day on a rotating basis. In 1997 campaign regions (*wilayah kampanye*) were introduced, adding territorial or geographical restrictions to the chronological ones.

Violations of election laws and regulations seem to have continued unabated, with very few prosecutions. The General Election Institute registered an increase in violations and election crimes from

607 in 1982 to 6,094 in 1987, of which only 28 were prosecuted.[25] The official figure for 1997 was 1,911 incidents.[26] It is impossible to judge the extent to which the tenfold increase between 1982 and 1987 was real or the result of more vigilant reporting and clearer standards resulting from the issuance of the detailed implementing regulations in 1985 (P.P. 35/1985). Still, there can be no debate about lax prosecution of violators, especially when they were government officials or members of Golkar.

A number of observers argued that the 1992 election was relatively improved when compared with previous New Order elections.[27] They claim it was implemented in a more neutral fashion, especially at the central and provincial levels of the bureaucracy.[28] There was less overt intervention by the armed forces in favor of Golkar, and less election-related violence accompanied the campaign. Whatever the improvements in 1992, they seem to have been lost in 1997. Election-related violence was the worst ever, as about 300 people died. The military gave more or less open support to Golkar, and there were numerous reports of double or multiple voting by civil servants, intimidation of voters, non-Golkar candidates and poll watchers, and "money politics" to benefit Golkar. The last stage of the vote count lacked transparency; five senior officials and Golkar leaders had access to the database but equal access was denied to leaders of the PPP and PDI.[29]

Votes and Seats

Thus far I have discussed the rules and norms that governed nominations, campaigning, voting, and counting. Another aspect was the procedure for translating the votes cast in the election into seats in the legislative body. As indicted, the PR formula, with an open list, was adopted with little controversy for the 1955 election.[30] It was arguably the only possible choice, given the variety and depth of sociocultural cleavages, the decentralization of power, and postrevolutionary participatory ethos. A PR system allowed for fairer representation and for a greater diversity of viewpoints to be expressed in the legislature and government; in the 257 elected legislative seats, twenty-seven parties and one individual were represented.[31]

However, PR-list electoral systems are frequently vilified for providing incentives for multiplication of parties, for parties becoming more ideologically oriented, and for granting parties too much control over the selection of legislators.[32] These sentiments were shared by some elements in the army, who in the early New Order period proposed switching to a single-member plurality system with smaller electoral districts than in 1955. But leaders of two major parties opposed it, fearing Java would be underrepresented and a diminution in party power.[33] A PR-list system was retained, but with some major modifications.

These changes can be described in terms of the five major decisions involved in devising any PR-list system: districting, formula, tiers, thresholds, and preferences for candidates.[34] The number of electoral districts was increased from fifteen to twenty-six (twenty-seven beginning in 1982 with the addition of East Timor), corresponding to the increased number of provinces since 1955, and a very different method of determining district magnitude (number of seats per district) was applied. In 1955 district magnitude was a simple function of the population of the electoral district divided by a common divisor (300,000). Reflecting the concentration of population at that time, this method resulted in allocating a combined 69.7 percent of the seats to four electoral districts (27 percent) on the island of Java. A few years later, major rebellions erupted outside Java in Sumatra and Sulawesi, protesting in part Java's preponderance in the national political economy. Not surprising, therefore, the New Order authorities sought for political reasons a different way of determining district magnitude, one that would give heavier representation to the provinces outside Java.

Their solution was to allocate seats to electoral districts according to three stipulations. First, each electoral district (i.e., province) was allocated seats equal to the total number of second-level administrative units (regencies and municipalities) within its boundaries. Since the number of seats open for election was more than the total number of administrative units, a second round was needed to allocate the remaining seats according to size of population. Using a representation ratio, one seat for 400,000 population, districts whose population was more than the number of its administrative units multiplied by 400,000 received additional seats. Third, the combined seat allocation for districts on Java and outside Java had to be equal. The effect of the application of these rules was overrepresentation (or malapportionment) in sixteen out of the twenty-seven electoral districts (59 percent), all of which were outside Java, and underrepresentation in every district on Java.[35]

New Order political architects may also have anticipated what soon became a reality. Given the generally lower level of development outside Java and the central government's control over resources, it would be easier for the government bureaucracy to mobilize votes for Golkar outside Java. Thus, malapportionment in favor of areas outside Java would enhance Golkar's success, because the quota of votes needed to win a seat would be lower in those areas.

The next task was distributing seats to parties on the basis of the votes they had obtained. The electoral formula known as the "largest-remainders using a Hare quota" used in 1955 for distributing seats among parties within each electoral district was carried over without an adjustment procedure or second tier of distribution to reduce distortions resulting from the allocation of seats.[36] As a result, the New Order's procedures allowed a "mechanical effect," to be explained shortly, that worked to the advantage of the largest party" (Golkar).

A fourth issue concerns legal threshold of exclusion, a means of sending a message that marginal parties are not considered suitable players in the legislative arena. No thresholds were utilized in the 1955 election; as mentioned, 172 parties or individuals contested the election and 28 obtained seats, with 12 of them (43 percent) winning only one seat. Unlike the usual pattern, where countries attempt to exclude in a nonpartisan fashion using an objective criterion such as percentage of the vote, the New Order electoral engineers chose to exclude parties and individual candidates on the basis of ideological and political criteria by interfering in the internal affairs of permitted parties and by creating Golkar as the sole channel for the political participation of members of the bureaucracy and retired military. The mechanism of exclusion became more direct in 1973, when nine parties were coercively fused into two. Even then, nominees from all three continued to be screened by security agencies, with PPP and PDI suffering the most disqualifications.[37]

A fifth decision pertained to the procedure used for selecting particular candidates to fill legislative seats. Apparently a combination between "closed-list" and "open-list" was utilized in 1955. It was closed in the sense that voters who voted for a party were not allowed to express any preference for individual candidates and legislative members were elected in the order specified on party lists. On the other hand, ballots used in 1955 were "open-list" in that self-nominated (without party identification) individuals were listed on the ballot in some districts. In addition, the ballots contained a place where voters could simultaneously nominate and express their preference by writing in the name of a party or person.[38]

The New Order abolished the opportunity for self-nomination and write-ins, resulting in a more consistent closed-list procedure. Not only were parties given complete control over the selection of legislators; there were also no sanctions for practicing deception with the party list. As Gaffar pointed out, "One of the peculiarities of Indonesian elections was that some candidates shown in the list did not really intend to be elected. They were listed morely [*sic*] to reflect the image of the party. This is especially the case of Golkar."[39]

Political Consequences of the Electoral System

An important theoretical question often asked about PR systems is if they create incentives for multiplying the number of parties contesting elections. This question concerns the "psychologcal effect" of electoral institutions. In the case of the electoral system created for the first election in 1955, with its allowance for self-nominated (nonparty) candidates and write-in ballots, the answer is clearly positive. But in the pseudodemocracy of the New Order, various controls, especially the law recognizing and permitting only three parties and election contestants, modified the incentive structure and blocked the effects normally detected in electoral and liberal democracies from occurring. Undoubtedly one effect of these restrictions was to foment schisms within the parties, most notably the defection of NU from the PPP in 1984 and the split in the PDI in 1996.

A related question is whether the combination of PR and large district magnitude tended to make parties more ideologically oriented. Although magnitudes ranged from 62 (East Java) to 4 (Bengkulu, East Timor, Central Sulawesi, and Southeast Sulawesi), presenting us with a potential case for testing this general hypothesis, the New Order's controls on the number of parties and limitations on ideologies precluded the expected increase in ideological orientation from occurring.

Still another theoretical question concerns the "mechanical effect" of PR and pertains to the relationship between the proportion of votes a party gets and the proportion of seats it wins in the legislature. "All electoral systems give an advantage to stronger parties but that bias is much less pronounced in PR systems."[40] One mechanism through which they confer advantage is through the decisive effect of district magnitude on proportionality.[41] This effect is examined in Chapter 4 for the last two New Order elections in 1992 and 1997. District magnitude (M) and the index of deviation from proportionality (D) were strongly and inversely correlated (−.69 in 1992 and −.61 in 1997). In other words, the fewer the number of seats in an electoral district, the higher the deviation between proportion of votes and proportion of seats (and vice versa). Deviation from proportionality always benefits larger parties and discriminates against smaller parties.

Afan Gaffar, citing Rae's argument that electoral systems tend especially to advantage the party obtaining the majority of votes (a mechanical effect), points out that the New Order electoral system advantaged Golkar, which obtained a majority in every district, and disadvantaged especially the PDI.[42]

Using for convenience the 1982 data. . . . Of 27 electoral districts PDI obtained one or more seats in only nine. PDI was denied seats in several districts even though it gained a substantial number of votes. In the province of North Sulawesi, for example, the PDI was denied seat [*sic*] even though the party was able to collect almost the same amount of votes with the Islamic party, that is, 6.11% and 6.77%, respectively. The PPP was awarded a seat allocated to the district. In the district in which the total allocation of seats was small the largest party (Golkar) swept an average of about 70% of the seats. Hence the contribution of the electoral system toward the hegemony of Golkar is very clear, and small parties, especially the PDI has difficulty to gain more influence.[43]

Besides a tendency toward lower magnitudes, the fifteen districts where PDI failed to gain a seat had two additional characteristics in common. They were all located outside Java and their populations were relatively small.

The mechanical effect of the New Order's PR-without-correction electoral system is reflected in Table 2.3. The first column under each party shows the proportion of the total vote the party received, the second column indicates the proportion of total seats the party was allocated, and the third column is the difference between the two or the size and direction of deviation from perfect proportionality. For example, in the 1971 election Golkar received 62.8 percent of the votes, but 65.2 percent of the seats, resulting in a positive deviation of 2.4 percentage points or approximately nine more seats than it would have been allotted had the electoral rules produced perfect proportionality. The two small parties, PPP and PDI, registered a negative deviation in every election (fewer seats than under perfect proportionality), whereas the large party, Golkar, registered a positive deviation in every election.

The foregoing analysis of the New Order electoral system supports several conclusions. In a departure from the electoral system used in 1955, the New Order introduced malapportionment or the overrepresentation of voters residing outside Java. Proportional representation with lists was utilized in both eras, but a change occurred from an open list in 1955 to a closed list during New Order elections. Certain psychological effects expected on theoretical grounds were muted or absent as a result of New Order controls on the number of parties and their ideologies. For example, the comparative theoretical literature hypothesizes that higher district magnitude will result in more competition among parties, partly because leaders of smaller parties will choose not to run candidates in districts where magnitude is low. This phenomenon was precluded from occurring because New Order authorities required each party to run candidates in every electoral district. However, evidence of the ex-

Table 2.3
Overall Deviation from Proportionality, 1971–1997

Year	Golkar			PPP			PDI		
	Votes	Seats	Dev.	Votes	Seats	Dev.	Votes	Seats	Dev.
1971	62.8	65.2	+2.4	27.2	26.8	-0.4	10.0	8.0	-2.0
1977	62.1	64.4	+2.3	29.3	27.5	-1.8	8.6	8.1	-0.5
1982	64.1	67.2	+3.1	28.0	26.1	-1.9	7.9	6.6	-1.3
1987	73.0	74.8	+1.8	16.0	15.3	-0.7	11.0	10.0	-1.0
1992	68.1	70.5	+2.4	17.0	15.5	-1.5	14.9	14.0	-0.9
1997	74.5	76.5	+2.0	22.4	20.9	-1.5	3.1	2.6	-0.5

Source: General Election Institute (LPU).

pected mechanical effects of PR was found to exist. For example, because of the large variation in the number of seats per electoral district (district magnitude) there were marked deviations from proportionality. Both the 1955 system and the New Order system advantaged the larger parties ("large" as measured by votes received). Golkar strategists were able to capitalize on malapportionment, on the deviation from proportionality, and on the lack of corrective mechanism to increase their seats in the legislature.

Finally, although these issues about votes and seats loom large in the comparative theoretical literature, it should be acknowledged that under the New Order's pseudodemocracy the number of seats won by the parties was not very important because it had no effect on the selection of the executive and little effect on government policies. Never during the entire New Order period did members of the legislature propose legislation, nor did they have authority over any "pork barrel" funds. As Mallarangeng points out,

Voting was more a symbolic expression than an opportunity to make strategic choices. . . . The most important aspect of the election as far as voters were concerned was each party's share of the vote. For the supporters of Golkar, meeting the target vote for the district was what counted. . . . For the supporters of the PPP and the PDI, the ultimate challenge was increasing their party's vote share while at the same time decreasing the vote share of Golkar.[44]

FACTORS EXPLAINING VOTERS' CHOICES

The 1955 Election

In his definitive studies of the 1955 election, Herbert Feith's primary concern was describing and explaining the election results (outcome).[45] He dealt with procedural aspects, the electoral institutions, and election administration only in passing. One significant finding was the unexpectedly high voter turnout that characterized all subsequent elections as well. Estimated at about 88 percent, it was higher than the turnout usually achieved in local (village head) elections.[46]

Feith offered a multifaceted explanation of this phenomenon. Many voters were afraid of the wrath of their village head, of other village councilors, and of party leaders who had canvassed for their votes if they did not go to the polls. But more important than fear was the powerful community obligation voters felt. In the years preceding the election, nationalist leaders had put forward two arguments in favor of holding elections. One stressed democratic ideology and national pride, and the other was more pragmatic, emphasizing that elections were necessary for the attainment of political stability. Once they arrived at the polls, the majority of voters had a significant degree of freedom of choice due to "competing obligations" arising from the plurality of parties with organized strength in most villages.[47]

The outcome of the election was inconclusive. About three-quarters of the total vote was divided among four parties, each receiving between 16 and 22 percent of the vote. Ironically the success of one of them, the Indonesian Communist Party (PKI), plus its success in the provincial elections in Java that followed in 1957, deeply alarmed its competitors as well as the army leadership. This fear played a big role in the demise of electoral democracy and its replacement by pseudo-democracy for the next forty-four years, until the 1999 election.

To explain the direction of the vote or reasons for the support of particular parties, Feith and other scholars have emphasized broad sociological characteristics. They argue that the Indonesian electorate was divided into competing social groups based on religion, ethnicity and region, and class and economic interest and that each of these was represented by a particular political party. The major sociocultural divide, which Clifford Geertz labeled *abangan* versus *santri*, referred to an animistic, nationalist, heavily Javanese ethnic orientation on the one hand and a more devout Islamic orientation on the other. Each of these divisions was then overlaid with divisions of somewhat lesser salience. One was class, affecting especially the *abangan* voters, with upper-class *abangan* tending to support the Indonesian National Party (PNI) but the lower class attracted more to the Indonesian Communist Party. Affecting the *santri* persuasion was a division between traditionalists, who tended to vote for the Awakening of the Islamic Teachers (NU), and modernists, who had more affinity with the Consultative Council of Indonesian Muslims (Masjumi). A third division was rooted in location or region. The PNI, PKI, and NU drew support disproportionately from the island of Java, whereas Masjumi was strongest outside of Java.[48] These divisions are revisited in Chapter 6 in the discussion of continuities between the 1955 and 1999 elections and in Chapter 7, where I investigate influences on the direction of the 1999 vote.

New Order Elections

1971 Election

Voter turnout was even higher than in 1955, reaching over 93 percent.[49] The New Order authorities effectively mobilized the bureaucracy and the army behind its new electoral organization, Golkar, which obtained over 60 percent of the vote in the election. Explanations for Golkar's predominance have stressed its identification as the government party, the combination of pressure, threat, and intimidation by the civilian bureaucracy and the military, the increased *abanganization* of the electorate compared to 1955, voters' identification of Golkar with the *abangan* worldview after the physical decimation of the PKI, and the negative vote of persons weary of the ideological conflict and polarization that had previously characterized political life.[50]

The apparent relevance of the *abangan* factor, the slightly stronger showing of NU compared to 1955, and the tendency for the PNI to attract more votes in areas of previous PKI strength suggested the continued relevance of the *abangan–santri* cleavage. The concentration of PNI support in Java indicated that regionalism had not disappeared.

1977 Election

The 1977 election was waged among three contestants, rather than ten as in 1971, because New Order authorities had forced a "simplification" of political life in 1973. There were no surprises, as the election was carefully managed. Golkar retained its predominant position with a proportion of the vote nationwide nearly identical to the previous election. However, the new Islamic Party garnered a larger percentage of the vote than its component parties combined did in 1971, and considerably more than PDI, the other fused party. It won a plurality of votes in two provinces, one of which was the capital, Jakarta. Two scholarly explanations of these results mentioned an anti-Golkar trend and growing Muslim opposition to the New Order.[51] Both pointed to the continued relevance of the *abangan–santri* divide.

1982 Election

The national-level results of the 1982 election were virtually identical with those of 1977. Golkar won 64 percent of the total vote, a majority in twenty-five out of twenty-seven provinces, and a plurality in Jakarta, thus avenging its defeat to PPP there in 1977. It lost only in Aceh, the northernmost province on the Island of Sumatra, obtaining 40 percent of the vote, behind the PPP with 59 percent. Examining the results by region, Suryadinata noted that Golkar's support was somewhat weaker in cities outside Java, and the PPP correspondingly stronger. He attributed this pattern to the stronger *santri* and weaker *abangan* political culture outside Java. He identified five factors to explain Golkar's dominance: (1) relative unity among the New Order elite during the campaign, (2) mobilization of masses by village heads who had been turned into civil servants in 1979, (3) improved civil–military relations resulting from the military's civic action programs, (4) government programs providing credits and subsidies for development projects, and (5) the internal or organizational weaknesses of PPP and PDI.[52]

1987 Election

The 1987 election results revealed "the first significant change in voting pattern established in 1971."[53] "Golkar strengthened its grip on power, the PPP took a nosedive, and the PDI came back to life after repeatedly losing ground in 1977 and 1982."[54] Golkar drew 73 percent of the vote, up nine percentage points, and for the first time won a majority in all provinces of Indonesia. This was especially surprising, considering that the military took a more neutral position and focused more on keeping the peace than on ensuring a Golkar victory. These gains were largely made at the expense of PPP, which had undergone internal turmoil for several years, reflected in the decision of NU in 1984 to renounce organized political activity and formally withdraw from PPP. This turmoil had been fomented by Law no. 3/1985 requiring that all parties adopt *Pancasila* as their sole ideology, thus depriving the previously Islam-based PPP of its unique appeal. The election authorities required PPP to switch its identifying symbol from the Ka'bah of Mecca to a star: "The NU leadership got out the vote for Golkar and in so doing increased its influence in the political system."[55]

Besides the dissension within PPP and the defection of NU, explanations of the outcome stressed Golkar's plentiful campaign war chest and its success in identifying itself with the New Order's development activity.[56] The improved showing of PDI, compared to the 1982 election, was attributed to internal consolidation of the party structure by the new general chairman, Soerjadi, and its appeal among the youth and among disadvantaged and lower-class voters in the cities.[57] Except for this mention of a class-related factor, the influence of sociological factors on voters' choices is thought to have weakened.

1992 Election

The 1992 election campaign took place in an atmosphere of relatively more openness, no doubt reflecting increased self-confidence of New Order authorities, and was marked by greater neutrality on the part of the army and somewhat reduced pressure on local government officials to deliver the vote to Golkar.[58] As a result, Golkar suffered a decline of nearly five percentage points in its share of the vote and PDI gained commensurately, which represented an improvement for PDI of 33 percent over the previous election. PDI seemed to have attracted the bulk of the 17 million new voters, who found PDI a potent symbol of opposition, especially with the active involvement of former President Soekarno's children, Gunther and Megawati, in PDI's campaign.[59] A generational cleavage appeared to have developed, especially in larger urban areas. There was also a striking regional trend: PPP gained ground in Java, but lost in Sumatra, Kalimantan, and Sulawesi. Explanations of this phenomenon mentioned PPP's success in Java in appealing to voters of the traditional *santri* persuasion, winning back many of those who had defected in 1987. But outside Java PDI success was attributed to its ability to attract voters across the *abangan–santri* divide who had become dissatisfied with Golkar, as well as to winning protest votes over issues specific to particular provinces.[60]

1997 Election

Compared to the five previous New Order elections, the last one in 1997 was remarkable in several ways, including "the altered political environment in which the elections took place, the increased intensity of the government victory effort, the changed character of the resistance to government control and manipulation, as well as the greatly increased election-related violence."[61] Although it produced a landslide for Golkar, which chalked up its largest margin ever (over 74 percent of the vote), Schiller argues that far from being a "useful fiction," the election either weakened government legitimacy or demonstrated its declining legitimacy.[62]

The government effort took two forms, not unlike previous elections. On the one hand, Golkar had huge resources available for conducting its campaign. They included "pre-campaign political activity, organizational support from the bureaucracy, biased media coverage, and Golkar's use of 'money politics' to win cadre and voter support." On the other hand, the type of electoral administration used to control the election process and manipulate the election outcome included "biased candidate screening, intimidation of voters, party cadre and election witnesses, campaign restrictions and reported electoral fraud." While most of these practices were evident in previous elections, in this election "both the total Golkar effort and the election manipulation appeared more intense."[63]

As mentioned, PDI had gained support rising from 7.9 percent in 1982 to 11 percent in 1987 and nearly 15 percent in 1992. Megawati was elected to the position of party chair in 1993, but in 1996 the government engineered a party congress to oust her and reinstate the former leader Suryadi. Megawati and her supporters refused to acknowledge the congress's decision and PDI was paralyzed by an internal split. A month later the most serious outbreak of violence in Jakarta in more than two decades occurred when Soerjadi supporters backed by the military and police forcefully evicted Megawati and her supporters, who were refusing to leave PDI's central headquarters. The clash turned into rioting in which at least five people died, over fifty buildings were burned or damaged, and hundreds of vehicles were destroyed. "Soerjadi's attempt to consolidate the party was unsuccessful, and at several events around the country he had to flee from angry crowds of Megawati supporters, who tended to regard him as a government puppet."[64] Megawati announced publicly that she would boycott the balloting and most of her supports either followed her example or voted for PPP. Consequently, the PDI share of the vote plummeted to 3 percent, down from nearly 15 percent in the previous election.

The direction of the vote seems to have been less influenced by sociocultural divisions in the electorate than by the structure of choice that had been engineered by the government:

The state had tremendous capacity to structure the climate for voter choice. Partly, this is due, as Liddle stresses, to the government's development record and to the fears of middle-class, especially Christian, Chinese, and other ethnic minority Indonesians, about the danger of a more open political system. Partly, it was also due to the high personal risk and limited possibility for gain that Indonesians saw from abstaining or from voting against the government party, and the even high risk from publicly urging an election boycott or supporting [another] political party. Indonesians knew that the government would win and that the other parties would not be able to make policies or dispense patronage. Many Indonesians also suspected that their ballots might not be secret and that abstentions or votes against the government might not be counted. Even without intimidation, those less-well-off Indonesians who were dependent on patrons for access to jobs and credit found it easy to listen to state-connected patrons who urged then to vote for the government party. In regions where the economy was backward and autonomous institutions absent, the government's clout was greatest.[65]

Patterns across the Six New Order Elections, 1971 to 1997

Comparing all six New Order elections, the outcomes of the first three elections were strikingly similar compared to the last three (see Table 2.1). Golkar's share of the vote averaged 63 percent in the first three elections and 71.9 percent in the latter three, an increase of more than 14 percent. There was also much more variation in PDI and PPP shares across the last three elections. Most notable was the collapse of PDI in 1997, when its share fell by 80 percent. PPP suffered a 43-percent loss in the 1987 election compared to 1982.

The national-level statistics disguise interesting patterns at the regional level, as shown in Table 2.2. One pattern is that interprovincial variation is much greater than interelection variation (same province across different elections). For example, there is much more variation among provinces in PPP's share of the vote in the 1982 election (ranging from a minimum of 0.2 percent in East Timor to a maximum of 59.1 in Aceh) than in PPP's interelection range in the province of Aceh (31.9 to 59.1). Thus, PPP's interprovincial range of 0.2 to 59.1 (equal to 58.9) is greater than the interelection range of 31.9 to 59.1 (equal to 27.2) for PPP in the province of Aceh.

A second pattern is relative continuity in size of party share across the six elections. For example, Golkar's support was strongest in Southeast Sulawesi in virtually every election, but it was weak or weakest in Aceh. Despite the weaknesses of the parties, owing in large part to their being created and manipulated by New Order authorities, this empirical pattern, together with the first one mentioned, provides a basis for an important inference: Party identification took root and was maintained in the electorate and in the institutions of administratively defined geographical areas during the pseudodemocracy of the New Order.

The only cross-temporal, comparative study of New Order elections was carried out by Andi Mallarangeng. He investigated the influences on the direction of the voting and on the extent of competition in four elections, 1977 to 1992. Using quantitative, socioeconomic, contextual measures at the second administrative level (regency and municipality), he built statistical (path) models for each party in each of the four elections, ranked the independent variables by their strength of influence in each model, and then compared the rankings across all four elections in order to search for patterns and trends over the fifteen-year period.[66] By using the statistical technique of multiple regression, he was able to gauge the independent effects of each variable while controlling for the effects of the others in his model. Mallarangeng's findings can be summarized as follows:

1. The strongest influence in all four elections on the direction of the vote (i.e., relative amount of support for a particular party) was the "party in the electorate," which he measured as support for the same party in the previous election.[67]

2. Urbanization had a positive influence on support for PPP and PDI, but a negative one on Golkar, meaning that PPP and PDI tended to draw more support in cities. Moreover, the influence of urbanization grew stronger over the fifteen-year period.

3. Islamicness exerted a positive influence on support for PPP, but had a weaker and negative influence on support for both Golkar and PDI. However, a weakening trend in the influence of Islamicness was discernable, suggesting a process of secularization or muting of the *abangan–santri* cleavage in the electorate.

4. Industrialization had a slight positive influence on support for both PPP and PDI, but a negative one on support for Golkar. We can infer that, similar to urbanization, industrialization is conducive to political pluralism.

5. Government spending in the years preceding an election tended to build support for Golkar.

6. Higher voter turnout rates tended to benefit Golkar, the government's electoral machine, while having a detrimental effect on both PPP and PDI.

7. Support for Golkar tended to be stronger outside the island of Java, whereas support for PDI and PPP tended to be stronger on Java.

CONCLUSION

The New Order electoral system and underlying political format were responses to an obsession with political order, stability, and economic growth. Ostensibly designed to meet the needs of an emergency situation, they were, nevertheless, maintained for six elections over twenty-seven years. A regime that was born out of a movement for a "total correction" of political life was gradually undermined by its own simplistic and static views of political order and the role of elections. Many among the political elite, increasingly educated and in tune with global influences, demanded more of the elections and used them to expose the weaknesses in the regime and its institutions.

In its report issued prior to the last New Order election in 1997, a team of researchers from the government's own Institute of Sciences (LIPI) identified three "distortions" in conduct of past elections. First, the government was too dominant, which was reflected in the structure of election committees. Every proposal for change in the structure was met with suspicion. Moreover, the government's control tightened over three rounds of revision in the Election Law, beginning in 1975. Second, elections could not be conducted fairly because of the bias, overtly and covertly, on the part of election administrators in favor of one contestant, Golkar. Golkar's six consecutive wins could not be separated from the intense involvement of the government bureaucracy, both in mobilizing voters and in manipulating the election machinery. Government officials at all levels served simultaneously as election officials and Golkar functionaries. Third, nongovernmental political parties with any aspirations that differed from the New Order mainstream were suspected of disloyalty and were psychologically, if not physically, traumatized.[68]

In the pseudodemocracy of the New Order, majoritarian aspects overwhelmed and undermined the consensus aspects, rendering the proportional system of representation ineffectual in bringing about an inclusionary ethos. From this perspective, Golkar's greatest margin ever and PDI's collapse in 1997 were deceptive. Rather than signifying heightened consensus, they were indications of growing majoritarianism and an exclusionary ethos. Despite certain institutions conducive to creating an inclusionary ethos (e.g., a proportional representation electoral system and a large, integrative party such as Golkar), the increasing autocratic behavior of the president and government control and manipulation of the electoral process produced an increasingly exclusionary ethos in a highly heterogeneous society, creating a volatile situation that threatened political stability.

In the six elections conducted by the New Order, the divisions in society based on religion, ethnicity and region, and economic interest (class) that structured partisan alignments and voter choice in the 1955 election were denied or repressed, but their effects did not disappear entirely. For example, PDI drew its support disproportionately from voters of the *abangan* religious orientation and from non-Muslims, whereas PPP vied to represent devout (*santri*) Muslims. But there was a trend of weakening influence of Islamicness on voting choices. Of course, most voters chose the government-backed Golkar, often for other reasons, such as the attraction of developmentalism and political stability, administrative pressures, and/or material benefit. Research across four of the six New Order elections suggested that a new cleavage, no doubt the consequence of the uneven spread of economic development, emerged to influence voting. It was the rural–urban divide and was reflected in stronger support for Golkar in rural areas, whereas PDI and PPP did relatively better in urban areas. Despite the controls on expression of political interests and the blurring of the social bases of the parties, the strong influence of the "party in the electorate" on the direction of the vote suggested that social-based voting was still the predominant influence on voting choices.

NOTES

1. Benedict R. Anderson, "Elections and Participation in Three Southeast Asian Countries," in *The Politics of Elections in Southeast Asia*, ed. R. H. Taylor (New York: Woodrow Wilson Center Press), 26.

2. Ibid, 27.

3. Ibid., 29.

4. Under proportional representation, parties are represented in the legislature in exact (or near exact) proportion to the vote they polled. In an open list system, voters may express a preference for one or more candidates within the party list they voted for.

5. National parties, regional parties, and space for write-ins were combined on each ballot.

6. Alfian, *Hasil Pemilihan Umum 1955* (Djarkarta: LEKNAS, 1971), 4, 9.

7. David Bourchier and John Legge, eds., *Democracy in Indonesia, 1950s and 1990s* (Clayton, Australia: Monash University, Centre of Southeast Asian Studies, 1994).

8. Law (Undang-Undang; U.U.) 15/1969, U.U. 4/1975, U.U. 2/1980, and U.U. 1/1985.

9. The most important are P.P. 35/1985, P.P. 43/1985, P.P. 37/1990, and P.P. 10/1995.

10. See, for example, BPHPR, "White Book on the 1992 General Election in Indonesia," Cornell University publication no. 23, Cornell Modern Indonesia Project, Ithaca, New York, 1994.

11. The legislature had a "reserved domain" or nonelected seats for the military.

12. Masashi Nishihara, *Golkar and the Indonesian Elections of 1971* (Ithaca, N.Y.: Cornell University, Cornell Modern Indonesia Project publication no. 58, 1972), 13. The structure was even more centralized than Nishihara may have realized. Although he correctly described the minister of home affairs as "ex officio" chairman of the LPU and local government chief executives as "ex officio" chairmen of local election committees, he failed to point out that these chief executives were chairmen who doubled as voting members (*ketua merangkap anggota*).

13. Due to its appointed seats in the legislatures, the military faction did not compete as a party in the elections.

14. BPHPR, "White Book."

15. Ibid.

16. Ibid.

17. Alexander Irwan and Edriana, *Pemilu: Pelanggaran Asas LUBER* (Jakarta: Pustaka Sinar Harapan, 1995), 18–22.

18. R. William Liddle, "The 1977 Indonesian Election and New Order Legitimacy," in *Southeast Asian Affairs 1978* (Singapore: Institute for Southeast Asia Studies, 1978).

19. Since the supervisory committees were placed administratively under the election committees at every level, rather than some more autonomous body, they probably had little effect on deviations and fraud that were implicitly or explicitly sanctioned by government officials.

20. *Pancasila* refers to five principles of "Belief in the One and Only God, Just and Civilized Humanity, the Unity of Indonesia, Democracy Guided by Inner Wisdom of Unanimity Arising Out of Deliberations among Representatives, and Social Justice for All the People of Indonesia." See *Indonesia 1990: An Official Handbook* (Jakarta: Department of Information, Republic of Indonesia 1990), 13.

21. Nishihara, *Golkar and the Indonesian Elections of 1971*, 24–28, Tables II, III, and IV.

22. Liddle, "The 1977 Indonesian Elections."

23. See the feature articles in *Editor* (Jakarta), September 14, 1991.

24. Jim Schiller, "The 1997 Indonesian Elections: 'Festival of Democracy' or Costly 'Fiction'?" Occasional paper no. 22, Centre for Asian-Pacific Initiatives, University of Victoria, Canada, 1999, 20.

25. See the feature articles in *Forum Keadilan* (Jakarta), May 28, 1992.

26. Aloysius Arena Ariwibowo, Andi Jauhari, Budi Setiawanto, Hermanus Prihatna, Rudy Moechtar, Sapto Heru Purnomojoyo, and Sri Muryono, *Pemilu 1997* (Jakarta: PT. Penakencana, 1997), 328 (note that I have been unable to locate official figures for the 1992 election).

27. For example, Gordon Hein pronounced it "the most trouble-free election in the country's history." See Gordon R. Hein, "Indonesia in 1992: Electoral Victory and Economic Adjustment for the New Order," *Asian Survey* 33, 2 (1993): 209.

28. Ramlan Surbakti, "Pemilihan Pada Pemilu 1992: Antara Kendala dan Peluang," paper delivered at the Seminar Nasional IX Asosiasi Ilmu Politik Indonesia, Surabaya, August 6–8, 1992.

29. Schiller, "The 1997 Indonesian Elections," 9–16; Stefan Eklof, "The 1997 General Election in Indonesia," *Asian Survey* 37, 12 (1997): 1187–1193; Komite Independen Pemantauan Pemilu (KIPP), *Laporan Hasil Pemantauan Pemilu 1997* (Jakarta: KIPP, 1997).

30. In electoral systems using the PR formula, seats are distributed (as opposed to plurality and majority formulae, which result in the election of individuals). The rationale underpinning all PR systems is to reduce the disparity between a party's share of the vote and its share of the seats. In a closed-list system, a voter expresses preference for a party (not an individual candidate), and seats are distributed in the order specified on the party list.

31. Alfian, *Hasil Pemilihan Umum 1955*.

32. Andre Blais and Louis Massicotte, "Electoral Systems," in *Comparing Democracies*, ed. Lawrence LeDuc, Richard G. Niemi, and Pippa Norris (Thousand Oaks, Calif.: Sage, 1996), 64–68.

33. Afan Gaffar, *Javanese Voters* (Yogyakarta: Gadjah Mada University Press, 1992), 64.

34. See Blais and Massicotte, "Electoral Systems," 57, who note, "There are many different ways of combining these variables, which explains why no PR systems are exactly alike."

35. Andi Alfian Mallarangeng, "Contextual Analysis on Indonesians' Electoral Behavior," Ph.D. diss., Northern Illinois University, 1997, 111; Gaffar, *Javanese Voters*, 89.

36. Mallarangeng, "Contextual Analysis," refers to the same formula as the "simple quota and largest remainders" formula. For an explanation of the formula, see Blais and Massicotte, "Electoral Systems," 60.

37. Gaffar, *Javanese Voters*, 71–81.

38. Alfian, *Hasil Pemilihan Umum 1955*.

39. Gaffar, *Javanese Voters*, 72.

40. Blais and Massicotte, "Electoral Systems," 69–70.

41. Douglas W. Rae, *The Political Consequences of Electoral Law* (New Haven: Yale University Press, 1967); Rein Taagepera and Matthew Soberg Shugart, *Seats and Votes: The Effects and Determinants of Electoral Systems* (New Haven: Yale University Press, 1989).

42. Golkar won a majority in every electoral district in the last three New Order elections (1987 to 1997). It was slightly less dominant in earlier elections, winning a majority in 88 to 93 percent of the districts.

43. Gaffar, *Javanese Voters*, 87. The disadvantage to PDI may have been slightly less than Gaffar writes. An official document from LPU indicates that PDI obtained one or more seats in eleven districts, not nine. See Ariwibowo et al., *Pemilu 1997*, 458.

44. Mallarangeng, "Contextual Analysis," 122–124.

45. Herbert Feith, *The Indonesian Elections of 1955* (Ithaca, N.Y.: Cornell Modern Indonesia Project, 1957) and *The Decline of Constitutional Democracy* (Ithaca, N.Y.: Cornell University Press, 1962).

46. Feith, *The Decline*, 429. About 2 percent were estimated to have died in the twelve to seventeen months between registration and election.

47. Ibid., 430–434.

48. Feith, *The Indonesian Elections*; chapters by Bernhard Dahm, "The Parties, the Masses and the Elections," and A. van Marle, "Indonesian Electoral Geography under Orla and Orba," in *Indonesia after the 1971 Elections*, ed. Oey Hong Lee (London: Oxford University Press, 1974).

49. Voting turnout increased from 87.9 percent to 93.4 percent. See Lembaga Pemilihan Umum, cited in Ariwibowo et al., *Pemilu 1997*, 23.

50. Jamie Mackie, "The Golkar Victory and Party—Aliran Alignments," in Lee, *Indonesia after the 1971 Elections*; R. William Liddle, "Evolution from Above: National Development and Local Leadership," *Journal of Asian Studies* 32 (1973); Ken Ward, *The 1971 Election in Indonesia: An East Java Case Study* (Cheltenham: Monash University Papers on Southeast Asia, 1974); Bernard Dahm and Ernst Utrecht, "The Military and the Elections," in Lee, *Indonesia*; Marle, in Lee, *Indonesia*.

51. Liddle, "The 1977 Indonesian Election"; Ernst Utrecht, "The Military and the 1977 Election," Occasional paper no. 3, James Cook University, Queensland, 1980.

52. Leo Suryadinata, *Political Parties and the 1982 General Election in Indonesia* (Singapore: Institute for Southeast Asian Studies, 1982). For a brief analysis, see Hein, "Indonesia in 1992."

53. R. William Liddle, "Indonesia in 1987: The New Order at the Height of Its Power," *Asian Survey* 28, 2 (1988): 182.

54. Blair A. King, "The 1992 General Election and Indonesia's Political Landscape," *Contemporary Southeast Asia* 14, 2 (1992): 160.

55. Liddle, "Indonesia in 1987," 184.

56. Ibrahim Ambong, "Pemilihan Umum 1987 dan Prospek Golkar," and Syamsuddin Haris, "PPP dan Pemilihan Umum 1987," in *Masa Depan Kehidupan Politik Indonesia*, ed. Alfian and S. Nazaruddin (Jakarta: Rajawali, 1988).

57. M. Riza Sihbudi, "PDI dan Pemilihan Umum 1987," in ibid.

58. Schiller, "The 1997 Indonesian Elections."

59. Suhaini Aznam, "No Surprises," *Far Eastern Economic Review*, 25 June 1992, 15.

60. King, "The 1992 General Election," 168.

61. Schiller, "The 1997 Indonesian Elections," 6.

62. Ibid.

63. Ibid., 9.

64. Eklof, "The 1997 General Election," 1184.

65. Schiller, "The 1997 General Election," 5–6.

66. Mallarangeng, "Contextual Analysis." Mallarangeng excluded the 1971 election because of the different party system in existence at that time and the 1997 election because of its "deviant" characteristics, including the collapse of PDI, apparent higher levels of spoiled ballots, election boycotting, and overt manipulation by the government.

67. A partial exception was found with PDI, as party in the electorate ranked second behind the influence of Java region in the 1982 election and second behind the influence of urbanization in the 1987 election.

68. Syamsuddin Haris, Arbi Sanit, Muhammad As Hikam, Alfitra Salamm, and Heru Cahyono, *Pemilihan Umum di Indonesia* (Jakarta: LIPI, 1997).

CHAPTER 3

The 1999 Electoral Reforms: Debate and Design

Serious discussion of fundamental reforms actually began as preparations were being made for the 1997 election. In early 1995 President Suharto called for research on the electoral system and instructed the Indonesian Institute of Sciences to undertake a study. The study produced a report that was submitted to him about a year later but was never published. As noted in Chapter 2, the report was highly critical and recommended some fundamental changes beginning with the 1997 election that would have had democratizing effects on the New Order.[1] Other studies were undertaken by independent groups.[2] All these studies contributed to the escalating criticism of the electoral system and widening discussion of proposals for reform that occurred in the mid-1990s.

As noted in the previous chapter, the 1997 election was badly flawed, seemingly marked by more violations of election law, fraud, and violence than ever. Apparently there was recognition at high levels in the government even before Suharto resigned that reforms were urgent. In early May 1998 the minister of home affairs, Hartono, appointed a team composed of expert staff and led by Ryaas Rasyid to propose changes in the laws and regulations governing the electoral system. After the transfer of power to Habibie and his announcement that new elections would be held as soon as possible, the new minister of interior, Syarwan Hamid, reaffirmed the appointments and mandated that the team submit proposals within two months. Ryaas Rasyid convened the team, publicly known as the "Team of Seven," for the first time on May 29, 1998.[3]

HABIBIE COMMITS TO
TRANSITION THROUGH REFORM

Almost immediately after he replaced Suharto as president on May 20, 1998, B. J. Habibie set about attempting to distance himself from the previous regime, in which he was key player for twenty years, and to gain legitimacy for his *reformasi* government. He shunned the legitimacy that would have come automatically from declaring himself a nonpartisan caretaker. Refusing to rule himself out as a candidate for "reelection," he sought to build legitimacy instead by announcing that he wanted to carry out new elections as soon as possible under new regulations. He asked the House of Representatives to call a special session of the Assembly later in the year because of its supreme authority to set Broad Guidelines for State Policy (GBHN), including schedules for elections and parameters for a new electoral system. With the economy severely contracted and incidents of social conflict mounting by the day, he had little choice. Virtually the entire political elite agreed on the necessity of a new general election as soon as possible and viewed it as a major, if not the primary, solution to the nation's ills. Until these elections could be held, however, Habibie had to gain approval for his democratic ideas from a House and Assembly whose members were beholden to the old authoritarian regime.

As president and titular head of Golkar, Habibie theoretically controlled both the House and the Assembly. Out of 500 seats in the House, Golkar controlled three-quarters of the elected seats, and the 75 appointed military appointees traditionally supported the government as well. The Assembly was composed of the House plus another 500 appointees of the government. But these representatives were more beholden to Suharto than to Habibie, who apparently felt the need to shore up support for his reformist agenda. Between June and mid-October 1998, 23 percent of the members of the Assembly were replaced.[4]

The process of replacement proceeded in phases and effected Golkar and the military factions the most. First, beginning in early June, calls came from a variety of sources for Assembly members who felt that they owed their selection in any way to corruption or nepotism (*korupsi, kolusi, nepotisme*; KKN) to submit their resignations. Among those responding were relatives of Suharto, a former Golkar secretary general, and the governor of Jambi province and his wife, who publicly resigned "to support the reformation movement and cleansing from the practices of KKN which is desired by the community."

The results of this voluntary phase must have been disappointing, because a couple of weeks later a second phase began as the first wave of recalls and terminations with honor began to be announced. Thirteen members of the Assembly sent a letter to President Habibie calling on him to replace Suharto appointees with "popular leaders and critics whose commitment to *reformasi* was not in doubt," and to consider appointing representatives from underrepresented groups in the community, such as the "handicapped, ethnic minorities, isolated communities, small farmers and laborers, women, pro-*reformasi* youth and students." They warned that failure to do so would "enable anti-*reformasi* and pro status quo forces to consolidate themselves, maintain their dominance, and force their will on the Assembly." They expressed their hope that "if the President can achieve a new breakthrough by reforming the Assembly, at least his image as a member of the status quo will be obliterated."[5] Harmoko, Assembly chairman, announced that these midterm replacements had special meaning because they were being done in the reformation era in order to insure that the Assembly was "truly established in accordance with the reformation spirit."[6]

About the same time, Habibie was consolidating his control over Golkar at a national party congress. One of his ministers, Akbar Tandjung, won a hotly contested vote and secured the leadership in a showdown hailed by many as a "triumph for Indonesia's democratic evolution" and as a step in "remaking the group into an independent political party shorn of organizational links with the bureaucracy and the military."[7] It greatly improved Habibie's ability to set the political agenda and remain in office until after the new election.

His proposals for reform of the electoral system were an important part of his effort to strengthen his legitimacy. These proposals took the form of three draft bills on political parties, the general election, and the composition of the legislative bodies at the national (House and Assembly) and regional (DPRD, DPRD II) levels. They were introduced in the House in August 1998 and eventually passed into law in modified form on January 28, 1999. Discussion in the House was interrupted by the special session of the Assembly in November, which laid down some general policies having the status of constitutional amendments.

Several of the Assembly's decisions dealt with reform of the electoral system and were important because they provided the general policy directions that guided the government and the House in crafting specific and detailed legislation, such as the three political laws. The Assembly codified President Habibie's plan to hold the next election in June 1999 and decreed that the election

- must be conducted by a free and independent (*bebas dan mandiri*) agency composed of representatives of both political parties and the government, and which is responsible to the president.

- must be held on a holiday.
- must be supervised by independent state agency (judiciary), political, and community institutions.
- may be monitored by community and international organizations.[8]

The Assembly also called for clearer separation of powers among the executive, legislative, and judiciary, limited the president and vice president to two terms of office, and revoked a 1978 MPR decision that had been used by Suharto to impose ideological uniformity on the political parties. In perhaps its most controversial decision, the Assembly recognized both elected and appointed (military) seats in the legislatures without specifying the number of seats, but stipulated that the number of appointed seats must be "decreased in stages as regulated by law."[9]

Thus, in accordance with these general policies, three new political laws were drafted by the government's Team of Seven with the objectives of facilitating multiple parties and freer and fairer elections, establishing a (primarily) single-member district-plurality (SMDP) electoral system, distinguishing more clearly the separate powers of the legislative bodies and the executive, empowering the sovereign Assembly (which selects and terminates the president), shifting more power from the executive to the legislatures, preparing the way for greater regional autonomy, and reducing the political role of the military, all democratizing changes intended to move Indonesia from a pseudodemocracy toward an electoral democracy.

This chapter will describe some of the major differences between the newly enacted electoral system and the previous one under Suharto (Chapter 2). Second, it will identify the most important or sensitive changes, tracing the public debate both within and outside the legislature as reported in the largely unfettered media. Particular attention will be given throughout to the bargaining, compromises, and modifications that occurred during the passage of the bill into law. What they tell us about the old and emergent political forces and about Indonesia's political evolution will be ventured in conclusion.

THE OLD AND THE NEW

Freedom to Organize Political Parties

During the last twenty-five years and five general elections (1977 to 1997) of the Suharto regime, only three political organizations (GOLKAR, PPP, and PDI) were recognized by law and allowed to contest the elections. Earlier, in 1973, the authorities required that nine parties fuse into two as part of the effort to simplify political life and weaken the parties. A 1998 Assembly decision and the 1999 law on political parties replaced the obligatory three-political-organization system with a voluntary, multiparty system. Whereas before the *Pancasila* was the sole philosophical basis for every party, under the new law parties were permitted to form around any principle and aspiration, provided it did not conflict with the *Pancasila*.[10] It became apparent that this was a difficult decision for the Suharto-era House, firmly socialized into "sole basis" thinking, because it was one of the four most contentious issues that could not be resolved at the committee level. Resolution eventually was achieved in mid-January through negotiations among the leaders of the four House factions.

Under the new law, obtaining legal recognition as a political party was a relatively easy task, requiring signatures of at least fifty citizens aged twenty-one or over and registration with a court and the Ministry of Justice, which was recorded publicly in the *Lembaran Negara* (government gazette). But only parties that met additional requirements were allowed to compete in the election as an antidote to ethnically and regionally based parties, not to mention fly-by-night ones. To qualify as an election contestant in 1999, a party had to have an organization established in one-third or nine of the provinces and half of the districts or municipalities in each of those provinces (hereafter, "qualified party"). Looking farther ahead to the election in 2004, the law instituted a threshold with delayed effect, requiring that in the 1999 election a party obtain at least 2 percent of the seats in the House or 3 percent of the seats in the regional legislatures, spread over at least half of the provinces and half of the districts. Thus, where previously the number of election contestants was stipulated by law, permitting only three, now they were limited on the basis of insufficient geographical coverage and depth or penetration of their organizations.

The government's initial proposal called for a threshold of 10 percent, but it encountered stiff opposition. The Team of Seven wanted to send a clear message that marginal parties are not considered suitable players in the legislative arena and to provide an incentive for mergers prior to the 2004 election. However, this proposal came under criticism for being higher than in every other country that utilizes a threshold except Turkey.[11] A second criticism was that a party falling under the threshold would be rendered a "lame duck" for five years in the current House, since it would be disqualified from competing in the next election. A representative of a lame duck party would be unable to represent constituents effectively, because he or she would know that he or she must change parties in order to run for reelection. This could also become an inducement for politicians to engage in electoral fraud. A third criticism concerned the seeming contradiction between a threshold requiring that parties prove they have nationwide support and another proposal for switching from the PR system to a constituency-based, district-plurality system. A major justification of the latter was giving greater voice to the "periphery," or facilitating expression of local interests and aspirations.[12]

Under the new law, political parties were recognized as being autonomous, and protected against government interference in their internal affairs. However, parties that violated the law could be frozen or disbanded, no longer by decree of the executive as happen in the past, but only by the Supreme Court after being convicted in a court of law. The old proscription on party organization and activism below the district level, known as the "floating mass," was canceled.[13] Parties were now allowed to organize all the way down to the village level. Canceled also was the much hated practice of screening party nominees by security agencies prior to the start of the election campaign, although certification from the police of noninvolvement in leftist organizations and subversive activity in 1965 was still required. Nor were members of the legislature subject any longer to midterm recall by their party for political reasons, a practice that was frequently used during the New Order to purge members who were too outspoken or independent of party leaders.

The new laws attempted to combat the influence of "money politics" in several ways. Positively, they provided for equal subsidization of qualified parties with public funds. This probably served as an incentive for party formation, especially since the law took effect during a time of severe economic contraction. Beginning with the 2004 election, however, each party passing the threshold is supposed to receive an amount that is a function of the number of votes it received in the previous election.

The law attempted to limit campaign finance by prohibiting individuals from contributing more than about $2,000 (Rp. 15 million) per year to a political party. Corporate entities were limited to about $20,000 (Rp. 150 billion). In order that the voters can know who and what interests support parties, each party was required to submit financial reports audited by public accountants, annually as well as before and after the election, to the General Election Commission (*Komisi Pemilihan Umum*; KPU).

Free and Fair Elections

New Order authorities, in their symbolic allegiance to democracy, had introduced four basic principles to guide the administration of elections in the past: direct voting (as opposed to indirect voting through a representative or intermediary), public participation (by everyone who meets minimal requirements), voluntary participation (without pressure, duress, or force), and secret balloting.[14] These principles were retained, but emphasis was placed on two additional ones: honesty and justice.

Virtually every election under Suharto was marked by widespread allegations and evidence of fraud and complaints that the playing field was tilted heavily in favor of Golkar.[15] Because all civil servants were required to belong to the Indonesian Civil Servants Corps (KORPRI) and the Corps collectively was a "pillar" of Golkar, individual civil servants and government officials were considered members and expected to support Golkar. Party functionaries were drawn heavily from the ranks of retired civil servants and military officers. Elections were under the complete control of the executive branch of government, members of which served concurrently as party officials. The General Election Institute, a structure within the Ministry of Home Affairs, was composed of ministers who actively campaigned for Golkar. Golkar had much greater access than other election contestants to government facilities, including the territorial administration. Government officials campaigned for Golkar under the guise of official duties, one important reason for disproportionately more media coverage of Golkar's campaign activities.

Two changes were intended to combat these problems. Civil servants retained the right to vote, but they no longer were permitted to join political organizations, engage in partisan political activity, run for office, or use government facilities to benefit a certain group. From the date a special government regulation took effect, the membership of civil servants in political parties was automatically terminated. Those who wished to continue as party members or functionaries were given three months to request permission from their immediate superiors. If granted, they were given a one-year leave of absence from the civil service and one year of severance pay. Anyone failing to request permission for continuing with party activity was to be dishonorably discharged from the civil service. This restriction on the political rights of civil servants was one of the most contentious issues in the reforms and will be discussed at greater length later. Second, the administration of the elections was placed under a powerful and semiindependent election commission. According to the new law, the commission worked in a "free and autonomous" manner and selected its leaders in democratic fashion from among its members. Among the commission's major duties were planning and preparing for elections, appointing and supervising temporary election implementing committees (explained shortly), determining the number of seats in legislatures at three levels to be decided by the election, determining the number of seats won

by each party, collecting and systematizing material and data on results of the election, and evaluating the general election system. The
commission was assisted by a permanent secretariat, a government
agency whose top two positions must be filled by career civil servants, not political appointees.

The government initially proposed that the commission be composed of representatives of the government, qualified parties, and
community members. In the legislative debate, the parties rejected
community members as a redundancy, arguing that the community
was sufficiently represented by the parties. But composing the commission of government and party representatives in equal numbers
ran into difficulty as well. Spokespersons for both old (PPP and PDI)
and new parties expressed concern that the government could domi-
nate the commission if the government representatives acted as a
block with the support of at least one party (e.g., Golkar). Eventually
agreement was reached on equal numbers of representatives of government, appointed by the president, and representatives of qualified political parties, all of whom serve five-year terms. High-level
government executives (i.e., directors general and above) were prohibited from serving as government representatives on the commission. But fears of government domination continued to be expressed
until the commission was seated and a party representative, Rudini
(a retired general and former minister of home affairs), was elected
to chair the commission.

To assist the election commission with the administration of an
election, the structure of temporary committees at five levels, which
paralleled and interfaced with the system of territorial administration
under the Department of Home Affairs, was retained (see Chapter 2).[16]
But under the new law this committee structure was somewhat less
centralized and less under the control of government executives than
in the past. Rather than each committee in this vast structure being
led by a government official, the new law provided for selection of
leaders in democratic fashion from among the committee members,
who consisted both of representatives of qualified parties and of the
government in unspecified proportions, except at the village level.
Each committee was established by the committee at the next higher
administrative level, but the relationship of higher- to lower-level
committees was technical and functional, not one of administrative
command. Each of the committees at the top four levels were to be
assisted by a secretariat staffed by government employees appointed
by the government executive at the same level.

The changes were more dramatic at the village and polling-station
levels, where in the past the majority of election regulation violations had occurred (see Chapter 2). The old voter registration com-

mittees (*pantarlih*), which were entirely composed of village official and partisan toward Golkar, were abolished. Second, the voting
implementation groups (KPPS) were to be composed entirely of representatives of parties. Third, leadership of the village implementation committees (PPS), although composed of representatives of both
parties and the local government, was no longer automatically vested
in local officials; rather, the committees were to pick their leaders
democratically.

The provisions for security and supervision were of particular
interest because of their potential role in handling irregularities and
minimizing fraud. Every election contestant had the right to del-
egate one person to witness the preparation, voting, and counting at
every polling station. The new law specifically invited domestic and
international election observers. At the central, provincial, and district levels the new law retained the network of supervisory committees (*panwas*), but placed them under the leadership of a judge
instead of a public prosecutor (member of the executive branch).
The other members differed as well, drawn neither from the government nor parties, but from the community and from higher education.[17] At the subdistrict level the committees were composed of only
representatives of the community and higher education. Whereas in
the past these committees were headed by members of the executive
branch (i.e., the attorney general or chief public prosecutor) and the
rules governing their work stipulated by the minister of home affairs, the new law placed them under the (semiautonomous) judiciary at each level and the Supreme Court was given the task of
regulating their work and relationships.

Real Legislatures

The reforms were also intended to enhance the representativeness, power, and accountability of the national and regional legislatures. Multiple parties were expected to better represent Indonesia's
diversity and to articulate a wider spectrum of ideologies and policy
platforms. Second, elected members should be more representative
and accountable than appointed ones. At the central-government
level the proportion of elected representatives in the House increased
from 85 percent to 92 percent. The sovereign Assembly was downsized from 1,000 to 695 (31 percent) and the proportion of directly
(66 percent) or indirectly (29 percent) elected representatives more
than doubled, from 43 percent to 95 percent.[18]

The Team of Seven initially proposed a radical change from a proportional to a mixed, predominately single-member district-plurality
system, which was intended to ensure that representatives would

be more responsive to the needs of the communities that elected them. This proposal was rejected. Adopted instead was a unique version of proportional representation by province combined with some elements of a district system, which the media labeled "PR Plus." Similar to the system used in previous elections in Indonesia, separate elections in effect were held in each of the twenty-seven provinces and seats were allocated to parties in proportion to their overall votes in each province. But rather than assigning seats to particular candidates based on parties' provincial vote totals and candidate priorities stated in party lists as in previous elections, candidates were supposed to be assigned to seats on the basis of how well the parties performed at the district level.[19] This issue regarding type of electoral system was one of the three most contentious issues in the political reforms and will be discussed at greater length later.

In the reformers' initial proposals, appointed representatives from the military were dropped 27 percent, from 75 to 55 seats (or from 15 percent of the old 500-member House to 10 percent of a new 550-member House). In the law that finally passed, however, military representation was cut more severely, by 49 percent, to 38 seats (about 8 percent of the total House, which was kept at 500 seats). Military representation has decreased by 50 percent at regional levels as well, dropping from 20 to 10 percent in the regional legislatures (DPRD and DPRD-II). This was another contentious issue to which I will return shortly. The reformers' proposal for an Assembly downsized 30 percent from 1,000 to 700 was left standing. In addition to the 500 members of the House, the new law called for 135 regional representatives (*utusan daerah*) and 65 group representatives (*utusan golongan*). Each of the twenty-seven regional legislatures elected five regional representatives, in contrast to the old system, under which these positions were appointed by the executive. With regard to the (appointed) group representatives, the law considered the 1999 election to be a transitional phase, in which the election commission was given the responsibility of determining which groups in society (based on gender, religion, function or occupation, etc.) were underrepresented, which organization(s) were legitimate representatives of these groups' interests, and how many representatives each organization was entitled to. In future elections, however, these determinations were to be the responsibility of the (outgoing) House. Unlike the old system of appointment by the executive, how these group representatives are selected will be an internal matter for the organizations concerned.

A number of changes were designed to empower the Assembly and the legislatures. The new law provided for greater separation of powers between the executive and the legislature. Since members of the House and regional legislatures represent political parties (except for appointees from the military) and civil servants are no longer allowed to serve as party representatives, members of the legislatures cannot serve concurrently as government officials.[20] Whereas previously the Assembly (which elects the president) and the House had joint or shared leaders, now they were separated, making it more difficult for the executive to control both of them. The regional legislatures were no longer component parts of regional governments, but rather friendly coequals of regional governments.

Second, the legislatures were given explicit powers they never had during Suharto's rule. The Assembly is no longer limited to quinquennial meetings and it is equipped with a permanent working body and secretariat.[21] The House of Representatives's capabilities were increased with additional standing commissions and new standing subcommissions.[22] In order to carry out its duties, the new law gives the House the rights to

1. Request information from the president.
2. Conduct investigations.
3. Revise draft or proposed laws.
4. Submit statements of opinion.
5. Submit draft or proposed laws.
6. Nominate a certain person for a particular position if permitted by law.
7. Determine the DPR's budget.

With new subpoena powers, the legislatures could require any state official, government official, or citizen to supply information.[23] Failure to respond was made punishable by a maximum sentence of one year in jail. Within months, the House began to exercise its new subpoena powers. For example, President Habibie was called to give testimony regarding his dramatic change in policy toward East Timor and again on his efforts to resolve the Bank Bali scandal. Perhaps most important, the law protected individual members of the Assembly and the legislatures from prosecution or recall for statements made in meetings related to their work as a member of one of these bodies.

Mechanisms to improve accountability were found in each of the three new political laws. As previously mentioned, a citizen should be able to learn about the contributors and financiers of any political party and legislative candidate. Parties are required to keep records of contributors and amounts contributed that are open to auditing by public accountants and must be submitted to the Supreme Court annually, as well as fifteen days before and thirty days after an election. Campaign finance is subject to separate record-keeping, but similar reporting and auditing requirements. Parties are prohibited from establishing commercial enterprises or holding shares in such. Stiff penalties are specified for violation of any of these regulations.[24] Although implementation of these provisions in the 1999 election left much to be desired, they did set higher goals and standards of accountability than ever before.

Also, many more citizens should be personally acquainted with a legislative representative. In formulating their list of candidates for the legislatures, central party leaders were obliged to take into consideration written proposals of local (i.e., district level) party leaders. They were also required to indicate on the (provincial) party list not only the name of each candidate, but also the locality from which he or she was nominated. Moreover, which candidates actually filled the seats earned by the parties on a provincial basis depended on how the parties performed at the local level. In these two ways the new law made the fortunes of a party somewhat more dependent on electoral support for their specific candidate at the local level.

Continuities in Electoral System Design

The laws that emerged from the policy process in the House maintained continuity with the previous New Order electoral system in several respects not yet mentioned. The number of electoral districts remained the same and no changes were made in the method of determining district magnitude (allocation of seats to districts), so districts outside the island of Java continued to be overrepresented. It is surprising how little attention was given to this issue, but this is understandable in light of rising levels of ethnic conflict and separatism in the regions. Apparently an unspoken consensus reigned against diluting the representation of provinces outside Java. The method of distributing seats to parties likewise remained the same, leaving the problem of deviation from proportionality unaddressed.

DEBATE ON MOST SENSITIVE ISSUES

Appointed Military Representatives (Reserved Domain)

The sociopolitical role of the Indonesian military (ABRI) has been one of the most frequently discussed topics in the literature on Indonesian politics since the military came to power in 1966. Suffice it to note here that civilianization of the government and subordination of the military to civilian authority was a key demand of the reformation movement. In 1998 electoral reform was under consideration at a time when expressions of popular anger against the military were a daily occurrence, when the reputation of the military was at an all-time low, and when the legitimacy of the military's sociopolitical role seemed weaker than at any time in recent memory. Military leaders were actively engaged in damage control, having publicly recognized the need for a redefinition of the military's dual function (*dwi fungsi*) doctrine.[25] In this context, military leaders agreed with a decrease in their representation in the Assembly and legislatures, as noted earlier. The debate was revealing of the diversity and strength of the feelings on this issue.

Initially, the government proposed reducing the size of the Assembly from 1,000 to 700 seats and increasing the seats in the legislature by 10 percent, bringing the total to 550, and a 10-percent quota on appointed seats reserved for the military (reserved domain) in the legislatures at all three levels. This represented a reduction in the proportion of total seats from 15 to 10 percent and in the number of seats from 75 to 55. These dimensions of the reserved domain were determined in negotiations between the government and the military and were based on a combination of political and economic criteria.[26]

Immediately after it was announced publicly, this plan to preserve a reserved domain for the military came under attack. Leading intellectuals criticized the plan on logical grounds. They pointed out the contradiction between reserved domains. in the legislatures and the military's doctrine of neutrality or standing above the political fray. They also noted the inequality or malapportionment resultant from giving less than a half million military personnel representation in the legislature equivalent to 33 million civilians.[27] A member of the Team of Seven conceded the points, but defended the plan on political grounds, noting that any proposal had to pass muster in a status quo–oriented (New Order) legislature. Too radical a change would negatively affect prospects for passage of other reform proposals. He invited the legislature to achieve a new consensus on fewer seats or on abolishing them altogether.[28]

Within the legislature, the Development Unity (PPP) faction took the most radical position, opposing military representation of any kind based on separation of powers (as part of the executive branch, the military does not belong in the legislative branch). Moreover, Article 27 of the Constitution reads, "All citizens have the same status before the law and government and are obliged to revere this law and this government with no exception."[29]

But a few weeks later, in mid-November, the sovereign Assembly decreed that "the appointment of members of the armed forces in the legislatures will be done reducing the total in stages as subsequently regulated by law."[30] Taking this decision as indicative of a "national consensus" in favor of a continuing but reduced presence of the military in the legislatures, the Development Unity faction modified its position, saying they would support the allocation of 2 percent of the seats in the legislatures. At the national level, this meant ten seats in the House.

Meanwhile, student demonstrations continued unabated, usually focused on two issues: removing the military appointees completely from the legislative assemblies and bringing Suharto and his family to justice for corruption. It appeared the role of the military was an even larger issue on the streets outside than within the legislature. Feeling the pressure from the students and seeking to reinvent themselves politically, Golkar began outbidding the government, to the chagrin of the military, which in the past had faithfully backed Golkar. Golkar proposed elimination of two-thirds of the current military seats in the House, dropping the number from seventy-five to twenty-five. Yet another variant came from two of the largest new parties, PAN and PKB, which proposed fifteen nonvoting seats.

When the debate resumed in January, it seemed that the political position of the military had continued to erode. The military faction in the House said they would no longer take a position on the matter, but would leave it entirely up to the other factions.[31] Also, interest seemed to have grown in finding some more objective formula to decide the issue. For example, if the new House was going to be equipped with forty standing subcommissions, would there not be a corresponding need for forty military representatives, one for each subcommission? In the end, as the negotiations approached the pre-established deadline of January 28, a more symbolic formula won the day and military representation was cut by half, from seventy-five to thirty-eight seats in the legislature and from 20 percent to 10 percent of the seats in the regional legislatures.

Proportional versus District-Plurality Electoral Systems

Perhaps the most dramatic change from the New Order electoral system was the proposal for a mixed, predominately district-plurality electoral system in which 76 percent of the seats in the legislature would have been allocated in single-seat districts according to the plurality principle and the remaining 24 percent distributed according to the current procedures of proportional representation. By proposing a combination, "district-plus" system, the Team of Seven hoped to make legislative members more accountable to geographical constituencies and less beholden to party leaders, while retaining an element of PR as a corrective against loss of representation suffered especially by small or minorities parties, which occurs in a pure, winner-take-all system. Months before the government's proposals were publicly announced, a lively debate on the pros and cons of the various types of electoral systems was carried out at seminars and in the media among intellectuals. This issue clearly dominated the debate on electoral reform carried on in the media.

Within a month after the government's district-plus proposal was conveyed to the legislature it became clear that it was in serious trouble. It was initially attacked, less in terms of the contending, underlying values (e.g., accountability versus representativeness) than in terms of its practicality. How could such a major departure from past practice be prepared and implemented by the government in the short time remaining to the election?[32] From the government reformers' point of view, this was a ruse; the real issue was that party leaders feared the loss of power that would occur if they could no longer determine the order of candidates in closed party lists. Meeting in mid-November, the Assembly's decision on the general election did not mention the issue. By the end of November, leaders of all four factions had decided against it, and for the first time in living memory the military faction sided with the parties against the government.[33]

But the issue remained on the table in modified form. Golkar, seeing an opportunity to don the *reformasi* mantel and supported by the military faction, proposed a new "variant" of PR that would use smaller electoral districts in order to improve the accountability of legislative members to voters. That is, instead of electoral districts being coterminous with the provinces, as they were during the New Order, Golkar and the military proposed using the over ten times more numerous second-level administrative units (regencies and municipalities), as in the government's district-plus proposal that had been rejected.

All factions had agreed to retain the proportional system, but they disagreed on the version (*varian sistem proporsional*), which concerned the size of the electoral districts. Golkar, borrowing an idea from the initial reform proposals, wanted to decrease the size of electoral districts (at which votes are translated into seats), making them coterminous with second-level (regency and municipality) rather than first-level (province) regional administrative territories. The small parties, PPP and PDI, wanted to retain the provincial districts, contending that they and other small parties would be disadvantaged by smaller electoral districts. Too many of the votes for their parties would be lost in the process of converting votes to seats and, because of its grip on the civil service, Golkar's dominance over local politics would be reinforced, tilting the playing field even more in favor of Golkar. In this way the issue of the version of proportional representation became linked with the issue of civil servants' involvement in partisan political activity.

One of the major criticisms of the government's proposal, coming from PPP and PDI factions and especially the new parties being organized outside the legislature, was that smaller (district) electoral districts would carry a greater risk of becoming political fiefdoms through reinforcement of existing local power structures. During the New Order most of these structures were dominated by government bureaucrats who were members of Golkar, which is evident from election results, especially outside Java and in large metropolitan areas. Thus, the critics argued, the proposed electoral system would reinforce Golkar predominance. Their suspicion was strengthened by state secretary and recently elected Golkar chairman Akbar Tandjung's expressed commitment to preserve the ruling party's close links to the government bureaucracy. But during the discussion of the district-plus proposal the Team of Seven rejected this criticism, pointing to their accompanying proposal for a prohibition on civil servants and members of the military joining parties and running for elected office. Reportedly, President Habibie was adamantly in favor of this prohibition.

The same parties raised a similar objection to the variant of PR advocated by Golkar with support from the military. They calculated that out of a total of 310 districts in Indonesia, 260 (84 percent) were too small in population to qualify for more than one seat in the legislature. Hence, the outcome would likely mirror the outcome of the government's district-plus system; in the vast majority of districts the seats would be won by the party achieving a mere plurality of votes. In the 1997 election the party winning a plurality everywhere was Golkar.[34] A related criticism was that a district-plurality system would be more susceptible to "money politics" and buying of votes, perhaps because in smaller electoral districts politicians' own funds can have greater impact. To address this criticism the bills proposed by the government's team included regulations on political finance that were much more comprehensive than those finally passed into law, as discussed earlier.

Another criticism was that the zero-sum, "winner take all" character of a district-plurality electoral system would be foreign to the history and traditions of Indonesia. As noted in Chapter 2, electoral systems utilized in both the late colonial and early republican periods were based on the principle of proportionality and were similar to the electoral system used in the Netherlands. The New Order likewise utilized a variant of PR; that is, representatives were chosen in multiple-member electoral districts (provinces), with voters choosing between parties rather than candidates. Because in this type of electoral system the seats awarded each party in the legislature are closely proportional to the votes it obtained nationwide, fewer votes are "wasted" and hence there is less likelihood of anyone feeling unrepresented. The reformers denied that the plurality and winner-take-all principles were foreign to Indonesia, citing the procedures for electing village heads in use for nearly two decades: If there is a sole candidate, an empty box must be provided for dissenting votes, and the empty box occasionally wins!

Yet another criticism was that the mixed district-plus system, with only 24-percent proportional representation nonconstituency seats, would be insufficiently compensatory and thus would not sufficiently correct the disproportionality arising from what was predominately a plurality system. If there were more than two parties or if a party's support was geographically concentrated, a mixed system relying so heavily (76 percent) on the plurality principle would produce outcomes of questionable legitimacy because of the disproportionality between party support (votes) and representation in the legislature (seats). The reformers responded by stressing that they were not proposing a system de novo; rather, they were working within certain conventions or were honoring some principles of the old electoral system. One of these was that every regency and city should have a minimum of one representative (seat), regardless of population size. A second principle was geographical balance or an equal number of seats between Java and Bali on the one hand and the other islands on the other.[35]

Political Rights of Civil Servants

The political bills submitted to the House of Representatives by Habibie's reform team contained a prohibition on civil servants being members, functionaries, or candidates of political parties. It was intended to correct what was perceived as a major problem in the New Order electoral system; namely, too little separation of powers, with personnel of the executive branch constantly taking sides and utilizing their positions to benefit Golkar. An estimated 10,000 Golkar officials were threatened with a choice: Resign from the party or resign from the civil service. With Golkar in control of 77 percent of the House, this proved to be the most intractable issue in the entire package of three reform bills. More than any other, this issue opened a fissure between Habibie's government and Golkar.

Months before the bill was introduced, differences of opinion on the issue were apparent at Golkar's extraordinary national congress held in July 1998. Akbar Tandjung, state secretary (minister) in Habibie's cabinet and representative of a stream within Golkar pushing to modernize the party and detach its links with the military, was elected general chairman over a retired general. New bylaws were passed that explicitly severed the relationship between the party and the "pillars" of the past, the military and the bureaucracy.[36] They reflected President Habibie's position that civil servants should not join parties or run for office.[37] Throughout the protracted struggle on this issue over the next several months he was unwavering in his position. He explicitly ordered the entire state apparatus, both civilian and military, directly and indirectly through the minister of home affairs and through the commander of the military, to remain neutral and nonpartisan in the coming election.[38]

As incoming general chairman of the party concerned with rebuilding the party and keeping it strong in a new, competitive political environment, Akbar Tandjung wanted to preserve the ruling party's close links to the government bureaucracy. At a meeting with reporters following the conference, Akbar said that new Golkar functionaries who also held structural positions in the bureaucracy (i.e., those carrying administrative authority) would be asked to choose one or the other, but he made no mention of the much larger number not holding structural positions. There was also another important exception: "This directive does not apply to ministers in the government, because they hold political positions."[39]

Following the congress, anti-Golkar sentiment was abundant. A group of academics and intellectuals concluded a two-day national dialogue with a statement warning that the government's forthcoming bills governing political parties and the election carried a "large social risk because they benefit Golkar which still owns a political machine throughout Indonesia."[40]

The leaders of eleven small parties met and announced they were establishing a party forum for purposes of "preventing Golkar from winning the coming election."[41] A special investigative report on the occasion of the twenty-seventh anniversary of the founding of the civil servants association, KORPRI, noted that despite the prohibition in the new bill on civil servants joining or serving as functionaries of political parties and Habibie's strong support for it, Golkar leaders remained silent, stubbornly sticking to their view that civil servants should express their political aspirations through Golkar.[42]

Within the legislature the debate continued in a special committee over the proposed clause, "Civil servants and members of the armed forces do not use their right to be elected." The Golkar faction argued that this wording infringed the rights of civil servants and offered less precise, substitute wording: "Civil servants can use their right of choice" (*hak pilihnya*). The military faction weighed in indirectly on behalf of Golkar by questioning the inequity in the proposed prohibition in light of the compensation given the military with a block of appointed seats. Should civil servants not be entitled to similar compensation? Both of the small parties, PPP and PDI, supported the government's proposed prohibition.[43]

Government spokesperson Ryaas Rasyid offered a compromise. A party may nominate a civil servant or soldier, provided he or she is terminated (with honor) from the civil service or military without right to a pension. But Golkar demurred, proposing instead that a civil servant or military nominee be given temporary leave or suspension rather than termination. PPP and PDI supported termination, but with pension. Speaking to the press after a committee discussion, Ryaas said the government was willing to compromise with Golkar, agreeing that civil servants take leave while retaining their civil servant status provided they relinquish their position and salary. He reiterated the government's position that neutrality of civil servants was needed to combat suspicion in some quarters that the new political bills served Golkar's interests: "A politically neutral bureaucracy more easily gives preference to the people's interest."[44]

After the beginning of the year, *reformasi* exponents outside the House intensified their pressure. Two major new parties issued a joint statement of concern over negotiations among status-quo-oriented groups to surmount the deadlock in the special committee over four unresolved issues, of which the political rights of civil servants and the military was one. They indicated their support for the government's proposal for neutralizing the civil service, as did the several student groups who staged demonstrations at the House building.[45]

Upon resumption of the special committee discussions, the PPP faction and the Golkar faction came immediately at loggerheads on the rights of civil servants and the variant of proportional representation (provincial versus district electoral districts). The two issues had become linked as the pressure mounted to achieve an agreement. Golkar threatened to settle the dispute by majority vote, which it clearly had the votes to win. PPP responded with its own threat of a walkout, confronting the legislature with the specter of producing a bill of questionable legitimacy.

As a way out, Golkar proposed that the articles in the two bills (on political parties and elections) pertaining to civil servants be omitted and relegated to a separate, comprehensive bill on the civil service. Initially, all the factions agreed until the realization began to spread that Golkar's gambit was premised on the assumption that such a comprehensive bill could not be processed through the normal legislative procedures in time for the election on June 7, 1999. In the meantime, the status quo would be maintained de facto, with civil servants free to join parties and become legislative candidates.[46]

Deadlock ensued, until the government offered to issue a presidential decision (*keputusan presiden*) in time to regulate civil servants' political activity in the coming election. The PPP faction agreed on condition that such a decision be issued by January 28 in order to ensure that civil servants were neutralized during the coming election campaign. But Golkar demurred, claiming a matter as important as abridging the "basic human rights" of civil servants to gather and organize politically should be regulated only through state law (*undang-undang*). If there was suspicion about civil servants improperly using state facilities to benefit one election contestant, Golkar argued, this problem should be handled through issuance of a presidential decision on use of state facilities, not by depriving civil servants of the rights enjoyed by other citizens.[47]

With the working committee deadlocked, voting ruled out, and the pressure of time mounting, about twenty leaders of the four legislative factions began meeting behind closed doors.[48] After several meetings that reportedly involved intense discussions and lobbying but never voting, they forged a series of compromises only two days before the January 28 deadline. The compromise involved deleting the problematic articles from the two bills and issuing simultaneously a special government regulation (*peraturan pemerintah*) on civil servants who join political parties.[49] Here the policy process becomes obscure to outside observers. The regulation was issued on January 26, the very same day that the compromise was reached, but it would become apparent two days later that either the agreement had been based on misunderstandings or that some parties to the agreement had changed their minds.[50]

The agreement almost unraveled just hours before the ratification of the entire package of political bills on January 28. The PPP faction interrupted a final hearing to ask for clarification on what they said were four substantive deviations in the government regulation from the compromise reached two days earlier. They threatened to walk out on the final ratification meeting for all three political bills unless revisions were made in the regulation so that it more faithfully reflected the earlier agreement.[51] Confronted with this ultimatum and counterthreats from Golkar, intense negotiations brokered by the government ensued among the factions. These resulted in an agreement on a tighter regulation that was issued the following day.[52] The final obstacle having been surmounted, the entire package of three political bills was ratified a few hours later.[53]

CONCLUSION

In Indonesia's transition from pseudodemocracy toward electoral democracy, the 1999 general election has been heralded as "the turning point or defining moment of the transition."[54] It took place under rules and procedures stipulated in three political laws passed earlier that year. The concern of this chapter has been to describe these laws and institutions, to explain how they differed from the previous ones that governed elections during Suharto's New Order, and to illumine the debates and politics behind their formulation and enactment (i.e., the policy process). The analysis provided lots of evidence of the "reform" mode of transition mentioned in Chapter 1. On the one hand, we noticed numerous examples of continuity with the electoral system of the previous regime. They included retention of closed-list PR and the formula for converting votes into seats, the multilevel network of temporary implementing and supervisory committees paralleling and interacting with the system of territorial administration, and reserved (downsized) domain for the military. On the other hand, we found many democratizing changes, several with far-reaching effects, such as multipartyism (in election contestants and in composition of election committees), independent election administration, neutralization of the bureaucracy that had been a pillar of Golkar support, and downsizing the Assembly while increasing the number and proportion of elected voices (seats).

In designing the new electoral system there was a surprising amount of genuine give and take and uncertainty about eventual outcomes. Taking place in a very dynamic political environment, the policy process in the House of Representatives became more important than it had been since the mid-1950s. The outcomes (laws) differed significantly from the bills introduced by the government. Examples include proportional representation when the government had proposed a mostly district-plurality system, and a decrease in the reserved domain for the military in the House from fifty-five to thirty-eight. No longer did the legislature function as a rubber stamp for executive decisions as it had during the New Order. And no longer did the government, Golkar, and the military form a united front against PPP and PDI. Examples here include the different positions on the district-plurality system (supported by the government but not by Golkar and the military), on the size of the reserved domain (Golkar wanted it smaller than the government and the military), and above all on the political status of civil servants (government and military against Golkar). There was no clear winner and all sides found compromise a necessity.

Outside the House of Representatives, dissatisfaction was expressed virtually everywhere by exponents of *reformasi*, including new parties, NGOs, and student groups. They were particularly aggrieved at the continuation, albeit downsized, of the reserved domain for the military and at the government's involvement in the new general election commission.[55] "A half-hearted reformation" (*reformasi setengah hati*) was a favorite epithet used in the press to describe the outcome.

The reforms owed much to the leadership of President Habibie and the deft and effective management of the policy process by the government team. Sensing accurately that his political future depended heavily on reform of the electoral system and carrying out an election as soon as possible, Habibie assembled a small group of skilled and politically astute assistants (Team of Seven), accepted their design and proposal, and then supported them throughout the legislative process. They accurately sensed that Golkar, severely weakened because of its identification with the New Order, could be successfully confronted on the issue of the political rights of civil servants. A couple of months before the bills were introduced in the House, Habibie and his close advisors (e.g., General Wiranto) orchestrated the takeover of Golkar's leadership by the reformist faction led by Akbar Tandjung and the resignation or recall of nearly 20 percent of the Assembly, removing those closest to Suharto and those likely to have been most recalcitrant toward reforms.[56] When this more receptive Assembly met in November, it threw its weight behind most of the reform proposals, such as the schedule for the election and the smaller reserved domain for the military. Then the government team effectively used this date and the threat of being forced to postpone the election to pressure the House into concluding its deliberations and ratifying the new electoral system by the government-designated deadline.

Golkar had the most to lose and, indeed, emerged from the process politically weaker than it went in. Although they controlled three-fourths of the votes in the House and occasionally threatened to call a vote, not a single issue was put to a vote. Majority rule was clearly trumped by small-party threats to walk out, which would have delegitimized the results. Despite its apparent victory in getting restrictions on the political rights of civil servants stricken from the law and relegated to a government regulation, the restriction survived nonetheless. Now, with the benefit of hindsight after Golkar's dramatic defeat in the election, it may have had the most far-reaching effect of all the changes. Apparently it dealt a mortal blow to "the culture of monoloyalty" that was so important to the maintenance of the New Order. Golkar's intransigence on the issue now appears in a more rational light.

Not only was majority rule laid aside in the policy process, the principle of one person–one vote was inoperative as well. Party discipline reigned supreme, as it had throughout the New Order. Reflecting on his experience, Andi Mallarengang, a member of the Team of Seven, wrote,

In general, the process was colored by party interest, which sometimes conflicted with the wishes of the society and with sound thinking. Decisions always awaited the word from party leaders. The process of assigning legislators occurred without regard for their autonomy as representatives of the people. Why? Because every time there was a debate, members of the House were not courageous to voice their own opinions, not to mention the aspirations of the people who elected them. They waited on the collective view of the party faction. In crucial matters, factions themselves lacked the courage to voice their collective opinion and awaited instructions from party leaders. . . . In the crucial situations, frequently the legislative session was postponed, because factions wanted to caucus first with their party. Finally, in the final moments, the party executives lobbied each other and the legislative decisions were made outside the legislature—by party executives who were not members of the House. This is what happened, extra-parliamentary decisions.[57]

We have noticed that the reformed electoral system was designed hurriedly and that the new laws were the result of a flurry of last-minute compromises. As a result, the laws provided only general principles; details about how exactly the system would work remained to be specified. So even though the focus of the next chapter is on implementation, analysis of the debate and design must be continued as well.

NOTES

1. A decrease in military representation in the DPR from 100 to 75 seats and a corresponding increase in elected seats in 1997 was in line with the recommendations of the study, although there is difference of opinion about the influence of the study on that decision. Compare Stefan Eklof, "The 1997 General Election in Indonesia," *Asian Survey* 37, 12 (1997): 1182 and Syamsuddin Haris, Arbi Sanit, Muhammad AS Hikam, Alfitra Salamm, and Heru Cahyono, *Pemilihan Umum di Indonesia* (Jakarta: LIPI, 1997), 1.

2. For example, Aloysius Arena Ariwibowo, Andi Jauhari, Budi Setiawanto, Hermanus Prihatna, Rudy Moechtar, Sapto Heru Purnomojoyo, and Sri Muryono, *Mendemokratiskan Pemilu* (Jakarta: Lembaga Studi dan Advokasi Masyarakat [ELSAM], 1996).

3. Andi Mallarangeng, team member, interview with author, February 21, 1999.

4. They consisted of 189 appointed members of the Assembly and 40 elected members who served in both the House and the Assembly. *Suara Pembaruan*, October 14, 1998.

5. *Suara Pembaruan*, June 26, 1998.

6. *Suara Pembaruan*, July 2, 1998; *Kompas On-Line*, July 2, 1998.

7. *The Straits Times*, July 12, 1998.

8. Ketetapan Majelis Permusyawaratan Rakyat Republik Indonesia (MPR RI), Nomor X/MPR/1998.

9. Ketetapan MPR RI Nomor XIV/MPR/1998.

10. However, the prohibition on communist parties remained in place and separatist parties were likewise outlawed. Former members of PKI and its affiliated mass organizations continued to be disenfranchised.

11. Andre Blais and Louis Massicotte, "Electoral Systems," in *Comparing Democracies*, ed. Lawrence LeDuc, Richard G. Niemi, and Pippa Norris (Thousand Oaks, Calif.: Sage, 1996), 2. "The best-known threshold is the German rule, which excludes from the Bundestag any party that fails to obtain 5 percent of the national vote or to elect three members in single-member districts. Turkey goes the farthest by demanding 10 percent of the national vote to secure a local seat, followed by Poland with a national threshold of 7 percent for national seats. All other countries require 5 percent or less of national or regional vote." The Indonesian team initially favored a 5-percent threshold, but President Habibie requested that it be raised to 10 percent.

12. From the point of view of democratic theory, there are preferable ways to guard against marginal parties and fragmentation of power in the DPR. For example, a system could be designed that allows voters to express degrees of preference through use of the cumulative vote, multiple ballots, approval voting, rank ordering of candidates or parties (the alternative vote), or single transferable vote. The reformers responded in two ways. On one hand they emphasized electoral conventions already well-rooted in the Indonesian electorate (e.g., voters' familiarity with showing their preference by punching each ballot only once). They also stressed the importance of simplicity and the trade-off between simplicity and the amount of information that voters are asked to provide.

13. The concept of floating mass referred to keeping the people unaffiliated with political parties and uninvolved in partisan politics except for a few weeks once every five years (i.e., during a general election) in order that they might concentrate on economic production.

14. *Langsung, umum, bebas, dan rahasia* (LUBER).

15. See, for example, BPHPR, "White Book on the 1992 General Election in Indonesia," Cornell University publication no. 73, Cornell Modern Indonesia Project, Ithaca, N.Y., 1994. Alexander Irwan and Edriana, *Pemilu: Pelanggaran Asas LUBER* (Jakarta: Pustaka Sinar Harapan, 1995).

16. A description of the administrative structure for the 1992 election can be found in my introduction in BPHPR, "White Book," which forms the

basis of comparison here. There was little change in the structure between 1992 and 1997.

17. The accompanying explanation of the bill defines the community representative as a local community leader, a religious functionary, a tradition or customary law functionary, or a cultural leader. Educational representative is defined as lecturer or student (as opposed to administrator).

18. The new law had set the number of Assembly representatives at 700, including 135 provincial delegates (*utusan daerah*), but the 5 provincial delegates from East Timor could not be chosen in September given the conditions there following the August 30 referendum. Thus, the actual number of provincial delegates was 130, and the total membership of the Assembly was 695.

19. The procedures on how seats were to be distributed to particular candidates within the total number earned by a party were not specified in sufficient detail in the new law, leaving the KPU to decide. The procedures actually used were as follows: Each party assigned its candidates to an individual district. Voters cast ballots for a party, rather than a candidate. Ballots included only the name and logos of the eligible parties. But at the same time the lists of which candidates had been assigned by the parties to given districts were made public in advance of election day and posted at the polling stations. Although candidates were matched to districts, there were no provincial or district residency requirements. Once the number of seats for each party had been determined, each party's seats were filled by the individual candidates assigned to the districts where that party fared best. Since there were two alternative ways of defining the latter (i.e., absolute number of votes received in a district versus the proportion [percentage] of total votes cast), the KPU decided to let each party choose which definition would apply to its results. Furthermore, the KPU decided to apply the district criterion only to candidates chosen through the application of "full quotas," but permitted the parties full discretion over the determination of candidates chosen through "largest remainders." In these ways the central party leaders were permitted much more discretion in filling their party's seats than intended in the new electoral law. For definitions and a fuller explanation complete with examples, see National Democratic Institute, "The New Legal Framework for Elections in Indonesia," report dated February 16, 1999.

20. An Assembly member may not serve concurrently as a state official, a government official with administrative authority, or a judiciary official. A House member may not serve concurrently in any government position, nor may a House member serve concurrently in a regional legislature and vice versa. A legislator may not serve concurrently as a member of two or more regional legislatures. U.U. 4/1999, Pasal 41.

21. As initially proposed by the reformers, the law would have required that the MPR meet annually to receive and evaluate an annual accountability speech from the president and to convey the people's aspirations and complaints. But the final form of the law left it up to the MPR to determine whether it will meet more than once every five years. Then, in its 1999

general session, the MPR passed a decree mandating annual sessions at which the president is obliged to present an annual report, but not to be held accountable. Had it decreed annual accountability, the MPR would have had the opportunity to reject the speech, rendering the president's political position untenable.

22. Although not specified in the law, media reports claimed agreement was reached on ten commissions and forty subcommissions.

23. U.U. 4/1999, Pasal 35.

24. For example, the violation of limits on contributions to parties or campaigns can result in a party being disqualified from competing in the election.

25. See "Paradigma Baru Peran ABRI," report dated Maret 1999, processed.

26. The Team of Seven initially proposed fifty-five appointed seats for the military in the DPR–MPR in return for abolishment of the military role (only elected seats) in the regional legislatures (DPRD, DPRD-II), based partly on the reasoning that the armed forces are guardians and protectors of national interests. Reportedly ABRI leaders initially agreed with the team, then later changed their minds after encountering strong opposition from the approximately 1,500 middle-level officers threatened with losing their jobs in the regional legislatures, for which they receive extra remuneration. Team members, interview with author, August 14, 1998.

27. "ABRI Diharapkan Tinggalkan Dwifungsil," *Kompas*, September 23, 1998; "Jangan Sampai ABRI Dipaksa 'Lengser' dari DPR," *Kompas*, October 6, 1998.

28. "Minimalkan Intervensi ABRI," *XPOS*, September 25, 1998.

29. "Indonesia Belum Siap Sistem Distrik," *Kompas*, October 15, 1998.

30. Ketetapan MPR 14/1998, Pasal 1, ayat 8.

31. "RUU Politik Memanas, Voting Mengancam," *Jawa Pos*, January 14, 1998.

32. "Pemerintah Bersikukuh Terapkan Sistem Distrik," *Jawa Pos*, October 22, 1998.

33. "Rancangan Undang-Undang Pemilu," *Kompas*, November 30, 1998.

34. "Pemerintah Buka Kemungkinan Kompromi," *Kompas*, December 4, 1998.

35. It is interesting to note that this dichotomy originated in the distinctions of the colonial period between "inner" and "outer" Indonesia, distinctions heavily criticized since independence as being Javacentric. Second, geographical balance of seats between Java–Bali and other islands results in malapportionment in favor of the other islands, since 60 percent of the population resides on Java–Bali.

36. "Habibie's Man Secures Top Party Post," *The Straits Times*, July 12, 1998.

37. "Dawn of a New Age," *Far Eastern Economic Review*, September 17, 1998.

38. "PNS dan ABRI Mutlak Netral," *Kompas*, January 6, 1999; "Ditindak, PNS yang Melanggar Netralitas," *Kompas*, January 7, 1999.

39. "Akbar Tandjung akan Segera Bertemu Gus Dur," *Kompas*, July 13, 1998.

40. "RUU Pemilu Perlu Konsensus Nasional," *Kompas*, July 24, 1998.

41. "11 Parpol Bentuk 'ForumPartai' Cegah Kemenangan Golkar," *Kompas*, July 31, 1998.

42. "Digugat, Monoloyalitas Pegawai Negeri Sipil," *Kompas*, November 29, 1998.

43. "Pemerintah Buka Kemungkinan Kompromi," *Kompas*, December 4, 1998.

44. Ibid.

45. "PAN dan PKB Buat Pernyataan Bersama," *Kompas*, January 6, 1999.

46. "Usul Golkar Ambangkan Status PNS," *Jawa Pos*, January 11, 1999.

47. "Syarwan Cari Terobosan soal PNS," *Jawa Pos*, January 12, 1999; "Pertahankan PNS Jadi Pengurus Parpol," *Jawa Pos*, January 13, 1999.

48. Time pressure was caused by a combination of a week-long recess, January 18–23, for celebration of the end of Ramadan and the high holiday Idul Fitri, and the deadline of January 28 for completion and ratification of the three political laws, which had been imposed by the government in relation to the time needed to prepare and conduct the election on June 7. Any change to the scheduled June 7 polls would have been a severe blow to Habibie's chances for reelection and likely would have led to fresh outbreaks of unrest across the country.

49. A government regulation carries more legal authority than a presidential decision in the Indonesian legal system, which helps to explain why Golkar acceded to the proposal.

50. Peraturan Pemerintah 5/1999 tentang Pegawai Negeri Sipil yang Menjadi Anggota Partai Politik.

51. Peraturan Pemerintah Republik Indonesia Nomor 5 Tahun 1999 tentang Pegawai Negeri Sipil yang Menjadi Anggota Partai Politik. Article 7, no. 1 read, "Civil Servants who have become members or functionaries of political parties at the moment this regulation takes effect are considered to have relinquished their membership and position." PPP demanded that "automatically" replace "are considered." No. 2 read, "must report to officials with authority," whereas PPP demanded "must request from their immediate superior and if permitted they much relinquish their government position." Article 8, no. 1 provided for severance pay of one year renewable up to five years. PPP demanded only one year (see the Penjelasan). Article 9, no. 1 read, "Civil servants who were terminated from their government position because of their membership in a political party, can return to their position if they relinquish their party membership." PPP contended this article was not part of the original agreement, but let it stand.

52. Peraturan Pemerintah Republik Indonesia Nomor 12 Tahun 1999 tentang Perubahan Atas Peraturan Pemerintah Nomor 5 Tahun 1999 tentang Pegawai Negeri Sipil yang Menjadi Anggota Partai Politik.

53. For accounts of the final day's events, see "Siap Disahkan," *Kompas*, January 29, 1999; "DPR Endorses Political Laws," *Tempo On-Line*, January 29, 1999.

54. R. William Liddle, "Indonesia's Democratic Transition: Playing by the Rules," in *The Architecture of Democracy*, ed. Andrew Reynolds (Oxford: Oxford University Press, 2001).

55. "RUU Politik Sangat Mengecewakan," *Kompas*, January 29, 1999. It should be noted that the government did not want to be so heavily involved. In early discussions with the Team of Seven, parties had rejected an offer of complete responsibility for conducting the election, so the initially proposed bill on the election called for tripartite control of the KPU among the government, political parties, and (nonpartisan) community leaders. However, the party factions in the House modified the proposal, contending that they were representative of the community so that separate representation was unnecessary.

56. The extent and importance of this winnowing in the House and Assembly for the success of the reform effort has been largely overlooked. For example, "Ironically, Indonesia's democratic future is being determined by a parliament (DPR) consisting almost entirely of Suharto-era appointees." *Van Zorge Report on Indonesia*, Issue VII, January 23, 1999.

57. Andi A. Mallarangeng, "Pengantar," in *UU Politik Buah Reformasi Setengah Hati*, ed. Thamrin Sonata (Jakarta: Yayasan Pariba, 1999), x–xi.

CHAPTER 4

Implementation of the 1999 Election

The passage of time and the benefit of hindsight provided by the publication of various studies, not to mention the political turmoil that marked the two years following the 1999 election, justify a reassessment of the election and make a more balanced one possible. A noticeable discrepancy exists between the overall judgment of domestic and foreign monitors that the goal of a free and fair election was largely achieved and the limitations identified in several detailed evaluations of the electoral institutions and processes. Indicative of the range of views are the following:

The elections went well, remarkably so in view of Indonesia's lack of experience with free elections, the short time available to organize them and the untested institutions to oversee them. The massive violence and widespread fraud which many had anticipated did not occur. . . . Indonesians knew that these elections represented a major turning point for their country and they pitched in enthusiastically to make them successful.[1]

The framework of regulations prepared for the 1999 Election were biased in favor of the status quo and did not reflect the message of the reformation.[2]

The study of five regions . . . proves that a shift in political conflict occurred. . . . In the 1999 Election, while various acts of political violence were still perpetrated by the state, the magnitude, scope, frequency and intensity of political violence committed by supporters of political parties and the general public were greater.[3]

In the assessment of elections, not only are the reference points important, but "the devil is in the details." This chapter continues the discussion on most of the topics begun in the previous one, but it does so from the vantage point of implementation and outcomes. I am most concerned with how the major innovations and institutions of the electoral reform were actually carried out, and what their effects were; I have not attempted to provide a comprehensive picture of the election or a discussion of every phase, as they are available elsewhere.[4] However, I begin with a brief overview intended for readers unfamiliar with the election.

OVERVIEW

The new political laws were finalized in late January, allowing just four months before election day on June 7 for preparation of the election. Forty-eight political parties qualified to contest the election at the end of March, and they immediately began campaigning unofficially. The General Election Commission (KPU), composed of government and party representatives, was appointed and began working in late March as well. Voter registration, which traditionally had occurred a year in advance of an election, finally got underway in May after two postponements due to insufficient preparation. Slow response from eligible citizens, who were supposed to take the initiative (unless they resided in isolated areas), in the context of the extremely truncated registration period, caused a regression to the (traditional) passive mode, whereby government officials assumed the responsibility of locating and registering eligible voters. About 85 percent of eligible voters were registered in advance and many others were allowed "instant registration" at the polling stations on election day.[5] The official campaign period, seventeen days long, began on May 19 and was structured by the election authorities in ways to minimize the potential for violence.

On election day, June 7, about 105 million voters cast legal ballots, or about 94 percent of those registered. More than 3 million Indonesians were directly involved from the polling site to the election commission in the administration and oversight of the election.[6] Each voter cast three ballots, for the legislature at each of three levels (except residents of Jakarta, where there were only two levels and absentee voters who cast only one for the national legislature), choosing among forty-eight parties on each ballot by punching a party symbol. The campaign and election day were surprisingly orderly, marked by much less violence than the election in 1997. However, security could not be guaranteed in two districts of Aceh, the northernmost province on Sumatra Island, and the election was permanently canceled there. The election had to be postponed in a handful of villages due to logistical difficulties in the provision of election materials. Hundreds of thousands of domestic election monitors were joined by thousands of international election monitors. They were united in their assessment that this was the freest and fairest election since 1955, notwithstanding thousands of documented violations of election laws and regulations. The announcement of official election results was delayed nearly two months, although unofficial results were known within a week and were confirmed by several parallel vote counts, helping to alleviate widespread concern that the results were being manipulated. A major cause of the delay was conflict within the election commission. Parties obtaining insufficient votes to get a seat in the House (but with enough votes on the commission to block a decision) banded together, refusing to certify the election, ostensibly awaiting investigation of election irregularities, but actually maneuvering to obtain seats nonetheless. With the commission deadlocked and the election supervisory committee recommending certification, President Habibie intervened and certified the election. Once the election was certified, conflict continued in the commission over vote-sharing agreements, which ultimately were disallowed. Seats were assigned to parties by quota and "largest remainder." Only six of the forty-eight parties reached the threshold of eligibility for future elections. Twenty-one parties obtained seats. Candidates were assigned to seats through a combination of party discretion (lists) and the number of votes won by parties in districts. Election results by party for the House are shown in Table 4.1.

The next step in the electoral process was forming the People's Consultative Assembly. It was composed of four types of representatives who differed in who they represented and how they were chosen: (1) the 462 members of the House elected in the general election, (2) the 38 appointed members of the House representing the military and the police, (3) 5 representatives from each province (total 130) elected by the newly elected provincial legislatures (DPRD), and (4) functional group representatives. Prohibited by the new law from being drawn from the executive or judiciary branches of government, the provincial representatives were elected by provincial legislatures in ways that reflected the partisan composition of the provincial legislatures.[7] Selection of the functional group representatives proved difficult and controversial. Meanwhile, the government of President Habibie had begun to unravel, battered by scandal, ineffectiveness in investigating and prosecuting principals of the previous regime for corruption, and the terror and abuse of human rights following the independence referendum in East Timor.

Table 4.1
Votes and Seats for the House of Representatives, 1999

Political Party	Total Votes	Total Votes (%)	Total Seats by Quota	Total Seats by Remainder	Total Seats	Total Seats (%)
PDI–P	35,706,618	33.73	135	18	153	33.12
Golkar	23,742,112	22.43	99	21	120	25.99
PKB	13,336,963	12.60	40	11	51	11.04
PPP	11,330,387	10.70	39	19	58	12.55
PAN	7,528,936	7.11	26	8	34	7.36
PBB	2,050,039	1.94	2	11	13	2.81
PK	1,436,670	1.36	1	6	7	1.52
PKP	1,065,810	1.01	-	4	4	0.87
PNU	679,174	0.64	-	5	5	1.08
PDI	655,048	0.62	-	2	2	0.43
PP	590,995	0.56	-	1	1	0.22

	Votes	%				%
PDKB	550,856	0.52	-	5	5	1.08
PPIIM	456,750	0.43	-	1	1	0.22
PDR	427,875	0.40	-	1	1	0.22
PSII	376,411	0.36	-	1	1	0.22
PNI FM	365,173	0.35	-	1	1	0.22
PBI	364,257	0.34	-	1	1	0.22
PNI MM	345,665	0.33	-	1	1	0.22
IPKI	328,440	0.31	-	1	1	0.22
PKU	300,049	0.28	-	1	1	0.22
PKD	216,663	0.20	-	1	1	0.22
Subtotal (excluding parties without seats)	**101,854,891**	**96.23**	**342**	**120**	**462**	**100**

Table 4.1 (*continued*)

Political Party	Total Votes	Total Votes (%)	Total Seats by Quota	Total Seats by Remainder	Total Seats	Total Seats (%)
PNI Supeni	376,928	0.36	-	-	-	-
KRISNA	369,747	0.35	-	-	-	-
KAMI	289,477	0.27	-	-	-	-
PUI	269,325	0.25	-	-	-	-
PAY	213,882	0.20	-	-	-	-
PR	208,765	0.20	-	-	-	-
MKGR	204,203	0.19	-	-	-	-
PIB	192,780	0.18	-	-	-	-
SUNI	180,170	0.17	-	-	-	-
PCD	167,975	0.16	-	-	-	-
PSII 1905	152,834	0.14	-	-	-	-
Masyumi Baru	152,419	0.14	-	-	-	-
PNBI	149,057	0.14	-	-	-	-

PUDI	140,978	0.13	-	-	-	-
PBN	111,621	0.11	-	-	-	-
PKM	104,643	0.10	-	-	-	-
PND	96,986	0.09	-	-	-	-
PADI	85,841	0.08	-	-	-	-
PRD	78,774	0.07	-	-	-	-
PPI	63,931	0.06	-	-	-	-
PID	62,903	0.06	-	-	-	-
MURBA	62,099	0.06	-	-	-	-
SPSI	61,101	0.06	-	-	-	-
PARI	54,677	0.05	-	-	-	-
PUMI	49,851	0.05	-	-	-	-
PSP	49,571	0.05	-	-	-	-
PILAR	40,508	0.04	-	-	-	-
TOTAL	**105,845,937**	**100**	**342**	**120**	**462**	**100**

Source: General Election Commission (KPU).

The House and Assembly were sworn in on schedule on October 1. Going into the general session of the Assembly, PDI-P, with a plurality of seats, claimed a mandate for its leader, Megawati. This claim was challenged by other parties, who found her uninterested in the bargaining process necessary to coalition building. Some conservative Muslims noted the disproportionately large numbers of non-Muslims in PDI-P and questioned whether a woman should be elected president. In the early sessions, PDI-P was outflanked on several procedural and organizational decisions. Amien Rais, the leader of PAN, was elected speaker of the Assembly and Akbar Tandjung, the leader of Golkar, was elected speaker of the House. The Assembly then rejected President Habibie's accounting for his 512 days in office, resulting in him withdrawing his candidacy for president. A coalition of moderate Islamic parties known as the "middle axis" proposed Abdurrahman Wahid (popularly known as Gus Dur) as a compromise candidate, although he was identified with PKB, which controlled only about 11 percent of the seats, one-third the number controlled by PDI-P. In a showdown between Megawati and Gus Dur, the Assembly voted 373 to 313 with five abstentions to elect Gus Dur to the presidency. Golkar and the military faction were crucial to his sixty-vote margin. Megawati supporters outside the Assembly were enraged and took to the streets in violent demonstrations in Jakarta and major provincial cities. The following day Megawati was elected vice president in a contest with the leader of PPP, Hamzah Haz. The 1999 election was completed on October 26 with the announcement of a thirty-five-person "National Unity Cabinet" drawn from PKB, PAN, PPP, PDI-P, Golkar, and the military.

MULTIPARTYISM

The new policy on parties was implemented consistent with the law; the government did not attempt to restrict the range of ideologies and principles (except communist and separatist) on which parties were declared. With greater freedoms of expression and organization than at any time during the New Order, 141 parties registered with the Department of Justice and were listed in the official government gazette.[8] Of this number, the three New Order parties and forty-five new ones passed a screening process certifying them as election contestants.

The screening process was controversial, less because of who was involved than how it was done. President Habibie appointed a special nonpartisan "Team of Eleven" for the task, composed mainly of academics and led by the widely respected Muslim scholar and educator, Nurcholish Majid. In order to qualify as an election contestant, the law required that a party have an organization in one-third of the provinces (nine), and in half of the districts in those provinces (six, on average). Moreover, the team had to complete the screening process in a month's time. Facing an impossible task, the team took shortcuts by drawing a sample of districts for verification visits by the team and by defining the presence of a party organization as two self-identified party officers (chair and secretary) in each party branch.[9] The process resulted in twelve of the disqualified parties protesting that their branch organizations had been by-passed in the sampling, while larger parties criticized the superficiality of the criterion of two self-identified officers without regard to office facilities or number of members. It should be noted that there was a material incentive for qualifying as an election contestant, especially at a time of severe economic depression. The Habibie government continued a practice begun under the New Order of subsidizing qualified parties in the amount equivalent to several hundred U.S. dollars each (Rp. 1,500,000).

As shown in Table 4.1, the outcome of the election was a somewhat less partisan fragmentation of the House than in 1955. The top four parties obtained 79 percent of the vote (cf. 77 percent in 1955), and the winning party obtained 33.7 percent of the vote (cf. 22.3 percent in 1955). Of the forty-eight parties contesting the 1999 election, twenty-one parties succeeded in obtaining at least one seat (cf. twenty-eight in 1955). Only six of the forty-eight parties passed the 2-percent threshold of seats needed to qualify for the next election, but those six parties combined captured 88.5 percent of the vote.

The stipulation of the law for parties with broad geographical support was reinforced by the election outcome. Each one of the five parties that far outdistanced the rest were truly national parties. PDI-P, with 33.7 percent of the vote, obtained a plurality in eleven out of twenty-seven provinces. Golkar drew 22.4 percent of the vote and won a plurality in fourteen provinces. PPP, with 10.7 percent, won a plurality in one province and placed second or third in eighteen provinces. PAN, with 7.1 percent, placed fourth or better in seventeen provinces. Although PKB placed third overall with 12.6 percent of the vote, its support was concentrated in populous East and Central Java, where it placed first and second, respectively.

The election outcome also vindicated parties that campaigned on broad, inclusive themes. While PKB, PPP, and PAN were clearly perceived as Islamic parties, all three campaigned on reformist themes, including democracy, tolerance, and human rights. Conversely, parties with avowedly Islamist agendas were marginalized, drawing under 10 percent of the vote, combined.

POLITICAL FINANCE

The new laws on political parties and elections placed limitations on the amount individuals and entities could contribute to parties and made vote buying and other forms of election fraud illegal and subject to criminal penalty. But these provisions were ineffective for a variety of reasons. Preelection reports were not submitted on schedule, they excluded the (critical) campaign period, and the audit work was clearly superficial, largely because most political parties did not have an appropriate bookkeeping system. When the election commission issued a cursory summary five days before the election, the report generated little news coverage or political attention. Although parties acknowledged violations in their postelection reports, the laws were not enforced.[10]

There were several causes of these deficiencies. The interrelationship between regulation of party campaign funds under the election law and regulation of financial activity of parties generally under the political party law remained ambiguous. It was unclear, for example, whether contributions made during the election period counted against the maximum total donation by an individual of $2,000 and by an entity of $20,000 to a party within the period of one year.

Second, the jurisdictional scope of the campaign finance regulations was unclear. The official campaign period was seventeen days (May 19 to June 5), but parties began campaign activities immediately upon being qualified to contest the elections in early March. Did the political finance provisions apply to money raised and spent during the official period only or to the longer period? As it turned out, the only audited reports required by the electoral commission before election day covered only the period from March 5 through May 18, the day before the official campaign began. Obviously, this effort had little effect on the overall objective of financial disclosure.

Third, the election law left to the commission determination of the limitations upon campaign funds that could be accepted by political parties. The commission interpreted this provision to mean limitation upon overall campaign spending by parties. On the day before the official campaign period began, the commission announced by decree that parties' national spending limits would be equivalent to $13.8 million and that specific limitations were set at every level of party organization, ranging from about $12,550 at the provincial level down to $125 at the village level. These limits, which contemplated national, top-heavy campaigns by the parties, needed clear reporting requirements and effective enforcement mechanisms for their implementation that were far beyond the capacity of the electoral and judicial institutions.

The election law required that political parties submit to the Supreme Court an audited financial report at the end of each year and fifteen days prior to and twenty-five days after the general election. As already noted, the preelection reports omitted the campaign period. Five days before the election the commission attempted financial disclosure with the issuance of a cursory summary (less than fifteen pages) of parties' financial activity based on audited reports. The report was distributed to the news media, but it generated little news coverage or political attention.

In its summary report, delayed until November, the commission reviewed the audited financial information it had received from the parties and offered some general and specific observations that served as self-criticisms of the weak political finance system in Indonesia in 1999. It acknowledged that most political parties did not have an appropriate bookkeeping system. Most parties did not record or report receipt of "in-kind" donations (goods or services), and failed to include spending by organizations that sponsored or supported parties. No party admitted spending over the commission's campaign spending limit, although many reported contributions exceeding legal limits and some refused to identify their donors by name.[11] Despite the commission's reports of acknowledged violations of contribution limitations and reporting requirements, neither the commission, the Central Election Supervisory Committee, the Supreme Court, or any prosecutors initiated any enforcement actions against the political parties, individuals, or entities involved.[12] Similarly, in its final report the Central Election Supervisory Committee (Panwaslu) noted a combined total of 140 violations involving "money politics." Only eighteen (13 percent) were forwarded to the police for investigation, and none were prosecuted.[13]

INDEPENDENT ELECTION ADMINISTRATION

A primary objective of electoral reform was to take election administration away from the executive branch and place it under a more neutral authority. As noted in Chapter 3, a powerful election commission was established, composed of representatives of the government and political parties, with responsibility for planning, implementing, and evaluating all stages of the general election. In addition, the Election Law had been loosely and often ambiguously drawn and it bestowed residual authority upon the commission, enabling it to formulate policy (legislate) on all matters insufficiently specified or omitted from the law, as well as supervisory authority over political party (election contestant) finances. The commission was equipped with a network of implementing committees (PPI, PPD-

I, PPD-II, PPK, PPS, KPPS), running from the central to the village levels, all of which were similarly composed of representatives of the government and the political parties, with leadership usually from the parties. Except for the lowest level (KPPS), these committees were assisted by the same secretariats in the regional government bureaucracy under the Ministry of Home Affairs, which had administered previous elections during the New Order. Not only were the same personnel involved, but wherever new electoral procedures were ambiguous or poorly understood there was a tendency to fall back on old operating procedures, which contributed to the relatively high incidence of procedural violations. The lack of an independent secretariat was an issue in the postelection reforms of the commission, as will be discussed in Chapter 8.

How well did the commission function? Controversy surrounded it from the very beginning, when a purported list of politically controversial candidates for the government positions on the commission was leaked to the press. But the government gave way to pressure with the actual appointment of well-respected nominees, including some of the most vocal and ardent reformers. The rules called for the commission to organize itself, and the noted human rights lawyer Adnan Buyung Nasution was the majority choice. But he stepped aside for the runner up, retired General Rudini, head of a small party and former minister of home affairs: "This was apparently part of the bargain leading to the appointment of real reformers to the KPU."[14]

One of its first major policy decisions sharply divided the commission and seemed to lay aside the fears of the political parties that the five government appointees and the Golkar representative would vote as a bloc. With several government representatives abstaining, the commission voted to allow its own members from political parties to campaign and be candidates, but it barred senior government officials including cabinet officers from the campaign. This action was directed against ministerial incumbents from Golkar. Although inconsistent and out of step with the practice in most democracies, where ministers are considered political appointments separate from the civil service, this action could be understood in light of past experience with the bureaucracy actively behind Golkar. President Habibie challenged this decision and it was referred to the Supreme Court, but the court returned it to the president, citing the Election Law, which gave him final authority. Eventually a compromise was reached, with the affected ministers taking formal leaves of absence during the campaign period.

The law also provided for a network of election supervisory committees (*panwas*), separate from the commission and its network, composed of a judge (except at the lowest level) along with representatives from higher education and the community. The difference between the two networks was that the supervisory committees were intended to be nonpartisan and hence did not include party representatives. However, the new law did not specify the powers of the supervisory committees, and even after a Supreme Court decree intended to clarify this prior to the election, their authority and enforcement powers remained vague. It was unclear, for example, whether the supervisory committees were linked in a hierarchical appeals structure, whether each committee had final jurisdiction in its respective region, and whether committee decisions were advisory or binding on implementation committees. The work of the committees was also seriously hampered by their dependence on insufficient and unreliable funding sources.[15] Beginning approximately with the counting phase, the election commission became increasingly polarized and dysfunctional. The decision rule which it had set for itself, consisting of a two-thirds majority needed to certify the election, was manipulated by the tiny parties who had failed at the polls to maintain their positions and power on the commission. Ostensibly protesting electoral fraud (but in reality attempting to protect their positions on the commission and leverage House seats), thirty-one of the tiny parties withheld their votes, thereby denying the commission the two-thirds majority it needed to certify the election. What made this behavior even more questionable was that the central-level party representatives were, in effect, overturning the decisions of their colleagues on lower-level committees (PPD-I, PPD-II, etc.) to certify the election.

In its final report, the central supervisory committee charged the commission with overreach and abuse of its authority. It cited the commission's decision allowing parties greater authority than the law allowed in determining their elected candidates.[16] Another example was the usurpation of authority over certain matters that logically belonged to the supervisory committees.[17] These problems helped propel reform of the election commission to top priority on the agenda of postelection electoral reforms, discussed in Chapter 8.

An important corollary to independent election administration was keeping civil servants from partisan political activity, such as using government facilities to benefit particular election contestants. Although the incidence of such practices was greatly reduced from 1997 levels, the problem remained a substantial one. The central supervisory committee recorded 236 cases of "deviations from the regulation on neutrality of the bureaucracy and government officials," which represented 6 percent of all deviations. Two of the most blatant and notorious cases, involving government officials using government programs to benefit certain parties, were the disbursement of Social Safety Net Program (JPS) funds under the Golkar banner and allocation of Farm Enterprise Credit (KUT) by functionaries of the People's Rule Party (PDR). The committee reported these cases to the Supreme Court, who alone had the authority to sanction the offending parties, but the court refused to consider them on technical grounds.

Many election monitors were impressed with how small a role the government bureaucracy played at the village level. This represented a sea change.[18] The Election Law mandated joint government and party representation in the implementation committees at all levels except the lowest one, the voting implementation groups that ran the polling stations. These groups were composed entirely of party representatives and members of the community. This change in institutional design had powerful effects. Unlike past (New Order) elections, where village election administration was firmly under the control of government officials and where the rights of witnesses from the political parties were frequently infringed, the management of polling stations was largely taken out of the hands of local governments and given over to civil society.

CONTROLLED AND PEACEFUL CAMPAIGN

Approaching the 1999 election campaign, fear of violence and social unrest was understandably widespread. The memory of the most violent campaign in Indonesia's history just two years earlier was still fresh. In-between, the country had been wracked by numerous outbreaks of ethnic, separatist, and religious violence. Informal campaign activities by supporters of various parties began months in advance of the formal campaign period, usually with little attempt by the authorities to stop or to prevent it.

The election commission took two steps to minimize the risks of violence. It set the formal campaign period at seventeen days, the shortest ever. Second, it continued the practice begun during the New Order of organizing the campaign into rounds, with parties taking turns on a rotating basis and with larger parties prevented from campaigning on the same days in order to minimize opportunities for conflict between their supporters. Under this system each party was limited to three days of activities involving masses of their supporters (e.g., television broadcasts and public rallies that often evolved into illegal motorized parades). The parties, particularly the larger ones, attempted to maintain discipline as well by training marshals and deploying them at rallies and along parade routes. These efforts paid off; the campaign was relatively peaceful and devoid of violence, except in a couple of districts in the province of

Aceh, where the campaign was effectively canceled. The most frequent violations of campaign regulations consisted of organizing mass parades, posting party symbols in the wrong places, supporters of one party destroying the campaign materials of a competitor party, and traffic violations (usually during motorized parades).

One of the weaknesses in the Election Law was the lack of specification of the circumstances under which parties should be held responsible for Election Law violations as opposed to their members and sympathizers (individuals). And since the only sanction the election supervisory committees could apply to offending political parties was a written warning—power to use stronger sanctions against parties having been reserved to the Supreme Court—the parties largely ignored the warnings of the committees. Thus, it was easier for the committees to discipline errant individuals than parties by reporting them to the police. However, such action usually ended in a warning or other resolution short of formal charges because all involved (committees, violators, police) tended to be residents of the same district. Five times more individuals than parties were charged with violations. Individuals often became scapegoats for party infractions because of the much greater complexity of referring cases to the Supreme Court and its reluctance or refusal to get involved in election cases.[19]

DELAYS IN DETERMINING ELECTION RESULTS

A major problem in the election administration was the inordinately long delay of nearly two months that occurred between election day and certification of the results. This was important because the longer the delay, the more suspicion tended to arise that the results were being manipulated, undercutting the legitimacy of the election. There were a variety of reasons and causes for the delay. On the administrative–technical side, one can begin with the magnitude of the task and the inexperience of the volunteer election workers. On election day, 112 million Indonesian voters went to more than 320,000 polling stations scattered over the vast archipelago nation. Election authorities had a scant four months to prepare an election that introduced many new procedures and forms. The vast majority of local election workers were inexperienced and most had received little training in advance. Due to the suspicion and doubt surrounding previous elections and the determination to achieve a high degree of legitimacy for this one, more transparent procedures, cross-checking, and consensus-building measures were required, all of which were time consuming. Counting and recounting was done manually and publicly at the polling-station level, where poll workers were sometimes overly meticulous.[20] Results were aggregated manually at several levels above, each level rechecking the reports of the units within its jurisdiction and delaying until its own report was complete before forwarding any results to the next level. Even though unofficial results were sent electronically once they reached the subdistrict level, official reporting moved much more slowly along a different channel.

At each level, political party representatives had to sign the official record (*berita acara*) indicating their agreement, giving them an opportunity to delay the reports until any problems they perceived were resolved to their satisfaction. While these instances were relatively infrequent given the number of polling stations, violations classified as "administrative" and "procedural" (*tata cara*) represented three-fourths of all those reported to the election supervisory committees.[21] The vast majority of disputes were resolved at the polling-station and village levels. Those that could not were referred to higher administrative levels. Many of them involved allegations of "criminal" (*pidana*) violations by parties.[22]

Over a week after the election some party representatives on election implementation committees in twelve provinces refused to certify the election results. Attempting to break the stalemate, the central supervisory committee sent a team to each province to investigate and make recommendations, a process taking most of another week. Meanwhile, the unofficial results, corroborated by several parallel vote counts conducted by monitoring groups, revealed that most of the forty-eight parties would fall short of enough votes to gain a seat. A number of them proposed *stembus akkord* (vote-sharing agreements) ex post facto. Controversy ensued in the commission, which stiffened the resolve of the losing parties to withhold certification of the election results.

When the election commission met in late July to certify the election results, twenty-six tiny parties refused to sign, preventing the commission from certifying the election. Convinced that further delay would cause a postponement of the Assembly meeting scheduled for November to elect a new president, seriously undermining the legitimacy of his government, President Habibie intervened and certified the election.

COMPROMISING: "PR PLUS"

The outcome of the election commission's decisions to give central party leaders considerable discretion in filling their party's seats (as in the old system) was a substantial diminution of the significance of the district element of Indonesia's new hybrid electoral system. It turned out that 97 out of 462 elected House seats (21 percent) "represent" districts other than those to which they were originally assigned. The national leaders of most parties chafed at the district element of the electoral system, which effectively reduced their power, so they worked to undermine that element.[23] There were several reasons. First, they sought to ensure that top party leaders got elected, whatever their performance in the district to which they had been assigned. Second, some parties had specific reasons for taking advantage of the flexibility permitted by the KPU in the process of determining elected candidates. For example, in response to the criticism it had received during the campaign for nominating a disproportionate number of non-Muslims, PDI-P took corrective action.[24]

MECHANICAL EFFECTS

Chapter 3 noted that several important decisions in the design of the electoral system were carried over from previous regimes. For example, the reformers in 1999 continued the malapportionment in favor of districts outside the island of Java that began under the New Order. Also, the method of distributing seats to parties known as the "largest remainders using a Hare Quota" has been used continuously, beginning in 1955. Since then there also has not been an adjustment procedure or second tier of distribution to reduce distortions. As a result, the old biases remained in the system in 1999.

Tables 4.2 and 4.3 show these effects, the former presenting the overall deviation from proportionality (i.e., difference between percentage of votes and percentage of seats) for the twenty-one parties that obtained seats. Parties that made a stronger showing in the areas of lower district magnitude outside of Java have a positive overall deviation (e.g., Golkar, +3.54; PPP, +1.85; PBB, +0.87). Table 4.3 gives the district magnitude (M) and index of deviation from proportionality (D) for each of the twenty-seven electoral districts (provinces) for 1999 as well as the two previous elections. The most dramatic change is the increase in D for every district; the average D increased from 5.2 in 1997 to 14.7 in 1999, reflecting the greater number of contestants (parties) and fragmentation of the vote in 1999. Thus, what was gained in representation from multipartyism during voting was partially eroded through the procedures used in assigning seats to parties.

CHARACTERISTICS OF HOUSE MEMBERS

The results of the election in terms of partisan composition of the House were noted earlier in the discussion of multipartyism. Inter-

Table 4.2
Overall Deviation from Proportionality, 1999 (%)

Party	Votes	Seats	Deviation
PDI-P	33.73	33.12	-0.61
GOLKAR	22.43	25.97	+3.54
PKB	12.60	11.01	-1.59
PPP	10.70	12.55	+1.85
PAN	7.11	7.36	+0.25
PBB	1.94	2.81	+0.87
PK	1.36	1.52	+0.16
PKP	1.01	0.87	-0.14
PNU	0.64	1.08	+0.44
PDI	0.62	0.43	-0.19

PP	0.56	0.22	-0.34
PDKB	0.52	1.08	+0.56
PPIIM	0.43	0.22	-0.21
PDR	0.40	0.22	-0.18
PSII	0.36	0.22	-0.14
PNI-FM	0.35	0.22	-0.13
PBI	0.34	0.22	-0.12
PNI-MM	0.33	0.22	-0.11
IPKI	0.31	0.22	-0.09
PKU	0.28	0.22	-0.06
PKD	0.20	0.22	+0.02

Source: General Election Commission (KPU).

Table 4.3
Electoral District Magnitude (M) and Index of Deviation from Proportionality (D), General Elections, 1992–1999

Province	1992		1997		1999	
	M	D	M	D	M	D
East Java	62	0.7	64	0.5	68	3.9
West Java	61	0.3	68	0.5	82	3.4
Central Java	57	0.7	59	0.7	60	4.6
South Sulawesi	23	2.4	23	5.2	24	8.5
North Sumatra	22	2.0	23	2.1	24	10.9
Jakarta	14	4.2	18	1.8	18	38.7
West Sumatra	14	3.5	14	1.7	14	11.1
South Sumatra	13	3.4	14	3.7	15	12.8
East Nusa Tenggara	12	1.9	13	4.1	13	11.1
Lampung	11	3.6	11	4.3	15	10.6
Aceh	10	5.1	10	5.2	12	16.2
South Kalimantan	10	1.2	10	4.9	11	11.8
Irian Jaya	9	2.4	10	3.6	13	13.5
Bali	8	5.3	9	6.8	9	8.6
West Kalimantan	8	3.4	8	5.3	9	16.8
Riau	7	5.0	8	4.8	10	12.8
West Nusa Tenggara	7	1.9	8	6.0	9	20.0
North Sulawesi	7	7.2	7	4.1	7	16.8
Jambi	6	9.6	6	7.4	6	19.6
Yogyakarta	6	8.1	7	8.6	6	13.5
Central Kalimantan	6	8.7	6	6.8	6	18.9
East Kalimantan	6	5.2	6	9.7	7	17.7
Maluku	5	10.0	5	7.0	6	18.9
Bengkulu	4	14.2	4	5.2	4	29.2
East Timor	4	9.2	4	11.5	4	13.5
Central Sulawesi	4	14.0	5	15.1	5	17.1
Southeast Sulawesi	4	5.6	5	2.8	5	17.6

Source: 1992 and 1997, General Election Institute; 1999, General Election Commission and International Foundation for Election Systems (Compiled).

Note: Correlations: 1992 = −.69, p <= .01; 1997 = −.61, p <= .01; 1999 = −.56, p <= .01.

esting as well were the personal characteristics of the legislators as a group and how these compared with previous legislatures. Compared with the House members chosen in the previous two elections, they were the youngest (Table 4.4). They had slightly less formal education than legislators in 1997, but more than those elected in 1992 (Table 4.5).

Occupational differences were more dramatic. In the two previous New Order legislatures the proportions of incumbent legislators, and especially civil servants, were considerably higher. The proportion of legislators from the private sector—consisting of entrepreneurs, professionals, and employees—jumped to 70 percent in 1999, compared to about 40 percent in the two previous legislatures (Table 4.6). We can infer that the legislators elected in 1999 had fewer direct connections with the government and that they are therefore likely to be supportive of more independence vis-à-vis the government.

The data on gender are surprising in light of the greater freedoms since 1998 and the heightened activity of women's groups. In contrast to expectations, the proportion of women joining the legislature fell from 15 percent in 1992 to 13 percent in 1997 and 9 percent in 1999.

We noted earlier that the unique PR-plus electoral system adopted in 1999 was supposed to result in legislators with stronger roots in their constituencies (districts). From this vantage point the evidence on place of residence paints a mixed picture. Half of the legislators in 1999 reported that they resided in the greater Jakarta metropolitan area.[25] Three-fourths resided on the island of Java, which was a slight decline from 83 percent in 1992 and a change in the right direction, but it was still disproportionately high, whether in terms of the distribution of population (60 percent live on Java) or House seats (50 percent from Java).

A cross-tabulation of occupation by party illumines the social bases of the parties in 1999 (Table 4.7). Not surprising, the most dramatic contrast was the high proportion of incumbents in Golkar's (65 percent) and PPP's (55.3 percent) legislative delegations, reflecting the seniority of these two parties with long experience during the New Order. Unexpectedly, however, incumbency in both Golkar and PPP increased over the last three elections. In Golkar the incumbency rates were 48 percent, 23 percent, and 65 percent for 1992, 1997, and 1999, respectively. The same indicator for PPP was as follows: 5 percent in 1992, 34 percent in 1997, and 55 percent in 1997.[26] Despite Golkar's and PPP's attempts to reposition themselves in the campaign as reformed parties, these data reveal one type of obstacle in that effort and show why they (especially Golkar) continued to be

Table 4.4
Members of the House of Representatives, by Age, 1992–1999 (%)

Age	1992 (n = 400)	1997 (n = 425)	1999 (n = 462)
Less than 35 years	2.9	2.6	3.7
35 to 49 years	33.8	36.3	38.9
50 years and above	63.3	61.1	57.4

Source: Kompas, October 1, 1999.

Table 4.5
Members of the House of Representatives, by Education, 1992–1999 (%)

Education	1992 (n = 400)	1997 (n = 425)	1999 (n = 462)
Elementary	1.0	0.0	0.0
Junior high school	0.8	0.9	0.4
High school	25.5	13.7	16.8
Academy	8.3	5.1	7.9
Baccalaureate	57.4	64.2	56.3
Graduate	7.0	15.1	18.6

Source: Kompas, October 1, 1999.

Table 4.6
Members of the House of Representatives, by Occupation, 1992–1999 (%)

Occupation	1992 (n = 400)	1997 (n = 425)	1999 (n = 462)
Incumbent	39.5	23.5	19.9
Private sector	40.4	39.2	69.9
Civil servant	12.5	28.9	4.1
Veteran	0.8	6.1	1.1
Retired civil servant	4.8	1.6	4.4
Military*	0.5	0.2	0.0
Housewife	1.5	0.5	0.6

Source: Kompas, October 1, 1999.
ªHeld elected seat.

Table 4.7
Occupation of Members of the House of Representatives, by Party, 1999 (%)

Occupation	PDI-P (n =153)	Golkar (n = 20)	PPP (n = 58)	PKB (n = 51)	PAN (n = 34)
Incumbent legislator[a]	0.0	65.0	55.3	3.9	0.0
Civil servant	3.9	4.2	1.7	2.0	5.9
Retired civil servant	6.5	2.5	3.4	7.8	2.9
Veteran	3.9	0.0	0.0	0.0	0.0
Employee (private sector)	8.5	1.7	3.4	0.0	0.0
Entrepreneur	47.1	21.7	22.4	29.4	47.1
Teacher	9.2	3.3	6.9	51.0	23.5
Lawyer	7.2	0.8	1.7	2.0	2.9
Reporter	4.6	0.0	0.0	2.0	8.8
Consultant	3.9	0.8	0.0	2.0	5.9
Other	5.2	0.0	5.2	0.0	3.0

Source: Kompas, October 1, 1999.
*National (DPR) or regional (DPRD).

perceived as status quo parties. Such large contingents of seasoned legislators may also help to explain their greater effectiveness than PDI-P in several key decisions of the Assembly in its 1999 session.

The obverse pattern was the importance of entrepreneurs in the delegations of the new parties, especially in PDI-P and PAN, where they consisted of a plurality (47.1 percent). Yet entrepreneurs were not only important in the delegations of new parties; they were the second largest group in Golkar and PPP as well. Private (likely Islamic) teachers were a majority in PKB's delegation, consistent with its identity as the political expression of the organization of Islamic teachers. Teachers were the second-largest group in PAN. Entrepreneurs and teachers are both occupations that value independence, initiative, and creativity. Their rise in the House would seem to bode well for the continuation of reform, while the sizeable group of incumbents suggests the status quo will have voices and defenders.

CONCLUSION

Public opinion polling conducted before and after the election indicated that the Indonesian electorate thought the 1999 election was well implemented. When asked how satisfied they were with the way elections were conducted, 88 percent of the respondents chose a positive answer.[27] When the same question was posed (but to different sample of respondents) about six months before the election, only about 36 percent answered positively, suggesting that the 1999 election dramatically changed perceptions about the conduct of elections in Indonesia. Responses to another question reinforces this inference. When asked, "Would you say that Indonesia is primarily a democracy today, or is it not primarily a democracy?" 89 percent answered affirmatively after the election, compared to 69 percent before. Several questions that were asked only in the postelection survey also reflect high regard for the election: A total of 84 percent said that they were "very satisfied" or "somewhat satisfied" with the results of the election overall, 83 percent "agreed completely" or "agreed somewhat" that the election was fair to all candidates and political parties, and 86 percent agreed that the count of the votes was honest. Among those who voted (96 percent), 90 percent had the impression that this election was administered "very well" or "fairly well."

In the nine months following the enactment of electoral reform in early 1999, the vast majority of the political elite were willing to play by most of the new rules of the political game, even though those rules introduced more uncertainty about outcomes than the elite had experienced in at least three decades. On the eve of election day, June 6, 1999, few Indonesians or foreign observers were willing to venture a prediction with any confidence. The uncertainty over who would be elected president continued all the way to the counting of the ballots on October 20.

Probably everyone had reservations about the new rules. Indeed, it was easy to find flaws in both design and implementation, as we have seen. Some individuals and groups sought to exploit the flaws and worked actively to modify or undermine the new rules and infant institutions. Examples include party leaders working to gut the district element in the hybrid electoral system and the concerted effort by small parties, who had been clearly beaten at the polls, to hold certification of the official election results hostage to their attempt to gain seats, nonetheless, by suddenly introducing new rules.

At the same time, there were strong pressures to implement the reforms. President Habibie took a personal interest in the reforms, apparently wanting to be remembered as the president who brought Indonesia out of an authoritarian past and into a democratic era.[28] Lacking the legitimacy of a genuine transitional administration in the context of a resurgence of student activism, Habibie had little choice but to implement the new system and hold the election on schedule (June 7, 1999). Habibie's political future and his hope for reelection were clearly tied to holding free and fair elections on schedule.

There was a tendency among members of the political elite to regard the election as a panacea; that is, to expect that it would decisively resolve the political conflicts that were apparent everywhere resulting from the disintegration of the New Order between forces defending the status quo and those committed to *reformasi.* Their expectation reminds us of Przeworski's theoretical formulation of democracy as "a particular system of processing and terminating inter-group conflicts." However, to what extent they realized and had accepted democracy as a process of "institutionalizing uncertainty"—a system of "terminating" rather than "resolving" conflicts in which "losers who play according to the rules do not forsake their right to keep playing"—was open to question.[29]

After the passage of the new political laws and the setting of the date for the election, doomsayers were raising tough questions: Can an election be organized under new rules and implemented in a sprawling country involving more than 100 million voters in only four months? With the (authoritarian) controls loosening on the expression of ethnic, religious, race, and class (SARA) sentiments and social tensions exacerbated by a severe economic depression, will staging a general election result in the eruption of a conflagration, causing in turn a return to authoritarian rule or disintegration of the

Indonesian nation-state? These scenarios failed to materialize, and the election—nine months long and interspersed with all sorts of problems and occasional chaos—went more smoothly than everyone expected.

NOTES

1. United States–Indonesia Society, "Parliamentary Elections in Indonesia," workshop proceedings, Washington, D.C., June 22, 1999.
2. Ellyasa K. H. Darwis, "Tiga Paket UU Politik Tahun 1999," in Komite Independen Pemantau Pemilu (KIPP), *Menata Reformasi Paska Pemilu 1999* (Jakarta: KIPP, 2000), 2.
3. Hermanwan Sulistyo, "Kesimpulan," in Komite Independen Pemantau Pemilu, *Kekerasan Politik Dalam Pemilu 1999* (Jakarta: KIPP, 2000), 157–158.
4. See Donald E. Weatherbee, "Indonesia: Electoral Politics in a Newly Emerging Democracy," in *How Asia Votes*, ed. John Fuhsheng Hsien and David Newman (New York: Seven Bridges Press, 2001).
5. Panita Pengawas Pemilihan Umum, *Pengawasan Pemilihan Umum 1999* (Jakarta: Panmas Pusat, 1999), 26.
6. Weatherbee, "Indonesia," 341.
7. Considering the severe cuts in the number of appointed seats for the military and police and the opportunity for 200 indirectly elected seats (i.e., 135 regional and 65 group representatives), the question arises whether (retired) military obtained some of these indirectly elected seats. Some evidence that they did not comes from the results of organizing the Assembly. Regional representatives were required to affiliate with one of the eleven blocs in the Assembly. None chose to affiliate with the military bloc. See National Democratic Institute (NDI), "The 1999 Presidential Election, MPR General Session and Post-Election Developments in Indonesia," November 28, 1999.
8. *Partai Partai Politik Indonesia* (Jakarta: Kompas, 1999), xi.
9. Nine provinces multiplied by six districts multiplied by 141 parties equals 7,614 potential party organizational units needing verification. This works out to about 28 per day per team member.
10. International Foundation for Election Systems (IFES), "Regulation of Political Finance in Indonesia," December 1999, unpublished manuscript.
11. Ibid. For example, PDI-P reported 586 unidentified donors, fourteen donations from individuals that exceeded the legal limit, four excessive contributions from business entities, and a $50,000 equivalent loan from an individual. Golkar acknowledged receiving three anonymous personal donations that were double or triple the limit and three contributions from corporations that exceeded the limit, and it failed to attach a list of donors to its final report as required by law. PKB reported receiving two donations from individuals that exceeded the legal limit and four excessive contributions from business entities. PPP reported contributions from 168 party executives that exceeded the legal limits. PAN reported receiving one individual donation that exceeded the limit. Most of the $74,000 reported received by PKP came from unidentified donors.

12. Ibid.

13. Panitia Pengawas Pemilihan Umum, *Pengawasan Pemilihan Umum 1999*. However, as will be noted, I found that one case was prosecuted in Sleman.

14. Weatherbee, "Indonesia."

15. For a critical evaluation of the supervisory committees and recommendations for their improvement, see Fredrick Rawski, "Draft Report on Panwaslu," July 23, 1999, unpublished manuscript.

16. This relates to the PR-plus system, under which each candidate had to stand from a particular (district) constituency and the winning candidates were determined by a combination of position on the party list and voting results at the constituency level.

17. Indicative was the commission's independent recording and publishing of election violations, which have little correspondence with those recorded and published by the central supervisory committee. Compare Komisi Pemilihan Umum (KPU), *Buku Evaluasi Pelanggaran dan Kecurangan Pemilihan Umum Tahun 1999* (Jakarta: KPU, 2000) and Panitia Pengawas Pemilihan Umum, *Pengawasan Pemilihan Umum 1999*.

18. In their study of violations in the 1992 election when village and polling-station election committees were dominated by government officials, Alexander Irwan and Edriana found that 618 out of 1,019 (61 percent) of violations were committed at the village (PPS) and polling station (KPPS) levels and more than half involved violations of the rights of political party witnesses. See *Pemilu: Pelanggaran Asas Luber* (Jakarta: Pustaka Sinar Harapan, 1995), 18–22.

19. Panita Pengawas Pemilihan Umum, *Pengawasan Pemilihan Umum 1999*.

20. At the polling station where I monitored the counting, each of the approximately 500 ballots were unfolded, displayed, choice announced orally, and tallied one by one, a process that consumed about four hours. Then a discrepancy of one vote (0.2 percent) resulted in a decision by the committee running the station to immediately conduct a complete recount, which they completed about midnight, bringing to an end their eighteen-hour workday.

21. These categories encompassed the following types of problems: discrepancy between number of ballots received and number of registered voters, unavailability of ballots for nonresidents with proof of registration elsewhere, insufficient indelible ink (used on fingers to prevent multiple voting), insufficient number of holograms (attached to official ballots), late arrival of election materials, unregistered voters with valid identification permitted to vote, election workers requiring voters to sign or address their ballots, barring of properly credentialed monitors, counting of votes at night under insufficient illumination for witnessing and monitoring, counting ballots at a different location, counting ballots without the presence of political party witnesses, and improper completion of reporting forms by election workers.

22. Included in this category were using government budgetary funds and development projects to benefit a particular party, bribing voters or purchasing votes, and receiving contributions above and beyond the limitations of the law.

23. The district element reduced central party leaders' power because had they strictly followed the law the designation of winning candidates would have been an objective, arithmetical exercise and some party officials would not have been seated in the House. In other words, political imperative often took priority over following the letter of the election regulations.

24. NDI, "The 1999 Presidential Election."

25. Greater Jakarta included Bogor, Tangerang, Bekasi, and Depok.

26. "Muka Lama: Birokrat; Muka Baru: Wirausahawan dan Guru," *Kompas*, October 1, 1999.

27. Steven Wagner for IFES, "Preliminary Summary of Public Opinion Preceding the Parliamentary Elections in Indonesia—1999," n.d.; Steven Wagner for IFES, "Survey of the Indonesian Electorate Following the June 1999 Elections," n.d. These surveys were intended to be representative of the entire adult population of Indonesia (over eighteen years of age) and claim a margin of sampling error of less than ±2.5 percent. I have combined responses to "completely satisfied" and "somewhat satisfied."

28. John McBeth, "Dawn of a New Age," *Far Eastern Economic Review*, September 17, 1998.

29. Adam Przeworski, "Problems in the Study of Transition to Democracy," in *Transitions from Authoritarian Rule: Comparative Perspectives*, ed. Guillermo O'Donnell, Philippe Schmitter, and Laurence Whitehead (Baltimore: Johns Hopkins University Press, 1986), 56–57.

CHAPTER 5

The Election in the Heartland of Java: A Case Study

This case study at the local level is intended to provide a detailed and comprehensive picture of how the electoral reforms affected the 1999 election in a particular place. It thus complements Chapter 4, illustrating many of the arguments and adding colorful details. The overall question guiding the study was this: In what specific ways was this election similar to and different from previous New Order elections?

Sleman is a district located in the special region and province of Yogyakarta, which is considered the heartland of the island of Java and the cultural center of Indonesia's largest ethnic group, the Javanese. Bordering the municipality and provincial capital, Yogyakarta, on the south and encompassing the highly fertile slopes of Indonesia's most active volcano, Mt. Merapi, on the north, Sleman is the most prosperous district in the province. Its economy is highly diversified, although the majority of Sleman's people are employed in agriculture. A major domestic and international tourist destination, Sleman sports a half-dozen five-star hotels, the world-renowned Prambanan Temple complex, and the only multimedia training center in Indonesia. With a population approaching 1 million and twenty-nine institutions of higher learning (twenty-seven private and two public), Sleman has the reputation of being an enlightened and dynamic area, modestly expressed in its official motto and acronym, "Sleman capable" (*SEMBADA*) (see the appendix to this chapter for additional statistics on Sleman).[1]

REGISTRATION OF PARTIES,
VOTERS, AND CANDIDATES

Forty-seven of the forty-eight parties authorized as election contestants by the Central Election Committee (PPI) registered to campaign in Sleman. The one that did not register turned out to be an extremely minor party in terms of both the district and the national voting results.[2] Every party that registered received a subsidy from the Sleman district government that was spread over two fiscal years (April through March). The subsidy totaled Rp. 13,700,000 (Rp. 291,489 per party) in 1998–1999 and Rp. 240,000,000 (Rp. 5,106,382 per party) in 1999–2000.[3] Apparently these subsidies were in addition to those received by provincial and national party organizations from the provincial and national governments.[4]

Voter registration got off to a slow start beginning April 5, apparently due to the change from passive to active mode in which prospective voters were required to take the initiative and to the truncated registration period compared to previous years. Concern about security was another factor, as the political unrest and rioting that rocked Jakarta and nearby Solo less than a year earlier was still fresh in people's memories. During the first week of registration villagers had to present themselves in person at the registration office set up by the village election committee (PPS), where they were required to show some form of identification such as a population registration card (KTP), marriage certificate, or driver's license. Then the PPS official filled out a form and gave the registrant a receipt. Since only a small proportion of eligible voters had registered themselves by the end of the first week, instructions came down from Jakarta for PPSs to switch to the passive mode. Beginning on April 13, PPS members went house to house identifying and registering eligible voters. Additional voters were added to the rolls through May 15, bringing total registration in Sleman to 553,587 persons or about 96 percent of all those eligible.

Unlike previous elections, when the PPSs were controlled by the village administration, which supplied the chairman and majority of members, in this election PPSs were allowed to have only one representative of the government, they were dominated by party representatives, and they chose their own chairpersons. They reported encountering two problems. Unlike previous years, when residency in the village was a criterion for membership and PPSs were composed of local leaders, under the new rules the major criterion for membership was being designated the representative of a particular political party. Usually, every party having an organizational structure (*kepengurusan*) in the village was entitled to a representative on the committee. But sometimes parties with supporters in the village but no formal organization were accommodated as well, and they sent representatives who were not residents. These nonresident PPS members were often poorly, if at all, acquainted with the community they were attempting to register, an obvious handicap in locating eligible voters, especially those omitted from the list of registered voters that had been prepared for the previous 1997 election.

Second, multiparty committees turned out to be a mixed blessing, beginning at the village level and at every higher level, including the General Election Commission (KPU). From a theoretical democratic perspective, they were supposed to provide checks and balances and ensure transparency, honesty, and fairness, but being competitors, the members of the multiparty committees often had difficulty working together. Thus, multiparty composition proved a recipe for inefficiency, which became apparent in the voter registration process.

Another kind of problem arose from the tardy and uneven distribution of election materials. Some PPSs failed to receive the official forms on which they were supposed to report registered voters. If they created their own forms, the authenticity came under question at higher levels of review. If they waited for the forms to arrive, they were late in meeting deadlines. Thus, delays arising from partisan antagonism were often exacerbated by this authenticity–time dilemma.

These problems reverberated in other aspects of the Sleman committee's preparation for the election and it found ways to short-cut what seemed like excessively complicated procedures mandated in the election regulations. After drawing up the provisional list of registered voters by April 18, election rules directed that it be sent to the committee at the next subdistrict level (PPK) for review and ratification before being posted publicly in the village for three days. At the end of that time the list was supposed to be revised, becoming the permanent list and taking into account any changes that seemed warranted from the process of public scrutiny. Then the cycle was to be repeated over the next six days, ending April 29. In practice, however, PPSs seldom posted either the provisional or the permanent list, removing the opportunity for scrutiny not only from the public, but also depriving the supervisory committees (*panwas*) one of their core functions. Moreover, the extension of the registration period by instruction from Jakarta until May 4 sent a signal that intermediate deadlines and procedures could be ignored.

Beginning with voter registration, the various phases of the election were monitored by a network of supervisory committees (*panwas* or *pengawas*) that were established at four administrative levels. At every third level (e.g., district of Sleman) the supervisory committee was composed of seventeen persons appointed by the chief judge of the district court from among persons considered to be nonpartisan leaders in the community or in local institutions of higher education. The *panwas* for the district of Sleman was inaugurated and began its work on April 8, guided by printed technical instructions sent from the provincial level (ultimately the central *panwas* in Jakarta) and assisted by a secretariat of ten employees of the district court. The fourth-level supervisory committees (*panwascam*) were established in similar manner, although there was more flexibility in composition. Committee heads did not have to be judges, nor did members have to be drawn from the higher-education community in areas where they were unavailable.

According to members of the Sleman *panwas*, their work was inhibited by apparent disregard of civil service rank in the appointment of leaders and corruption of funds allocated for the work of the committee. The chief judge of the district court appointed a judge to head the *panwas's* secretariat (tasked with operations) who was more senior than the judge he appointed to chair the *panwas* (tasked with policy and administrative decisions). *Panwas* members were convinced this aberrant procedure was intended to facilitate the skimming of funds allocated for the election, because the secretariat failed to assist the work of the committee even in basic operations (e.g., no recordkeeping or filing system), and the senior judge heading the secretariat would not recognize the administrative authority of the *panwas* chairman.

These problems were local manifestations of a basic contradiction and weakness that permeated every level of the election organization. While executive authority was vested in independent committees (consistent with *reformasi*), they were assisted operationally by secretariats composed of the same individuals who were involved in the implementation of previous (New Order) elections. However, in Sleman most of the time these bureaucrats refrained from active partisanship on behalf of Golkar, the party identified with the government. More often they remained silent and passive, which may also have been motivated by fear of causing a disturbance. Examples included the passivity of the police while observing blatant violations of campaign regulations, and the silence of hamlet leaders at the "money politics" trial described later.

To monitor the registration process, the Sleman *panwas* organized itself into four teams, with each team responsible for several of the seventeen subdistricts in Sleman. Then each team paid a visit to the subdistrict committees (PPK and *panwascam*), as well as to several village-level voting committees (PPS) chosen at random. This seemed the best way to approach the Herculean task they faced: the need to monitor and supervise a total of eighty-six PPS and 1,345 polling stations (TPS).

The Sleman committees (PPD-II, Panwas-II) were also involved with the certification of candidates who had been nominated for the district legislature. This was no small task, involving certification of about one-third of the 725 candidates on party lists for all three legislatures (DPR, DPRD-I, DPRD-II). Problems occurred with five cases. In one case the local head of the People's Rule Party, who was listed at the top of his party's list for the district legislature, was found to have been listed as a local officer of the National Mandate Party (PAN) during party registration. Other parties clamored for the disqualification of the entire PDR list on the basis that it had been submitted under the chairman's fraudulent signature. The problem was resolved without disqualification of the entire PDR list by the presumed head agreeing to withdraw his PDR candidacy. In another two cases accusations of flawed character were raised by members of the respective subdistrict constituency. One case concerned termination of employment with the police and the other involved chronic alcoholism. The fourth case involved a nominee who had been convicted of a felony (theft). All four cases resulted in withdrawal of nominations.

The case of the nominee accused of alcoholism had another dimension. The accusation had been made in a letter sent in the name of the subdistrict supervisory committee to the provincial election committee (PPD). When the nominee found out, he threatened to kill whomever sent the letter. The subdistrict committee reported the threat to the police and the Sleman *panwas* sent a letter of warning to the nominee's party. Meanwhile, the police summoned the district party leader and instructed him to help control the nominee. They also quietly intensified the security around the threatened committee members.

THE CAMPAIGN

As in previous elections, the campaign was highly regulated. The election commission issued detailed regulations, running sixteen pages in length.[5] These were in addition to the regulations that had been laid down in the Law on Political Parties and the Law on General Elections, which dealt with the most serious violations (*pidana*). The regulations included the permissible "forms" (*bentuk*) of campaigning (e.g., dialogues, monologues, limited public meetings, radio and television broadcasts, public distribution of partisan materials, public display of partisan materials), the "style" (*tata cara penyelenggaraan*) of campaigning (e.g., parties have equal rights and obligations; everyone must maintain security, order, national unity, and integrity; prohibition on negative campaigning), and the campaign schedule (e.g., May 19 through June 4, mass meetings only between 9:00 A.M. and 6:00 P.M., at least five radio or television broadcasts per party). Included as well was a section containing fourteen prohibitions and five types of sanctions, ranging from written warning to progressive (district, province, nationwide) cessation of campaign activity.

Sleman election authorities sought additional methods to structure the campaign in ways they thought would minimize conflict among the supporters of different parties. First, the period was divided into two rounds of eight days each. Second, the district was divided into two zones, east and west. Each party was assigned two specific days of campaigning, one in each round, and they were split between the two zones. Third, in order to accommodate all forty-eight parties, six parties were scheduled every day (simultaneously), three in the eastern zone and three in the western zone. In the final step, the assignment of specific parties to specific dates, more subjective or political considerations came into play. Each of the eight parties perceived to have the most supporters was assigned a different day. These parties were Golkar, PKB, PK, PPP, PDI-P, PAN, PBB, and PKP. In sum, all legal public campaign activity had its prearranged time and place; any activities outside these specifications was a violation and subject to sanctions.

There were other constraints as well. If a party wanted to utilize its scheduled opportunity to campaign, it was supposed to notify the police and the district election committee (PPD-II) in writing three days in advance. They were asked to specify the place, time, estimated number of participants, and form or type of activity. Parades and convoys with motorized vehicles were prohibited.

In order to instruct party activists and to ensure that the rules were well socialized, the Sleman government called a meeting of local party leaders and police in advance of the start of the campaign period. All assented to an agreement with seven clauses, including "all activities would be in accordance with religious teachings, ethics and courtesy," "never disturb another party's activities," and "maintain unity and harmony of the community." All were warned that they shared the responsibility for upholding the agreement.

Despite all this advance planning, it turned out that many of the regulations were honored about as often in the breech. Parties frequently failed to give advance notice of their planned activities. The larger parties, especially, could not or would not contain their activities within the predetermined zone as well as the district boundary. Virtually all parties violated the prohibition against motorized parades, during which their supporters engaged in various traffic violations and endangered the safety of others using the same roads. In fact, these parades were the predominant form of campaigning.

Various forms of political violence occurred, but fortunately none was lethal. A particularly difficult problem to manage was the bands of youthful PDI-P and PPP marshals armed with swords, spears, and clubs. Despite their blatant violation of the law prohibiting the carrying of sharp weapons, the authorities were reluctant to intervene for a variety of reasons, including being outnumbered and fear of provoking a riot. Another form was the destruction of rival party flags, posters, and command posts. The alleged perpetrators in most of these cases were supporters of PPP, and it was a PPP nominee who threatened to kill, as described earlier. A number of cases of negative campaigning occurred, usually taking the form of anonymous pamphlets insulting Golkar.

The campaign served to expose those tiny new parties that had entered the campaign largely for the money. Indonesian National Party of Supeni (PNI-Supeni), the Republic Party (PR), and the Deliberation, Work and Cooperation Party of the Republic (MKGR) were three parties that failed to organize any public campaign activities on their scheduled days. During their attempts to monitor campaign activities, members of the supervisory committee found that the leader of PNI-Supeni had listed the telephone number of his brother-in-law, but he was residing elsewhere out of telephone contact. The office of the Republic Party in Sleman was housed in a temporary shelter with bamboo walls and a dirt floor, and lacked a telephone or any office equipment. A neighbor reported that the party leader was not readily accessible because he lived some distance away in another subdistrict. The MKGR scheduled a rally for 2:00 P.M. on May 22 in the subdistrict of Kalasan, but no one showed up except the party's subdistrict leader and two members of the supervisory committee, who had come to monitor. He explained that he was the sole party member in the subdistrict and carried out all tasks and roles by himself, from making posters to serving as the party's candidate for the Sleman legislature (DPRD-II).

The campaign period ended on Friday, June 4, and was followed by a two-day calm period (*masa tenang*). Friday night virtually all partisan posters, banners, flags, and other attributes posted in a public place or publicly visible were removed, except for some "command posts" (*posko*), the elevated, bamboo meeting places that had been erected, usually by youthful PDI-P supporters. Fearing that they could easily be incited to riot, election officials tolerated this infraction of the rules. The calm period was a continuation of the practice used in previous elections under the New Order and reflected the concern of election authorities with keeping emotions stirred by partisan activity under control. According to the election supervisory committee, the worst violations of election rules occurring during the calm period were instances of "money politics" and most implicated Golkar. A man was found handing out Rp. 50,000 bills (about $8) to village heads, along with a picture of a ballot being punched for Golkar in the subdistricts of Pakem and Turi.[6] A supporter of Golkar in one village and a supporter of PKB in another were reported to have handed out Rp. 10,000 bills (about $1.25) for the promise of a vote. In a meeting of the Family Welfare Movement (PKK) in Pendowoharjo village, a subdistrict of Sleman, Golkar supporters were reported to have distributed detergent and money to women in attendance. In Umbulmartani village, a subdistrict of Ngemplak, Golkar sponsored a short course on making traditional medicine, which was accompanied with practice in how to punch a ballot for Golkar and a Rp. 12,000 (about $1.50) honorarium for all participants.[7]

One of these offenders was charged with a criminal offense under the Election Law and was finally brought to trial before a three-judge panel in Sleman district court over a year later.[8] If convicted, the election law provided for a maximum sentence of three years in jail. In the testimony from two PDI-P marshals (*satgas*) and three hamlet leaders (*kepala dusun*) on the opening day, the crime was described as follows: The accused visited hamlet leaders, bringing them a supply of mock ballots that had been punched for Golkar and asking them to distribute the copies to voters in their respective hamlets. He also gave them an envelope containing Rp. 50,000. About forty spectators came to watch the proceedings and most of them were known as PDI-P partisans. The accused was eventually convicted, but the sentence was unavailable. This is the only case of election law violation to be prosecuted in Sleman.

In their final report on election violations, the election monitoring committee for the province of Yogyakarta (MPP Walhi DIY), a federation of independent monitoring groups, found that 124 cases of election-rule violations occurred in the district of Sleman. About one-third of these were noncriminal violations committed by local election committees, apparently as a result of insufficient understanding of election regulations.[9]

VOTING AND COUNTING

Overall, the casting of ballots proceeded smoothly at the 1,345 polling stations in the district. In terms of voter turnout, the election in Sleman was a clear success, with 96 percent of the registered voters casting their ballots. At every polling station about a dozen local people volunteered their labor, from early morning until late at night. Others contributed food for poll workers and materials needed for erecting the polling stations because the government provided a subsidy of only Rp. 40,000 (about $5) per station. Unlike past elections, party witnesses and independent monitors were present at every station. Serious violations resulting in calls for repolling did not occur. Nevertheless, the election supervisory committee noted the frequent occurrence of small infractions. Polling stations opened late, after 8:00 A.M., because the polling station committees (KPPS) were unprepared. Materials used at the stations were deficient (e.g., insufficient ballots, low-quality indelible ink that faded too quickly).

The counting process was more problematic, as serious delays occurred nearly everywhere in the district. Provisional subdistrict results were reported almost immediately by telephone directly to the Joint Operations Media Center, which had been set up in Jakarta by the General Election Commission. However, the processing of official results up the regular administrative channel was badly delayed and not announced until August 1, nearly two months after the election. A number of reasons were given for the delay. Little training was given to poll workers. The counting at the polling-station and village levels was all done manually, a tedious and boring process for poll workers. On the average and with no mistakes, initial counting took about ten hours.[10] If counting began immediately after the polls closed at 2:00 P.M. and a one-hour break was taken for dinner and evening prayer, poll workers finished their task at 11:00 P.M., approximately a sixteen-hour work day. Also, there were no minimum requirements for poll workers. Many were inexperienced and had been given too little training in advance. The forms that had to be completed by the polling-station committees were quite complicated. They had to account for every ballot received, damaged, used, and left over. At a polling station monitored by the author, the committee found their tabulations were in error by 1 out of over 500 ballots cast (less than 0.2 percent), but because they wanted to do their job perfectly (and without any basis for suspicion), they decided to completely recount the ballots, which took them far into the night. At the next two levels of reporting and aggregation (village, subdistrict), election officials waited on complete reporting from below before forwarding results to the next level. In such a system, it is easy to understand how delays accumulated.

At the subdistrict and district levels, a potential cause of delay was the requirement that party representatives certify the results in their respective area. If they had complaints about the administration of the election or doubted the validity of the results, they could cause delay by withholding their signatures until the problem had been addressed to their satisfaction.

Table 5.1 shows the direction of the vote in Sleman and includes comparative indicators on the province of Yogyakarta and for the nation as a whole. It is interesting to note that the reform parties (PDI-P, PAN, and PKB) received more support in Sleman than at the provincial and national levels. This is especially the case with PAN, which can probably be explained by the fact that PAN's general chairman, Amien Rais, resided in Sleman. The higher support for reform parties was largely at the expense of Golkar, which did worse in Sleman than in the province and nationwide.

Focusing only on Sleman, very slight differences are apparent in the results for the three legislatures. Only PKB and PPP registered slight improvement in their relative support for the provincial (DPRD-I) and district (DPRD-II) legislatures. Another finding (not shown in Table 5.1) is a slight drop-off in total number of votes cast for provincial and for district legislatures. That is, 521,266 votes were cast for the DPR, 518,113 for the DPRD-I, and 516,614 for the DPRD-II, or a decline of about 1 percent between votes for the DPR and votes for the DPRD-II.

These small discrepancies were likely caused by implementation of the election regulations regarding voting away from home. Voters who registered to vote outside their district or city (administrative level II) of residence but within their province (level I) were allowed to vote for national (DPR) and provincial (DPRD-I) legislatures, but not for district or city legislature (DPRD-II). Similarly, voters registered outside their province of residence were allowed to vote for the national legislature but not provincial and district or city legislatures. As a center of higher education with a large student population originating from all over Indonesia, Sleman had a relatively large student population who may have been subject to these regulations, preventing them from casting one or two of the three ballots. Large numbers of student voters may also have been a factor helping to explain why reform parties obtained proportionately more support in Sleman than in the province of Yogyakarta.

ALLOCATING SEATS AND DETERMINING REPRESENTATIVES

In contrast to New Order elections, this phase of the election proved to be one of the most conflictual and difficult in Sleman. To understand why, it is useful to note that at each of the three administrative levels, authority over the final vote count and the allocation of seats to parties was supposed to be the responsibility of the corresponding elec-

Table 5.1
Direction of the Vote in Sleman District, Yogyakarta Province, and Indonesia

| Party | Sleman District | | | Yogyakarta Province | Indonesia Nationwide |
	DPR	DPRD-I	DPRD-II	DPR	DPR
PDI-P	36.4	36.2	35.8	35.7	33.7
PAN	19.3	18.8	18.7	17.3	7.1
PKB	14.0	14.3	14.3	14.3	12.6
Golkar	11.8	11.7	11.7	14.3	22.4
PPP	5.3	5.5	5.7	4.9	10.7

Source: General Election Commission (KPU).

tion committee (i.e., PPI, PPD-I, PPD-II). In their effort to distinguish themselves in a crowded field of forty-eight parties, party leaders at all three levels were often more concerned about advancing their own personal interests than their common interest in upholding the rules of the political game. But their behavior was also partly a response to uncertainty in the legal environment, as the General Election Commission issued some rules late, abruptly changed rules on several occasions, and even promulgated contradictory rules.

In Sleman, controversy erupted over the legality of vote pooling (*stembus akkords*; SA) in awarding six seats on the basis of "largest remainders."[11] The commission was late in establishing ground rules for such accords. Then it extended the deadline to June 4 or three days before the election, so one source of controversy concerned the deadline for declaration of SA. Two out of six SAs in Sleman had been first concluded at the national level for the DPR prior to the extended deadline. But four were only local agreements (DPRD-II) that had been declared after the deadline. Controversy swirled, especially about the legality of the latter, causing local election officials to seek guidance from higher levels.

But the General Election Commission twice reversed its decisions, adding fuel to the fire. On July 21 the commission advised provincial officials in Yogyakarta that only SAs concluded among national party leaders were valid for allocation of seats in the regional legislatures. The first reversal came on August 4, when the commission ruled that local SAs were valid internal affairs of the parties. Moreover, whether a local SA had been concluded after June 4 was immaterial. A radiogram dated August 10 canceling the August 4 instruction was the second reversal.

In an effort to end the uncertainly over SAs in Sleman, local election officials (i.e., PPD-II and *panwas*) met August 11 and found other deficiencies in the local SAs. Some lacked signatures of parties supposed to be involved. Some bore signatures of party functionaries other than the local chairperson of the party concerned. Finally, some parties had already withdrawn from local SAs. The officials concluded their deliberations by deciding to disallow local SAs in the awarding of the last six seats. Their action foreshadowed the decision on August 30 by the commission to break the deadlock at the national level by abolishing all SAs.

CONCLUSION

The election in Sleman district went remarkably smoothly considering the political uncertainty over the previous year, the crowded field of forty-seven contestants, and new rules that were handed down only several months before. Compared with previous elections, the citizenry was more involved, indicated not only by voting turnout, but also by the thousands who attended campaign rallies and served voluntarily as election workers, party witnesses, or independent monitors at polling places. Their actions reflected a collective realization, at least among a significant portion of the population, about the importance of this election for political reform and democratization in Indonesia.[12]

Community and government leaders cooperated to prevent conflict from erupting and to maintain social harmony. To this end, they continued a number of the practices that had been introduced in the previous, authoritarian New Order era, such as a short sixteen-day campaign, structuring the campaign according to rounds and requiring that the keenest competitors campaign on different days, requiring advance notification of public meetings, and a period of calm between the campaign and election day. Still, small-scale conflict erupted here and there and hundreds of minor and dozens of major election violations occurred. There were times when the authorities either could not or would not enforce the rules, with the motorized parades and *poskos* left standing during the quiet period and election day as good examples. But in previous elections sanctions were rarely applied because the government and its party, Golkar, were the biggest violators. Now the lax enforcement and reluctance to prosecute were more the result of inadequately specified rules, ambiguous responsibility, and fragmentation of authority.

The Sleman experience showed that the design of the electoral system has important consequences. The modified proportional representation system adopted in the 1999 Election Law required that a legislative candidate be identified with a particular constituency. In Sleman the scrutiny of subdistrict constituencies raised questions that ultimately resulted in the denial of five nominations. This showed that a necessary function in the electoral process, previously carried out behind closed doors by government security and intelligence agencies, could be implemented much more democratically.

The electoral law and the implementing regulations issued by the General Election Commission and the Supreme Court contained ambiguities and limitations that tended to weaken the legitimacy of the election. One example was the reversal by the commission in first allowing and then disallowing vote-pooling arrangements. Another was the powerlessness of the supervisory committees. Formally they had authority in all but criminal matters (e.g., attempts to buy and sell votes), but they were given no means of enforcing sanctions on violators.

In its concluding report, the Sleman supervisory committee identified these weaknesses in the election: deficiencies in election workers, unsatisfactory facilities and infrastructure, uncertainty in regulations and insufficient implementing regulations, lack of transparency in managing funds for the election at several levels of the bureaucracy, weaknesses in the ability of political parties to provide political education for their followers, and insufficient consciousness on the part of some citizens and party leaders about the real meaning and function of an election campaign. To remedy these weaknesses, the committee recommended (1) the establishment of specific, minimum qualifications for election workers, (2) more satisfactory administrative support in the form of computers, guide books containing election regulations, and large, blank tabulation sheets, (3) improvements in the design, method, materials used, and intensity of briefing and training activities for election workers, and (4) that parties provide more and better political education for their supporters.

We conclude with the proverbial "half full or half empty" situation. Despite some major similarities with previous, New Order elections (e.g., short and highly structured campaign period, mobilization of voters during the last half of the registration period, inability or unwillingness to prosecute Election Law violators), the differences, many of which were inspired by *reformasi*, were far greater. They provide reasons for finding the glass of electoral reform half filled.

APPENDIX

Sleman in Statistics, 1996–1998

Administrative areas: Seventeen subdistricts (*kecamatan*), eighty-six villages (*desa*), 1,212 *dusun*, 2,866 *rukun warga*, 6,961 *rukun tetangga*

Area: 57,482 hectares (18 percent of the province of Yogyakarta)

Average annual rate of population growth: 1.19 percent

Population density: 1,391 per square kilometer

Population living in rural areas: 51.91 percent, residing in fifty-four villages

Population living in urban areas: 48.09 percent, residing in thirty-two villages

Infant mortality rate: 8 per 1,000

Child mortality rate (under five years of age): 0.63 per 1,000

Life expectancy: seventy-three years

Regional Gross Product by Economic Sector, 1998 (based on market prices)

Sector	Rupiah (millions)	Percentage
Agriculture	474.9	17.7
Mining	11.1	0.4
Manufacturing	407.3	15.2
Electricity, gas, water	24.2	0.9
Construction	251.9	9.4
Trade, hotel, restaurant	519.0	19.3
Transportation and communication	258.3	9.6
Finance, rent	287.9	10.7
Services	453.4	16.9
Total	2,688.1	100.0

Sources: Ir. Sutrisno, MES (Chairman, BAPPEDA Sleman), "Peta dan Potensi Wilayah KKN di Kabupaten Dati II Sleman," 1996; BPS and BAPPEDA Kabupaten Sleman, *Buku Saku Statistik Kabupaten Sleman 1998*, Sleman, September 1999.

NOTES

1. SEMBADA refers to *Sehat, Elok, Makmur, Berbudaya, Aman, Dinamis, Agamis* (healthy, beautiful, wealthy, civilized, secure, dynamic, religious).

2. In Sleman, Masyumi Baru received under 700 votes and nationally it received 0.14 percent. To understand how a new, locally unregistered party could still receive about 700 votes in Sleman, one must recall that Masjumi was one of the "big four" parties in the 1955 election. If Masjumi Baru leaders hoped name recognition would bring them votes, their strategy proved effective. There is a Pearson's correlation coefficient of .63 between areas of Masjumi strength in the 1955 election and areas of Masjumi Baru strength in 1999.

3. Supardjo, head of election subsection (Kasubsie Pemilu) of the Sleman Social–Political office (Kantor Sospol), interview with author, May 16, 2000.

4. The central government provided Rp. 150,000,000 for every party. In addition, the Yogyakarta provincial government reportedly contributed Rp. 10,000,000 per party, but these reports could not be confirmed.

5. Keputusan Komisi Pemilihan Umum Indonesia no. 13/1999 tentang Tata Cara dan Jadwal Waktu Kampanye Pemilihan Umum.

6. *Kedaulatan Rakyat*, June 9, 1999.

7. Based on notes of the junior author, who was a member of the Sleman supervisory committee.

8. *Kedaulatan Rakyat*, June 9, 1999. Case 44/Pid.B/2000, in which the accused was Sadputra Wahyu Giri.

9. *Kedaulatan Rakyat*, June 12, 1999.

10. An average of 412 voters each cast three ballots at the polling station or a total of 1,236 ballots. If opening, displaying, and tallying each ballot consumed thirty seconds, it would have taken over three hours to count them, provided no mistakes were made.

11. The electoral district for the DPR and the DPRD-I was the province, but for the DPRD-II it was the district and municipality. Each electoral district had a quota equal to the total population divided by the number of seats available (e.g., 824,266/45 = 18,317 in Sleman). Parties earned one seat for each quota of votes received and remaining seats were then allocated to parties on the basis of the largest vote remainders. A *stembus akkord* is a voluntary agreement among parties to combine their remainders in order to improve their chances of obtaining seats.

12. We recognize that some people had other motivations for participation in the election, such as "going along to get along" and seizing the opportunity provided by the campaign for letting off steam or creating public disturbance.

CHAPTER 6

The Democratic Elections of 1955 and 1999: Similarities and Continuities

This chapter begins the task of explaining the influences on voting choices in the 1999 election. Many observers have drawn comparisons with Indonesia's first election, held in 1955. Although separated by forty-four years, the most recent election is widely believed to have had more in common with the first election than with any of the ensuing six elections conducted during Suharto's pseudodemocracy.

Commonality can refer to similarities, which in turn are of different types and causes. We can delineate intentional or planned similarities that occur anywhere elections are administered in democratic fashion (e.g., voter registration in advance, casting secret ballots). This type can be differentiated from similarities that occurred coincidently, such as the two-month delay between election day and announcement of official results, which occurred in both the 1955 and 1999 elections.

Talk about commonality may also assert something deeper, that there were certain continuities between the two elections If this is what is being suggested (or implied), what is alleged to have been transmitted or bequeathed across forty-four years from the 1955 election to the 1999 election? An even more perplexing question is this: What is the best way to investigate and substantiate continuity? If the alleged continuity resides in the thinking or behavior of individuals, then our investigation would of necessity be limited to voters who voted in both elections, virtually all of whom are now over sixty years of age. Relative to the total voting population of 106 million in 1999, it would be a very small and unrepresentative sample indeed!

SIMILARITIES

Perhaps the most obvious similarities were the freedom of the press, the freedom to organize parties, and the large number of election contestants. Both elections were multiparty to the extreme. In 1955, out of over 100 election contestants (parties, groups, individuals), 28 parties won seats, compared to 48 contestants and 21 winning seats in 1999.

There were also similarities in economic and political environments. In both eras, expectations toward the election ran high. Many of the political elite tended to view the election as a panacea. The election was regarded as a way out of an unsatisfactory general economic and political situation and as a means of national reconciliation. In 1955 the situation was viewed as affected by "recurring cabinet crises, army challenges to government authority, corruption, political nepotism, party bickering and above all the impotence of government in the face of the enormous tasks facing it in every direction."[1] This description applied forty-four years later as well, except for recurrent cabinet crises, which no longer applied because of the change to presidential government in the late 1950s. Another difference was that the political environment had been more impacted by sudden economic depression that began in 1997, ignited by the Asian financial crisis. Political stakes were high in both elections, yet no one was able to predict the outcome with any accuracy.

There were a number of parallels as well in election administration. Both were conducted under new electoral laws. In the debate over the electoral law in 1953, proportional representation was adopted without opposition. But in 1998–1999, while the end product was basically a PR system, it was preceded by a lengthy debate in which the government proposed switching to a plurality (district) system. Arguably, both electoral systems had a "hybrid" or combination element. The electoral law of 1953 made provision for a candidate to be elected, regardless of the order in which his name was placed on his party's list, if he obtained by the write-in vote system 50 percent of his party's quotient of votes in any district. As it turned out, not one representative was elected by the write-in system. In 1999 proportional representation by province was combined with assignment of candidates to districts, and some importance was given to district-level results. Vote-pooling arrangements (*stembus akkords*) were permitted and utilized in 1955. In 1999 they were initially allowed, then abruptly canceled when controversy erupted, which could have been avoided had the General Election Commission issued the regulations governing them in a timely manner.

The electoral administration in both eras achieved a high degree of impartiality, in part by granting large roles to multiparty election committees at all levels of election administration. However, adherence to the multiparty format turned into a two-edged sword in both eras; perhaps more than any other aspect, it brought criticism of the electoral system as being democratically perfectionist, overcomplicated, and consequently slow and expensive. In several ways the administration in 1999 was more democratic. When the Central Election Commission was first constituted in 1953, representation from parties in opposition to the government was excluded. Only three days before election day it gained five new members from parties hitherto unrepresented. In 1955 the multiparty election committees at the district and subdistrict levels were chaired by the top executive officer (*bupati, camat*), whereas in 1999 the committees elected their leaders from among party representatives. In both elections the village-level multiparty committee were autonomous and not directly linked to general civil administration.

In both eras slippage occurred in adhering to designated time tables and many technical regulations were issued at the last minute. Three different cabinets were involved in the earlier election. The Election Law was passed and campaigning began under the Wilopo cabinet in mid-1953. But it was under the succeeding Ali Sastroamidjojo cabinet that organizing for the election began and the initial phases of the election were implemented, such as voter registration, submission by the parties of candidate lists, and scheduling of the election for September 29, 1955. When the Burhanuddin Harahap cabinet assumed office on August 12, it immediately faced the question of whether it could or would hold the elections on the date set down by the previous cabinet, but its affirmative answer was delayed until September 8. In the three weeks that remained, a tremendous amount of work had to be done.

The 1999 election was scheduled for June 7, 1999, about four months in advance. Although the government of President Habibie inherited considerable election infrastructure from the previous 1997 election, the organization and rules governing the 1999 election were very different, requiring time for retraining and socialization. Moreover, the number of voters had more than doubled since 1955. As a result, it proved impossible to adhere to the initial schedule in virtually every phase of the election, and the government deliberated postponement until late April or about six weeks before the scheduled election day. Like the Central Election Committee of 1955, the General Election Commission (KPU) of 1999 issued many last-minute (even retroactive) regulations.

With regard to the election campaigns, both were accompanied by widespread fear of violence and political instability, which by and large did not materialize. A related commonality was the sparseness of campaign appeals based on regional and ethnic feeling, and a virtual absence of anti-Chinese appeals. However, this should not be understood to mean that the elections were unaffected by regional rebellions. For example, political instability dampened voting turnout in south and southeast Sulawesi in 1955 and several districts of Aceh in 1999. Perhaps the greatest difference in the two campaigns was in the pattern of party appeals. Due to the communications revolution, the increase in mass media, and higher levels of education and literacy in 1999, there was more similarity between party appeals nationwide and the issues of political debate in Jakarta.

In both elections voting turnout was relatively high and the casting and counting of ballots was carried out mostly in accordance with international standards of transparency, accuracy, and fairness. Voting turnout or the proportion of registered voters participating in the election was estimated at 92 percent in 1955 and 93 percent in 1999.[2] As mentioned, in both elections a two-month delay occurred between election day and the announcement of official results. In both, as well, over a third of representatives were residents of Jakarta.[3]

CONTINUITIES IN THE BASES OF PARTY SUPPORT

On the basis of analysis of the 1999 voting results, some scholars have postulated "broad continuity" with the outcome of the election of 1955.[4] What could this mean? Not that the same election contestants won a similar share of the vote, because in 1999 successful parties (i.e., those winning seats in the legislature or DPR) all had different names, different organizations, different officers and personnel, and a different proportion of the vote. Not that individuals living during both elections tended to vote for similar parties, because even if we knew how they voted, they would form a minuscule and unrepresentative sample. Rather, what is being asserted is that voters with certain characteristics (preferences, attitudes) supported certain parties in each election, revealing or articulating sociocultural divisions in the electorate. These divisions, first noticeable in the 1955 election, reemerged in the 1999 election. What were these patterns?

Four "big" parties emerged from the 1955 election, together attracting 77 percent of the vote. PNI, widely associated with Soekarno, Indonesia's charismatic founding father and head of state at the time of the election, drew support heavily from bureaucrats, nominal or syncretic (*abangan*) Muslims, and some non-Muslims and ethnic minorities and obtained 22 percent of the total vote. Another *abangan* party, PKI, won 16 percent of the vote, attracting mainly workers and peasants on Java.

The party of Islamic modernism, Masjumi, drew 21 percent and ran strongest outside Java.[5] NU, associated with a more traditional variant of Islam, garnered 18.4 percent of the vote, mainly from Java.[6]

There were also six "medium" parties, to use Feith's classification.[7] These included four religious parties. Two were Islamic—PSII (Islamic Association Party) and Perti (Islamic Education Party)—and two were Christian—Parkindo (Indonesian Christian Party) and Katolik (Catholic Party). The two nonreligious parties were PSI (Indonesian Socialist Party) and IPKI (League for the Upholding of Indonesian Independence).

Thus, overall, the 1955 election outcome revealed at least two clear patterns in the electorate. One was a near even balance between voters supporting nationalist and religiously inclusive parties (PNI, PKI, PSI, and IPKI), which, combined, obtained 42 percent of the vote, and those supporting Islamic parties (Masjumi, NU, PSII, Perti), which, together, received 44 percent of the vote. The second pattern was division within each of these two camps. The nationalist, religiously inclusive camp was divided on a class basis, with PKI as the main party of the lower class and PNI more upper class. The more devout Muslims, commonly labeled *santri*, were fractured between those choosing Masjumi (21 percent), the party most clearly identified with Islamic modernism, and those preferring parties associated with the traditional variant of Islam, namely, NU, PSII, and Perti (23 percent combined).

The assertion of "broad continuity" between the two elections implies that the 1999 results reflect similar patterns. However, there would seem to be formidable obstacles to any effort at demonstrating empirically that the 1999 results fit the 1955 patterns. As mentioned, the parties in 1999 had different names, organizations, officers and personnel, and proportions of the vote. The top six parties in 1999 and their respective shares of the vote were as follows:

PDI-P (Indonesian Democracy Party of Struggle)	34 percent
Golkar (Golongan Karya, Functional Groups)	22 percent
PKB (National Awakening Party)	13 percent
PPP (Development Unity Party)	11 percent
PAN (National Message Party)	7 percent
PBB (Star and Moon Party)	2 percent

Another obstacle is that none of the six parties wanted to be labeled "secular" or nonreligious. The majority of each party's supporters were Muslims, and the leaders of all six parties claimed to be practicing devout Muslims. For example, all had made the pilgrimage to Mecca. Only PPP and PBB campaigned on exclusivistic, Islamic themes. Combined, they attracted only 13 percent of the vote, far below the 44 percent obtained by the top four Islamic parties in 1955. Finally, the 1999 results suggest that the cleavage between traditional and modernist Muslims was much less pronounced, as 13 percent of the vote went to PKB (traditionalist) and 9 percent to PAN and PBB combined (modernist). PPP is widely thought to have bridged this cleavage, attracting votes from both traditionalists and modernists. Thus, unless stronger logical and empirical evidence can be found, the "broad continuity" thesis is unpersuasive and unsupported.

Hypotheses

This chapter proposes another approach to the problem of empirical evidence relevant to the "broad continuity" thesis. Essentially, it involves generating hypotheses about common ideological, social, and religious bases of party support in the two elections and then testing the hypotheses empirically by measuring association between areas of support for parties using data on voting at the district level (regencies and municipalities).

In both the 1955 and 1999 elections, the party most closely associated with (first) President Soekarno and representative of the nationalist, nonconfessional political orientation won the most votes. PNI won 22 percent of the vote in 1955, and in 1999 PDI-P, led by Soekarno's daughter Megawati, received 34 percent of the vote. We would expect, therefore, that they drew support from the same areas, which will be reflected in a positive correlation between support for PDI-P in 1999 and support for PNI in 1955 (hypothesis 1).

Because of its inclusive ideology, appeal to lower-class groups (e.g., urban workers, persons in the informal economic sector), and strength in particular regions (e.g., central and east Java, Bali), conventional wisdom on the election is that PDI-P appealed to voters who would have been attracted to PKI had it existed in 1999. Persons disposed toward this assumption infer, in effect, that PDI-P drew support from areas of PKI strength in 1955 (hypothesis 2).

A third intriguing question pertains to sources of support for the "reformed" Golkar party, which did not exist in 1955. Before the election, Golkar's prospects (or lack thereof) was one of the most controversial and hotly debated issues about the election, resulting in widely different predictions. We now know the magnitude of support for Golkar fell from 74 percent of the vote in 1997 to 22 percent in 1999, a 70-percent drop, but we know much less about the sources of that 22-percent support. At the time the 1999 election was carried out, President Habibie was the titular head of Golkar and its presidential candidate. As the founder and long-time chairman of the Association of Indonesian Islamic Intellectuals (ICMI), he was also associated with Islamic modernism. Moreover, Akbar Tandjung, a former leader of the modernist HMI (Islamic Students' Association), had risen to leadership of the party. For these reasons, we might expect that Golkar drew some support from areas where Masjumi and PSII did well in 1955 (hypothesis 3).

But Golkar can reasonably be expected to have drawn from two other areas as well. Because the bureaucracy served as one pillar of Golkar support under the Suharto regime and PNI likewise drew a large amount of its support from the bureaucracy, we might expect a positive correlation between support for Golkar and support for PNI (hypothesis 4). Also, in elections conducted by the Suharto regime, Golkar tended to monopolize the vote in areas that previously were communist strongholds, as voters sought to vote safely. It is reasonable to expect some residue of this pattern, or that Golkar drew support from areas where PKI had been strong in 1955 (hypothesis 5).

Fourth, parties based on Islamic traditionalism, especially strong in central and east Java, did well in both elections. As noted earlier, NU garnered 18 percent of the vote in 1955. However, it abandoned its role as a political party (i.e., component of PPP) in the early 1980s and PKB was founded in 1998 as the receptacle for the political aspirations of members of NU. A year later, PKB won 12 percent of the vote and one of its founders and the long-time chairman of NU, Abdurrahman Wahid, was elected to the presidency. Thus, we would expect a strong positive correlation between the vote for PKB in 1999 and the vote for NU in 1955 (hypothesis 6).

PPP was born through a fusion of four Islamic parties in 1973, a product of New Order social engineering. As the only permitted vehicle for Islamic political aspirations from then until 1998, we can expect that it drew support from areas of both traditional and modernist political orientation and that a positive correlation exists between votes for PPP and votes for any of the 1955 Islamic parties (hypothesis 7).

Finally, Masjumi, the party of Islamic modernists, won 21 percent of the vote in 1955, taking a close second place behind PNI. While modernist Muslims again vigorously organized and campaigned in 1999, they were less unified and apparently divided among PPP, PAN, PBB, and PK. Although PAN tried to appeal to a broader constituency, its leader, Amien Rais, was clearly identified with Islamic modernism. We would expect all of these Islamic parties to have drawn support from areas where Masjumi did well in 1955 (hypothesis 8).

Data and Methodology

The investigation of these hypotheses will focus on analysis of voting results at the district (*kabupaten, kotamadya*) level. There are a number of advantages in utilizing disaggregated information. Because there are more units of observation than in analyses based on national totals or on provincial aggregations, there is less loss of information and more precision in analysis. More powerful analytic techniques appropriate to the interval level of measurement can be utilized. It is also easier to detect any systematic biases in the data and to calculate margins of error or the probability of the findings occurring by chance. As far as is known, there are no published studies on the 1955 election that utilize nationwide voting results at the local level.[8]

The data used here describe voting behavior of groups of people living within defined territorial areas, rather than individuals. Very few of those people—only those over sixty years of age in 1999— could have voted in both the 1955 and 1999 elections, making collection and use of individual-level data highly problematic. The methodological assumption undergirding this analysis is that different individuals grouped by similar characteristics (e.g., modernist Muslims in Sleman district) at two different points in time (1955 and 1999) behaved or chose similarly (e.g., voted for the party perceived to best represent modernist Muslims, Masjumi in 1955 and PAN in 1999).

The 1955 voting results are drawn from the most comprehensive source available. Although not without some limitations, it contains the number of legal or valid votes cast for each party in each of 188 administrative districts (regencies and municipalities).[9] The 1999 voting results are the official returns for the national legislature (DPR) obtained from the Indonesia Election Committee). This source contains the number of legal or valid votes cast for each party in each of 326 regencies and municipalities.

In the forty-four years that passed between the two elections, the number of districts increased by over 70 percent. Thus, the first task in the analysis was to reconstruct the administrative boundaries (i.e., units of observation or data aggregation) used in 1999 in order to make them as geographically identical as possible to those used in 1955 (see Appendix A to this chapter). The next step involved combining the votes received by each party in 1999 in two or more districts and excluding a few districts (those missing or omitted in the 1955 data set; see Appendix B to this chapter). For example, the number of votes for PPP in 1999 in the municipalities of Banda Aceh and Sabang were combined with the votes for PPP in the regency of Aceh Besar because in 1955 these two cities had not yet been separated administratively from the surrounding regency. It should be noted that this task was informed by study of maps showing administrative boundaries and by expert advice, and that reconstruction by aggregating or combining was given priority over reconstruction by exclusion or omission because there was less loss of information.

Once the 1999 administrative boundaries had been reconstructed, the second task was merging the two data sets, or adding the 1955 variables to the (reconstructed) 1999 data set. Third, in order to control for differences in population size among the units, simple percentage indicators were computed by dividing the number of votes listed for each party by the total number of legal votes cast in each district. Finally, Pearson bi-variate correlation coefficients were calculated. On the basis of covariation (or lack thereof) between the number of votes for particular parties across the two elections, inferences can be drawn about likely continuities between the two elections. Table 6.1 is inclusive in the sense that all statistically significant relationships (coefficients) are reported. It is exclusive in the sense that only statistically significant relationships are reported.

In order to keep the presentation from becoming cluttered and overly detailed, only the results of the analysis of the top six parties in 1999 are presented. These six parties combined garnered 88.51 percent of the total votes, and only these six parties passed the 2-percent threshold of legislative seats required to qualify for the next general election in 2004.

Findings

Table 6.1 presents evidence on all of the hypotheses. The coefficients indicate the strength of covariation between areas of support for each of the six 1999 parties and each of the 1955 parties. The higher a coefficient is (the closer it is to 1.0 or −1.0), the stronger the association between areas of support for the two parties.

Note the (positive) coefficients between PDI-P and three 1955 parties that were nationalist and religiously inclusive, PNI (.59), PSI (.48), and PKI (.38). The relationship with PNI supports hypothesis 1 and the relationship with PKI supports hypothesis 2. With PDI-P drawing support from both areas of former PNI and PKI strength, the class division in the nationalist and religiously inclusive (*abangan*) camp appears to have disappeared. However, these three positive

Table 6.1
Relationship between Support for Parties, 1955 and 1999

1999 Party	1955 Party	Positive	1955 Party	Negative
PDI-P	PNI	.59	Masjumi	-.52
	PSI	.48	Perti	-.36
	PKI	.38	PSII	-.21
			NU	-.21
Golkar	PSII	.45	NU	-.44
	Parkindo	.39	PNI	-.38
	Masjumi	.26	PKI	-.35
PKB	NU	.84	Masjumi	-.36
	PKI	.22	Parkindo	-.26
	PNI	.20	PSII	-.21
			Perti	-.20
PPP	Masjumi	.42	PNI	-.27
	Perti	.36	PKI	-.24
			Katolik	-.20
PAN	Masjumi	.53	PNI	-.30
	Perti	.43	Parkindo	-.25
			NU	-.21
PBB	Masjumi	.39	n.s.	n.s.
	Perti	.24		
	IPKI	.20		

Sources: 1955 data, Alfian, *Hasil Pemilihan Umum 1955* (Jakarta: LEKNAS, 1971). Indonesia Election Commission.

Note: Numbers are Pearson correlation coefficients significant at the .005 level in a two-tailed test. Based on votes for DPR.

n.s. = not significant.

coefficients, along with the negative coefficients (or inverse relationship) between PDI-P and each of the four Islamic parties, Masjumi, Perti, PSII, and NU, indicate that the basic cleavage in the Indonesian electorate between areas supporting nationalist and religiously inclusive parties (*abangan*) and areas supporting Islamic parties (*santri*) has not disappeared.

The coefficients of .45 between Golkar and PSII and .31 between Golkar and Masjumi support hypothesis 3. However, the negative correlations of −.38 with PNI and −.35 with PKI were unexpected and are contradictory to hypotheses 4 and 5.

The .84 coefficient between PKB and NU supports hypothesis 6, and the negative correlations between PKB and Masjumi (−.36), between PKB and PSII (−.21), and between PKB and Perti (−.20) reflect the division between traditional and modernist Islamic orientations. The small correlations of PKB with PKI (.22) and with PNI (.20) were unexpected. They indicate PKB had some success, more than any other Islamic party, in bridging the basic cleavage in the electorate between *abangan* and *santri* orientations. An adequate explanation of how it did so requires further research, but two ideas seem plausible. They may reflect a high degree of Islamization and ideological homogenization in areas of previous PKI and PNI support. Second, the relationship with areas of former PKI support may derive from a similar social base of support or the fact that both parties had strong appeal among poor peasants and lower-class voters.[10]

As suggested in hypothesis 7, PPP drew support from both the traditionalist (Perti, .36) and modernist (Masjumi, .44) Islamic persuasions, but it had little appeal across religious lines (Katolik, −.20) or in areas where nationalist, religiously inclusive parties were popular in 1955; that is, areas of PNI (−.27) and PKI (−.24) strength.

Hypothesis 8 about the areas of support for PAN and PBB is likewise supported. Both found support in areas of former Masjumi strength (.53 and .39, respectively), although the .43 coefficient between PAN and Perti indicates that PAN appealed to a larger and wider Islamic spectrum, especially in Sumatra. This is consistent with the fact that PAN's vote surpassed the vote for PBB in every district of Sumatra in 1999 except one. Support for PAN was weak in areas of former PNI (−.30), Parkindo (−.25), and NU (−.21) strength in 1955.

Regional Differences: Central and East Java

Indonesia is a huge and varied country with a maldistributed population. Over 63 percent of the electorate in 1999 resided on the island of Java, which consists of only about 7 percent of the land area. This imbalance, plus the higher reliability of the 1955 data for two electoral districts on Java, Central Java (includes Yogyakarta) and East Java (see Appendix B to this chapter), raises the question about regional differences. Table 6.2 provides the correlation coefficients based on the voting results for only these three areas of Java, which in 1999 accounted for 37 percent of the total vote. In the following discussion of the findings, "Java" refers to these areas and excludes Jakarta and West Java.

Table 6.2
Relationship between Support for Parties in Central and East Java, 1955 and 1999

1999 Party	1955 Party	Positive	1955 Party	Negative
PDI-P	PKI	.59	NU	-.81
	PNI	.39	Perti	-.40
	Parkindo	.33*		
Golkar	PKI	.50	NU	-.63
PKB	NU	.77	PKI	-.51
	Perti	.32*	Parkindo	-.33
			Katolik	-.32*
PPP	NU	.47	PKI	-.33
PAN	Katolik	.78	NU	-.53
	Parkindo	.50		
	IPKI	.38		
	Masjumi	.34		
PBB	Katolik	.59	NU.	-.39.
	Parkindo	.45		

Sources: 1955 data, Alfian, *Hasil Pemilihan Umum 1955* (Jakarta: LEKNAS, 1971); 1999 data, Indonesia Election Commission.

Note: Numbers are Pearson correlation coefficients significant at the .005 level in a two-tailed test. Based on votes for DPR (N = 70).

*Significant at the .007 level.

Several differences with the national patterns are apparent. PDI-P received support in Protestant areas (.33). As suggested in hypothesis 5, Golkar attracted voters in areas of previous PKI strength (.50). The nationwide correlation between PKB and PKI disappears. Note as well that PPP retained support in some NU (.47) areas and, as a consequence, the coefficient between NU and PKB declines slightly (.77).

The correlation between PAN and Masjumi weakens, and that between PBB and Masjumi disappears. It is difficult to interpret the correlations with Katolik and Parkindo, except possibly that, coincidentally, they all drew support from the urban areas of Java.

SUMMARY AND CONCLUSION

The overall objective of this chapter was to investigate commonalities between Indonesia's first parliamentary election in 1955 and the most recent election in 1999. Commonalities were defined as consisting of similarities and continuities. Although I began by identifying a variety of similarities, the focus was on continuities in outcome. The methodological difficulties attendant to finding empirical evidence pertaining to the "broad continuity" thesis in election outcomes were noted and at least partially overcome by measuring the association between areas of support for particular parties in 1955 and 1999.

The analysis uncovered empirical support for six out of the eight hypotheses. Two out of eight were declined. The hypotheses and the findings can be summarized as follows:

Hypothesis 1: The higher the vote for PNI in 1955, the higher the vote for PDI-P in 1999—Supported.

Hypothesis 2: The higher the vote for PKI in 1955, the higher the vote for PDI-P in 1999—Supported.

Hypothesis 3: The higher the vote for Masjumi or PSII in 1955, the higher the vote for Golkar in 1999—Supported (but declined for Java).

Hypothesis 4: The higher the vote for PNI in 1955, the higher the vote for Golkar in 1999—Declined.

Hypothesis 5: The higher the vote for PKI in 1955, the higher the vote for Golkar in 1999—Declined (but supported for Java).

Hypothesis 6: The higher the vote for NU in 1955, the higher the vote for PKB in 1999—Supported.

Hypothesis 7: The higher the vote for any of the Islamic parties (Masjumi, Perti, NU) in 1955, the higher the vote for PPP in 1999—Supported.

Hypothesis 8: The higher the vote for Masjumi in 1955, the higher the vote for PAN or PBB in 1999—Supported.

It is important to note that, except as noted with hypotheses 3 and 5, these are nationwide findings and patterns based on statistical analysis of election returns for the vast majority of districts and cities throughout Indonesia. Second, limitations in the data include omissions and underreporting, especially in West Java and eastern Indonesia. Hence, it is altogether possible that the national patterns did not hold in some regions.

The empirical evidence provided here in the form of significant statistical correlations between areas of support for particular 1955 parties and areas of support for particular 1999 parties, as specified in the six supported hypotheses, makes a strong case for broad continuity in election outcomes. This continuity has two dimensions, one being the reemergence in the 1999 election of the basic cleavage in the electorate between areas supporting nationalist, religiously inclusive parties and areas supporting Islamic parties, commonly known as the *abangan* and *santri* divisions. The other dimension is the reemergence of a division within the Islamic community between traditional and modernist orientations. But the modernists are much more divided than in 1955, which is reflected in the relationship between Masjumi support and support for four parties in 1999 (Golkar, PPP, PAN, and PBB). Also, with the prohibition and eradication of PKI beginning in 1965, the lower-class division in the *abangan* camp that existed in 1955 is no longer organizationally articulated.

These findings suggest that attempts of the New Order for over thirty years and across six elections to blunt these social divisions through fusion of parties, enforcement of a sole ideological basis (*Pancasila*) for every political organization, and the attempt to build a predominate party system with Golkar and its platform of developmentalism in the lead, have largely failed. At the same time, it should be recognized that the divisions in the electorate as reflected in the pattern of voting in 1999 are not as deep or as pronounced as they were in 1955.

This analysis also helps to clarify the sources of support for the "reformed" Golkar party. The evidence here suggests that Golkar was able to reposition itself and won the support of many modernist Muslims who lived in areas of previous Masjumi and PSII strength. In its efforts to become an integrative party, it was more successful in drawing support from Christian areas, as evidenced by the .39 coefficient with Parkindo, than it was in attracting voters across the *santri–abangan* divide.[11]

Other evidence of failure in the New Order's attempts at political engineering can be found in the lack of correlation between areas of PDI-P support in 1999 and Parkindo and Katolik support in 1955. In 1973, five parties were forced to fuse into the Indonesian Democratic Party, which split in 1996 with the establishment of the Indonesian Democratic Party of Struggle. Had the fusion outlived the New Order, a correlation would have been found between PDI-P and Katolik and between PDI-P and Parkindo. An exception to this nationwide pattern occurred in Java, where there is evidence that PDI-P attracted support in areas of former Parkindo strength (.33).

APPENDIX A: GEOGRAPHICAL EQUIVALENCES
USED IN COMPARISON

1955 Regencies and Cities	1999 Regencies and Cities
Aceh Selatan	Aceh Selatan + Sungkil
Aceh Tengah	Aceh Tengah + Aceh Tenggara
Aceh Besar	Aceh Besar + Banda Aceh + Sabang
Aceh Barat	Aceh Barat + Simeulue
Tapanuli Utara	Tapanuli Utara + Dairi + Toba Samosir
Tapanuli Tengah	Tapanuli Tengah + Sibolga
Tapanuli Selatan	Tapanuli Selatan + Mandailing Natal
Asahan	Asahan + Tanjung Balai
Simalungun	Simalungun + Pemantangsiantar
Deli Serdang	Deli Serdang + Tebingtinggi
Langkat	Langkat + Binjai
Solok	Solok + Solok City
Sawah Lunto	Sawah Lunto + Sawah Lunto City
Padang Pariaman	Padang Pariaman + Padang Panjang
Limapuluh Kota	Limapuluh Kota + Payakumbuh
Indragiri Ulu	Indragiri Ulu + Indragiri Ilir
Kampar	Kampar + Pekan Baru
Kepulauan Riau	Kepulauan Riau + Batam
Bengkalis	Bengkalis + Dumai
Bangka	Bangka + Pangkal Pinang
Lampung Selatan	L. Selatan + Tjg.Krg./Bdr.Lpg. + L.Barat + Tenggamus
Lampung Tengah	L. Tengah + Metro + L.Timur
Lampung Utara	L. Utara + Tulang Bawang
Purwakarta	Purwakarta + Subang
Sukabumi	Sukabumi + Sukabumi City
Tanggerang	Tanggerang + Tanggerang City
Bekasi	Bekasi + Bekasi City
Serang	Serang + Cilegon

1955 Regencies and Cities	1999 Regencies and Cities
Bogor	Bogor + Depok
Pekalongan	Pekalongan + Batang
Magelang	Magelang + Magelang City
Semarang	Semarang + Salatiga
Blitar	Blitar + Blitar City
Pasuruan	Pasuruan + Pasuruan City
Probolinggo	Probolinggo + Probolinggo City
Mojokerto	Mojokerto + Mojokerto City
Badung	Badung + Den Pasar
Lombok Barat	Lombok Barat + Mataram
Kupang	Kupang + Kupang City
Sambas	Sambas + Bengkayang
Kutai	Kutai + Pasir + Balikpapan + Samarinda
Bulong	Bulong + Tarakan
Minahasa	Minahasa + Bitung
Poso	Poso + Luwuk/Banggai
Donggala	Donggala + Bual Toli-Toli + Palu
Maluku Utara	Maluku Utara + Halmahera Tengah + Ternate

Regencies or cities not listed were either equivalent or missing in the 1955 data source (see note 9). Data for Pidie, Aceh (district) was unavailable in 1999 data source.

APPENDIX B

How reliable are the data on which this chapter is based? As indicated, this chapter utilizes 1955 voting results compiled by Alfian, the only comprehensive source of 1955 voting results disaggregated to the regency and city level. This source provides full or partial results for 188 regencis and cities. All the other sources of voting data against which Alfian's data might be compared are much more aggregated, usually specified by electoral district (N = 15). So the only practical way of answering the question of reliability is to compare the data from Alfian with another, more aggregated data set. The comparison here utilized the official election returns found in Feith's monograph, and the comparison was limited to the ten parties that obtained the most votes and collectively accounted for about 88 percent of the total vote.[12]

To compare these two data sets, the Alfian set was first aggregated by electoral district and then both data sets were arrayed on the same spreadsheet of 300 cells (ten columns for parties and fifteen rows for electoral districts, times two data sets). This procedure showed agreement between the two data sets in 154 cells (51 percent). Of the 146 cells (49 percent) in which there was disagreement, Feith's figures were higher in 120 cells (40 percent) and Alfian's were higher in 26 cells (9 percent). Summing the discrepancies in these cells indicated that the Alfian source is short (underreported) by about 5,877,000 votes or 18 percent (with Feith's total, the combined vote for ten parties of 33,086,949, as the denominator).

The apparent underreporting in the Alfian data set does not by itself render these data useless. More important for analysis is the question of whether the underreporting seems random or systematic. Randomly distributed errors are less bothersome, because they are expected and managed through calculation of probability and "confidence intervals." But in the Alfian data set the problem is more complicated. Systematic bias exists and should be taken into account in utilizing these data. One type of systematic bias is geographical, as shown in the following list:

Electoral District	Alfian's Figures Relative to Feith's (percent)
North Sumatra	same (indicates a less than 0.1-percent difference)
Central Sumatra	11.5 less
South Sumatra	1.0 more
Jakarta	same
West Java	66.2 less
Central Java	0.2 less
East Java	0.4 less
Nusa Tenggara Barat	same
Nusa Tenggara Timur	3.2 more
West Kalimantan	same

South Kalimantan	100.0 less (missing in Alfian)
East Kalimantan	same
North Sulawesi	21.5 less
South Sulawesi	91.6 less
Maluku	same

As can be seen from the electoral districts where Alfian's figures are "less," omissions and underreporting were high in Central Sumatra (11.51%), West Java (66.2%), South Kalimantan (100%), North Sulawesi (21.5%), and South Sulawesi (91.6%). With three out of these five areas in Kalimantan and Sulawesi, one might be tempted to conclude that Alfian's data are biased against eastern Indonesia. However, because of its greater population, Alfian's omissions on West Java actually represent about two-thirds of the total difference in votes between the two sources.

Analytically distinct but empirically mixed with geographical bias is ideological or party bias. If the difference between the two data sets in the total vote for each party is expressed as a percentage of Feith's total for each party, the parties' position above and below the "average" (overall) level of 18 percent underreported is as follows: Perti +18 (equal to Feith's figures), Katolik +17, PNI +17, IPKI +16, PKI +4, Parkindo +4, NU 0, PSI −14, Masjumi −16, and PSII −34. These statistics can be interpreted as showing a continuum from nil (+18) to increasing degrees of underreporting or bias (high negative value), which obtains, especially, for three parties, PSI, Masjumi, and PSII. Perhaps the best illustration of mixed geographical and ideological bias is the case of Masjumi, which won a plurality of votes in Central Sumatra, West Java, South Sulawesi, and North Sulawesi, all areas in the Alfian data set where omissions or underreporting tended to be high.

In sum, comparison of the Alfian and Feith data sets on the 1955 election has identified omissions and underreporting that varies systematically by geographical area (in favor of Sumatra and Central and East Java and against West Java, South Kalimantan, and Sulawesi) and party (in favor of Perti, Katolik, and PNI and against PSII, Masjumi, and PSI). These biases need to be kept in mind when interpreting the correlation coefficients in Table 6.1. For example, the coefficients involving Masjumi are more likely to be underestimates than those for PNI. These limitations in the Alfian data set have to be weighed against its great strength as the sole source of comprehensive disaggregated returns for the 1955 election. It should go without saying that this chapter is premised on the author's position that these flaws are manageable, not fatal.

NOTES

1. Herbert Feith, *The Indonesian Elections of 1955*, (Ithaca, N.Y.: Cornell Modern Indonesia Project, 1957), 5.

2. The estimate for 1955 is taken from ibid., 50. For 1999, it comes from the KPU as cited in the *Jakarta Post*, July 16, 1999, p. 2.

3. Feith, *Indonesian Elections*, 88, estimates 34 percent in 1955, and I calculated 42 percent in 1999 using biodata from the General Election Commission.

4. For example, R. William Liddle, "Indonesia in 1999: Democracy Restored," *Asian Survey* 40, 1 (2000); Donald E. Weatherbee, "Indonesia: Electoral Politics in a Newly Emerging Democracy" in *How Asia Votes*, ed. John Fuhsheng Hsien and David Newman (New York: Seven Bridges Press, 2001).

5. Muslim modernists reject all of the Sunni jurisprudential schools in favor of direct interpretation by the faithful of the Qur'an and Hadith.

6. Muslim traditionalists adhere to the Syafi'i jurisprudential school within Sunni Islam.

7. Feith, *Indonesian Elections*.

8. Feith's (ibid.) pioneering study of the 1955 election includes Table 6 (p. 85), showing voting results for twenty residencies in Java. However, he notes that he compiled the table from press reports and cautions that it "contains considerable inaccuracies."

9. Alfian, *Hasil Pemilihan Umum 1955* (Jakarta: LEKNAS, 1971). Compared to the official 1955 election results (specified according to fifteen much larger electoral districts) in Feith, *Indonesian Elections*, omissions and underreporting of the results in Alfian's book total approximately 18 percent of total votes cast. However, the deficiencies are distributed unevenly, with the greatest (worst) in West Java, South Kalimantan, and North and South Sulawesi (see Appendix B to this chapter). This degree of unreliability in the database is managed here in two ways: (1) using only nationwide results based on analysis of all units of observation (N = 188) combined, and (2) reporting only correlation coefficients that attain a more rigorous level of statistical significance than is customary in this type of research (i.e., .005 rather than .05).

10. A post–1999 election survey of 2,990 voters in Java conducted by LP3ES found that those voting for PKB had less formal education than those voting for any other party. "Rakyat, Partai Politik dan Pemilu III," *Kompas*, June 14, 1999. Second, the correlation was discussed with several rural sociologists or community organizers who have had considerable experience working in poor rural villages in central Java. They found it plausible, noting that during the (authoritarian) New Order villagers in areas of former PKI strength tended to vote for Golkar, the government party, acquiescing to pressure by local officials and seeking to evade suspicion. But once the pressure weakened after the 1997 election and many local officials abandoned Golkar, the villagers tended to follow the lead of the local *kiai* (Islamic scholar), whose influence has been growing in rural Java. Robert W. Hefner, "Islamizing Java? Religion and Politics in Rural East Java," *Journal*

of Asian Studies 45, 3 (1987): 533–554. *Kiai* belong to NU, which officially backed PKB in the 1999 election.

11. If the level of significance required for reporting a coefficient in Table 6.1 is relaxed slightly (from .005 to .008), a coefficient of .19 enters between Golkar and Katolik, further evidence of Golkar's integrative capabilities with Christian communities in 1999. This relationship comes largely from East Nusa Tenggara, where Golkar won 41 percent of the vote in 1999 and Katolik took 41 percent of the vote in 1955.

12. Alfian, *Hasil Pemilihan Umum 1955*; Feith, *Indonesian Elections.*

CHAPTER 7

Social Influences
on 1999 Voting Choices

This chapter seeks to explain the direction of the vote or the underlying bases of voting choice in the 1999 election. As in the 1955 election, voters chose parties, not individual candidates. Chapter 6 found empirical evidence of continuity between the party systems of 1955 and 1999, meaning there was correspondence between areas of support for certain parties in the two elections. Considering these patterns together with the influence of the "party in the electorate" during New Order elections mentioned in Chapter 2, we can infer that many voters identified with a particular party over time (across elections) and hypothesize that party identification was a determinant of voting choice in 1999. How strong it was relative to other influences will be explored through multivariate analysis in this chapter.

As discussed in previous chapters, in 1955 the Indonesian electorate was thought to have been divided along religious, ethnic and regional, and class and economic interest lines, and these cleavages furnished both a base of voting support and a set of political interests that parties vied to represent. After Suharto came to power in the 1960s, his New Order government attempted with some success to modify the cleavage structure. We also noted a secular tendency in Western democracies toward decline in social-based voting. The question thus arises, to what extent did sociological characteristics influence voting choice in the 1999 election?

This chapter identifies and measures social-based and other contextual influences on Indonesians' voting choices in the 1999 election. It demonstrates that over half (on average) of the variation among districts in the votes for the five main parties (PDI-P, Golkar, PKB, PPP, and PAN) can be explained with statistical (regression) models using social and contextual variables. It thus provides evidence of the important role of the community context in individuals' voting choices and estimates the relative weights that ought to be attributed to explanations based on social characteristics versus those based on psychological or attitudinal ones derived through surveys of individual voters.

OBJECTIVES AND METHODOLOGY

In this chapter I first build quantitative indicators of the social context within which Indonesians cast their ballots and then use them to construct statistical models that measure the effects of these contextual variables on the voting for particular parties (direction of the vote). Virtually every previous study of Indonesian voting patterns that uses quantitative election returns is marked by one or more of several limitations. They fail to disaggregate below the provincial level. In a country where more voters cast ballots in each of three provinces than did voters in the entire country of Australia, and where nine or one-third of all provinces exceeded 2 million voters each, a great deal of variation within provinces is obscured by using provincial aggregates. Second, bivariate analysis is the norm; seldom have election analysts attempted multivariate analysis, which better captures the complexity of the empirical world and enables more accurate testing of alternative explanations (hypotheses). Third, they are based on a sample of cases that either have no pretense of representativeness (e.g., convenience sample) or, if they claim to be representative of some larger population, they contain a high margin of error.[1]

The methodology employed here largely overcomes these limitations. It utilizes a database in which the second-level administrative districts, consisting both of regencies (*kabupaten*) and cities (*kota*), are the units of data collection and analysis. Since these units are much smaller and over ten times more numerous than provinces, much more variation is retained and the larger number of cases allows more precise and powerful multivariate analysis, including factor analysis and multiple regression analysis. In addition, the database consists not of a sample, but of 94 percent of the population.[2] Also, socioeconomic data used to characterize the context were missing for about 15 percent of all districts (cases), usually because some regencies were split or some regency capitals were given equal, second-level administrative status (*kotamadya*) between the time the contextual data were generated (1983 to 1995) and the 1999 elections. These have been handled by inserting estimated values on the indicators that adhere to the following guidelines: (1) if a new regency was created from a larger one, duplicate figures were used; (2) if a new city was previously a part of a regency, estimates were made, taking into consideration figures for the regency and for other cities in the province; and (3) if data were otherwise missing, averages (means) for regencies or cities (whichever appropriate) in the province were used. Analysis based partially on careful estimates was considered preferable to excluding cases with missing data, because the latter would have decreased the number of cases (N) and introduced regional bias by giving greater weight to the data on Java and Bali, which were seldom missing.

Undergirding the analysis are several premises. I assume that socioeconomic traits of area units (or groups of people living within defined territorial boundaries of regencies and cities) affect the behavior of individuals within those units, consciously or unconsciously, and thus help to explain the electoral outcomes in those areas. However, since the unit of measurement is the group rather than the individual, inferences and conclusions should be drawn about the probable collective behavior of individuals in groups, not about individual behavior. In short, voters' choices are determined more by their sensitivity to their social milieu than by the individual voter's (rational) calculus. This limitation—the inability of grouped data to measure attitudes or opinions of individuals—is less restricting in a more group- and communal-oriented society like Indonesia than it would be in an individualistic society like the United States.

Second, I utilize publicly available, aggregate, and contextual data describing districts, which were collected or generated and published by Indonesian government agencies (e.g., population census). Hence, although these data have been carefully inspected and cleaned prior to their use here, certain limitations remain, especially the constraints imposed by the availability of data. An example is the time discrepancy between indicators built from the 1990 census and the 1999 voting returns. Due to the nonexistence of a census in 1999, indicators from the 1990 census were constructed and intermingled with 1999 voting results in statistical analyses. Such a procedure is common in quantitative social science and can be defended in terms of cost effectiveness, the high degree of stability in these indicators over time, and the robustness of regression analysis. Second, because the geographical distribution of the units of observation (regencies and cities or municipalities, both of which I refer to as "districts") differ from the geographical distribution of the voters, the regressions were rerun using a population-weighted data file and

the results compared. Since the differences were very minor (a testi-
monial to the robustness of regression analysis), I decided to avoid
unnecessary complexity and report the results obtained without
weighting. Insofar as the procedures and calculations used here are
logical and statistically sound, I am able to establish the degree to
which electoral outcomes can be explained by general factors or traits
common to all of them. The variance left unexplained by the models, the residual, represents the outside limit that can be attributed
to individual calculus, the unique characteristics of particular areas, and measurement error.

I seek to explain electoral outcomes (dependent variables), which
are operationalized in two ways. First, the "effective number of parties" is measured by the Rae fractionalization index and relates to
such important theoretical issues as type of party system and extent
of party competition.[3] Second, the direction of the vote is simply the
vote obtained by each party in the election as a percentage of the
total number of valid votes cast. It is important to note that all the
indicators and measurements control for differences among districts
in the size of population. By measuring electoral outcomes in these
two ways for each district and then relating these measures to other
social and contextual characteristics of the district, this analysis provides fresh insights about electoral behavior in 1999.

PATTERNS IN THE SOCIOECONOMIC CONTEXT

The review of previous studies on Indonesian elections in Chapter 2 identified aspects of the socioeconomic context that were
thought to have influenced voting choice in previous elections. The
next step was to measure or operationalize these aspects and assess
their relative strength. Several steps were involved. First, twenty-
four indicators were constructed using various kinds of data collected or generated by Indonesia's Central Bureau of Statistics (Biro
Pusat Statistik; BPS).[4] Second, they were reduced to six meaningful
and statistically independent factors or dimensions of common variation using factor analysis.[5] The indicators with their respective factor loadings are shown in Table 7.1.[6]

The first and strongest factor can be interpreted to represent the
theoretical dimension of *urbanization* (F1), because indicators pertaining to larger manufacturing firms, population living in urban
areas, population with television, population density, and, negatively,
the percentage of the employed population working in agriculture
have their highest loading on this factor. The second factor, on which
measures about the civil service, government expenditure, and ex-

Table 7.1
Factor Loadings of Twenty-Four Indicators of Context on Six Factors

Indicator	F1	F2	F3	F4	F5	F6
1.1 Workers in med./lg mfg firms, 1992,p.c.	.86					
1.2 Lg/med mfg firms 1992,p.c.		.83				
1.3 Employed industry, rural, 1990 (%)	.76					-.32
1.4 Employed in agriculture, 1990 (%)	-.67					
1.5 Employed in agriculture, rural, 1990 (%)	-.63				.35	
1.6 Urban population, 1990 (%)	.57					.37
1.7 Households with TV, 1990 (%)	.55					.30
1.8 Population density, 1999 (%)	.54					
1.9 Tertiary school graduates, 1990 (%)	.48			-.32		
2.1 Gov't devel. expend. 1994–1995 p.c.		.89				
2.2 Civil servants 1989 p.c.		.85				
2.3 Real estate tax collected 1994–1995 p.c.			.83			
2.4 Subsidy receipts 1994–1995 p.c.		.75				
3.1 Christians, 1980 (%)			-.90			
3.2 Muslims, 1980 (%)			.90			
4.1 Illiterate females, 1990 (%)				.98		
4.2 Illiterate total, 1990 (%)				.97		
4.3 Pop > 10 yrs. w/o prim'y educ, 1990 (%)				.71		
5.1 Farmers controlling >2 ha. 1983(%)					.84	
5.2 Land owned, 1983 average						.80
5.3 Religion teachers/primary teachers,1990		.35	-.33	-.56		
6.1 Employed industry, total, 1990 (%)						.89
6.2 Gov't own revenue 1994–1995 p.c.	.32	.31				.53
6.3 Farmers controlling <.5 ha. 1983 (%)					-.33	.52
Percentage of variance	35.5	18.9	7.5	6.5	5.6	4.2

tractive capability load heaviest, represents a theoretical dimension which can be labeled *government activity* (F2). The third factor can be designated *Islamicness* (F3) dimension, and is measured by the proportion of Muslim population and an indicator of piety or ortho- doxy of religious practice in the area; namely, religion teachers in elementary schools as a percentage of public school teachers. Both indicators load positively on the factor, justifying its label. As would be expected, the loading for Christians on this factor is strong and negative (–.90).[7] Two indicators of illiteracy and one of lack of pri- mary education load on the fourth factor, which can be designated *illiteracy* (F4). Indicators of access to large amounts of land ($\geq$ 2 hectares) and the average size of owned land holdings load on the fifth factor, which can be labeled *relative inequality* (F5). Where land hold- ings are larger, population density tends to be lower, which can explain the negative loading of religion teachers on this factor. The three indi- cators that load on the sixth factor—employment in (mostly small) in- dustry, locally generated public revenue, and farmers with very small land holdings—are likely to be high in areas that have a relatively high level of *development* (F6), and will be labeled accordingly.

Thus far, factor analysis has assisted in the simplification of data and the construction of multiple item scales (F1, F2, etc.), which are more valid and reliable than single-item scales. From the twenty- four indicators, factor analysis identified six underlying dimensions of the socioeconomic context. In a subsequent step, a score on each of the six factors was computed for each district. In other words, the six dimensions derived from analysis of all the cases combined were subsequently used to weight and combine the values of each case on the twenty-four indicators. Using these six factor scores to mea- sure the socioeconomic context has the methodological advantage of increasing the reliability of the multivariate analysis below in two ways. First, the confidence interval for any one factor is greater than for any of the individual indicators of which they are composed (i.e., fewer random errors, less measurement error, and less influ- enced by missing data). Second, the factors are almost uncorrelated with one another (due to oblimin rotation), upholding the impor- tant statistical assumption of multiple regression of no multicolline- arity among the factor scores (independent variables).

EXPLAINING THE EFFECTIVE NUMBER OF PARTIES

As discussed, one of the dependent variables in this analysis is the fractionalization of the vote as measured by the Rae fractional- ization index (F-index) or the "effective number of parties" (N-index) derived from it.[8] Being more intuitively understandable, the latter will be used here. On the (nationwide) average, there were 3.98 effective parties in districts in the 1999 election, up from 1.51 in 1997, when two of the three parties allowed were heavily constrained by New Order authorities. However, in 1999 there was considerable interdistrict variation in the N-index, as reflected in the range, a minimum of 1.31 and a maximum of 8.00, and the large standard deviation of 1.29. How can this variation be explained? Why did some areas have more effective parties than other areas?

Several hypotheses come to mind. We might expect that urbanization and education had a positive influence on the effective number of parties based on the theoretical understanding that urbanization is often accompanied by greater social and political pluralism. More competing social groups furnish bases of voting support for more parties. Education tends to increase independent thinking, including rational assessment of political parties, and political participation of all types. We might also expect a residue or legacy of the traditions formed during the last two New Order elections with regard to the effective number of parties (within the legal limitation of three parties). In other words, districts having a higher effective number of parties during New Order elections would have higher levels in 1999 as well.[9] Finally, remembering the diversity of the population, we would expect regional effects or differences related to particular histories, culture, and ethnicity.[10]

Table 7.2 reports the best linear model that could be built from the data available for this study for (statistically) explaining the effective number of parties. The explanatory power of each independent variable relative to and controlling for the effects of the others can be ascertained by comparing the (standardized) *beta* coefficients in the third column. The explanatory variables are listed in descending order of influence.

The two strongest influences were the tradition of effective parties during the last decade of the New Order (.479) and illiteracy (−.370). That is, those regencies and cities with a tradition of more effective parties tended to have more effective parties in the 1999 election as well. Those areas with higher levels of literacy (or less illiteracy) tended to have more effective parties. This finding well illustrates how the New Order, by its success in nearly eradicating illiteracy through universal access to basic education, unwittingly contributed to the demise of monolithic party politics in 1999 once the controls had been relaxed. The number of parties also tended to be higher in Sumatra, for several reasons.[11] Golkar maintained much of its strength there, but PDI-P also made inroads, especially in areas of PNI strength in 1955. Masjumi had dominated in Sumatra in 1955, but in 1999 those areas were seriously split between PPP, PAN, and PBB.

Table 7.2
Model of Influences on Effective Number of Parties, 1999 Election

Independent Variable	b	B (*beta*)	T	Significance of T
1. Tradition during New Order	.372	.479	9.542	.000
2. Illiteracy (F4)	-.044	-.370	7.042	.000
3. Sumatra region	.058	.217	4.269	.000
4. Relative inequality (F5)	.020	.184	3.817	.000
5. Urbanization (F1)	-.017	-.134	-2.683	.008
6. Islamicness (F3)	.011	.107	2.286	.023
(Constant)	.540		36.646	.000

Note: R^2 = .45, S.E.E. = .090, F = 39, Significance = .0005.

Contrary to expectations, urbanization had a slight negative impact (–.134). Perhaps urban tendencies toward political pluralism were offset by greater exposure to the mass media campaigns of a few wealthy parties, and thus greater concentration of the vote in those parties as well. Islamicness was a positive stimulus to more effective parties, which is reflected in the *beta* of .107. Relative inequality also had an impact (.184), suggesting that areas with wealthier farmers were fertile ground for new parties.

Ethnicity

Ethnic factors markedly influenced voting behavior in 1999 and need to be explicitly addressed. Consider the provinces of Bali and South Sulawesi, which had (district average) 1.59 and 2.03 effective parties, respectively, among the lowest in the entire country. In Bali the top party (PDI-P) got 79 percent of the vote, more than double its national average, the second party (Golkar) took 10.4 percent, and the third party (PKB) 1.7 percent. This lopsided pattern had little to do with illiteracy, urbanization, or the tradition of effective parties. It had everything to do with the fact that the Balinese voted as Balinese, who saw a vote to PDI-P as not just a rejection of the "status quo," but as an expression of their ethnic identity and perceived interests at that point in time. As Hindus they were a small minority in Indonesia, and numerically a declining one. To the normal sensitivities of a minority were added a perceived special relationship with PDI-P based on Megawati's (PDI-P chairperson) Balinese grandmother. An incident during the campaign further solidified the relationship. Government minister and PPP politician A. M. Saifuddin claimed that Megawati was evidently a Hindu and therefore unfit to be president. An islandwide apoplexy ensued, ranging from demands for Saifuddin's dismissal to threats of secession. In short, the politics of Balinese identity in context led to a greater proportional Golkar collapse in Bali than anywhere else, exclusively to the benefit of PDI-P.[12]

The players were different but the underlying dynamic much the same in South Sulawesi. Golkar got 66.5 percent, close to three times its national average, followed by 8.4 percent for PPP and 6.6 percent for PDI-P. Clearly Golkar held its ground there better than anywhere else. Why? Again, the factors mentioned in the nationwide model (i.e., tradition, illiteracy, urbanization, Islamicness, inequality) are clearly insufficient. More important, President Habibie being a native son, the Buginese and Makasarese had come to associate his fortunes with their ethnic identities and perceived interests. In short, having someone perceived as one of them ascend to the highest office and stay there was reason to put aside any inclination to protest longtime Golkar domination by voting for other parties.

Acknowledging the importance of ethnic factors for election outcomes is one thing, but measuring them and integrating them into the analysis here that seeks to uncover nationwide patterns is quite another. The variance left unexplained by the models, the residual, represents the outside limit that can be attributed to these difficult-to-measure factors and the unique characteristics of particular areas.

EXPLAINING THE DIRECTION OF THE VOTE

The following sections present for each of the five main parties the best nationwide linear model that could be constructed with the data available for this analysis. Each model was built through an iterative process that began by regressing a party's vote on the scores of the six contextual factors identified, several dummy variables denoting region, and indicators from the 1955 and the 1997 elections. None of the initial models were optimum; many different combinations of independent variables were fitted to the data.[13]

Indonesia Democracy Party of Struggle (PDI-P)

The existing scholarly literature and conventional wisdom about PDI-P's overall plurality in the election pose alternative hypotheses that can be tested here. First, the PDI-P vote was widely considered a protest vote, a vote against the status quo. Hence, we might hypothesize that high densities of civil servants, more tax extraction, higher government expenditures—all indicators of a high government profile—were counterproductive as far as support for the government party (Golkar) was concerned, producing instead higher levels of voting for PDI-P. Conversely, with 22 percent of the total vote going to Golkar, it seems plausible that PDI-P may have had difficulty making inroads in areas of higher government activity, as the bureaucracy was in a position to dispense and target resources strategically to the advantage of Golkar and to the disadvantage of PDI-P.

Second, the PDI-P vote was strongest in the districts of Java and Bali (although it did well nationwide), and it was especially strong in the large metropolitan areas. A variety of reasons have been offered by observers. The PDI-P leader, Megawati Soekarnoputri, was revered in part because of her mixed Javanese and Balinese ethnic ancestry. Being the daughter of Indonesia's independence leader and first president, Soekarno, enhanced her "revolutionary" credentials and legitimacy, and her party was viewed by many as a continuation of the Indonesian National Party, founded by her father.

During the campaign PDI-P became known for its attraction to young people, the militancy of its youthful cadre, and its ability to mobilize mass rallies and parades in the largest cities on Java. More than any of the other major parties, PDI-P campaigned on rectifying social and economic inequalities and combating corruption, themes that reverberated well among the underclass and in areas of previous PKI support.

These hypotheses are put to the test in Table 7.3. Recall the previous chapter, where evidence of a positive relationship was found between areas supporting the Indonesian National Party or the Indonesian Communist Party in 1955 and areas supporting PDI-P in 1999. Here those relationships are subjected to more rigorous testing in regression analysis, enabling us to (statistically) isolate their effects, measuring each one while simultaneously controlling for the effects of the other eight independent variables in the model. Comparing the magnitude of the *betas* in Table 7.3, the PNI–1955 (.404) had the strongest influence and PKI–1955 (.291) ranked fourth. The regional variable, Java–Bali (.382) had the second strongest influence. As expected, there is a strong negative influence from Islamicness (–.329), indicating that the more Islamic the area, the less the vote for PDI-P, and reflecting the continuing reality of the basic division in the electorate between nationalist–religiously inclusive orientation and orthodox Muslim orientation. PDI-P made inroads into areas that in 1997 voted strongly for Golkar (.245) and PDI (.144).[14] It also benefited from areas where relative inequality was higher (.168), from more urbanized areas (.132), and from areas of lower illiteracy (–.132). This negative influence of illiteracy should be interpreted in relation to the positive effect of urbanization; that is, illiteracy was lower in the large urbanized areas where PDI-P ran strong. Overall, these findings are remarkably confirmatory of our expectations and supportive of our hypotheses about the influences on voting choices for PDI-P. In light of the contradictory hypotheses about the effects of government activity, it is interesting that no influence could be found.

Functional Groups (Golkar)

Prior to the election, predictions about the extent of support for Golkar varied widely. Similar to the debate about PDI-P, observers disagreed about the effect of government activity on the prospects for Golkar in the election. Some thought it would be counterproductive, as it was often accompanied by allegations and evidence of corruption, collusion, and nepotism. Other observers argued that higher levels of government presence and activism would enhance

Table 7.3
Model of Influences on Indonesian Democracy Party of Struggle, 1999 Election

Independent Variable	b	B (beta)	T	Significance of T
1. PNI–1955	.004	.404	8.562	.000
2. Java–Bali Region	.133	.382	5.357	.000
3. Islamicness (F3)	-.046	-.329	-7.899	.000
4. PKI–1955	.004	.291	6.623	.000
5. Golkar–1997	.003	.245	4.327	.000
6. Relative inequality (F5).	.026	.168	3.715	.000
7. PDI–1997	.009	.144	2.983	.003
8.5. Illiteracy (F4)	-.023	-.132	-3.121	.002
8.5. Urbanization (F1)	.024	.132	3.029	.003
(Constant)	-.146		-2.449	.015

Note: R^2 = .69, S.E.E. = .098, F = 63, Significance = .0005.

Golkar's prospects in the election, contending that Golkar's "channel B" (bureaucracy) remained a formidable electoral machine, even if "channel A" (armed forces) had been largely neutralized and many of those in "channel G" (young party cadre) had deserted the party. Golkar's hold on the bureaucracy and support in the electorate was acknowledged to have weakened in Java–Bali, especially in the large cities, but it was thought to have remained largely intact in rural areas of previous PKI strength, as voters in those areas were in the habit of demonstrating loyalty to the government, as well as in areas outside Java where the bureaucracy's profile tended to be higher and civil society weaker. Also, observers had identified a "greening" underway in Golkar for at least a decade, as the party sought to neutralize threats to its dominance from modernist orthodox Muslims. Entering the campaign behind two leaders with strong modernist Muslim credentials, President Habibie and Chairman Akbar Tandjung, Golkar sought to reposition itself by attracting modernist Muslims.

The model for Golkar is presented in Table 7.4. By far the strongest influence on Golkar's support was regional; Golkar did especially well in eastern Indonesia (.631), as compared to Java–Bali and Sumatra. Another strong influence came from areas that voted heavily for Golkar in the 1997 election (.411), suggesting that its formidable organization and status as party in the electorate remained in place in many areas. The party's appeal to modernist Muslims met with some success, indicated by the *betas* with areas of previous Masjumi support in 1955 (.173) and Islamicness (.136). Finally, areas of higher relative inequality were disadvantageous for Golkar (–.164); we can infer that poor and lower-class voters preferred other parties (e.g., PDI-P, PKB). Thus, except for the surprising lack of influence, neither positive nor negative (counterproductive), from government activity, the regression results support the hypotheses.

National Awakening Party (PKB)

Keeping in mind its recent founding in 1998 by and for members of the Awakening of the Islamic Teachers, we expected the foremost influence on the PKB would be religion. Other noticeable but secondary influences would include region, because the vast majority of NU members reside in Java, urbanization (negative), because most NU members live in rural areas, illiteracy (positive), which is higher in rural areas, and positive effects from areas where NU and PKI attracted votes in 1955 (recall correlations in the previous chapter).

The evidence pertaining to these hypotheses is presented in Table 7.5. Similar to the model for PDI-P, the strongest influence emanates

Table 7.4
Model of Influences on Functional Groups' Party, 1999 Election

Independent Variable	b	B (*beta*)	T	Significance of T
1. Eastern region	.240	.631	15.857	.000
2. Golkar–1997	.005	.411	10.171	.000
3. Masjumi–1955	.002	.173	4.192	.000
4. Relative inequality (F5)	-.030	-.164	- 4.232	.000
5. Islamicness (F3)	.020	.136	3.222	.001
(Constant)	-.241		-6.470	.000

Note: R^2 = .69, S.E.E. = .1012, F = 120, Significance = .0005.

Table 7.5
Model of Influences on National Awakening Party, 1999 Election

Independent Variable	b	B (*beta*)	T	Significance of T
1. NU–1955	.003	.400	9.855	.000
2.Java–Bali region	.089	.339	6.902	.000
3. PPP–1997	.003	.280	5.427	.000
4. Illiteracy (F4)	.028	.215	5.023	.000
5. Urbanization (F1)	-.020	-.152	-2.960	.003
6. Municipality status	.047	.145	2.287	.023
7. Development (F6)	-.017	-.094	-2.107	.036
8. Government activity (F2)	.009	-.082	-2.148	.033
(Constant)	-.048		-4.443	.000

Note: R^2 = .72, S.E.E. = .069, F = 84, Significance = .0005.

from voting patterns in the 1955 election, but here it was from areas that previously supported NU (.400). PKB also benefited from areas of PPP strength in 1997 (.280). In other words, this is evidence that some PPP voters in 1997 switched to PKB in 1999. PPP, it will be recalled, was a fusion of four Islamic parties in 1973 and was considered the vehicle of orthodox Muslim aspirations until 1999. It is noteworthy that we find an Islamic connection through PPP rather than through the contextual Islamicness factor (F3). There was also a strong regional effect; the party's attraction was stronger in Java–Bali (.339). The level of illiteracy had a positive effect on the vote for PKB (.215), and the level of development a slight negative one (−.072), indicating that the party appealed to poor and lower-class voters. The weak inverse relationship with government activity (−.082) seems consistent with this pattern, as it would have been lower in more impoverished areas. Finally, as expected, large metropolitan areas had a negative influence on the PKB vote (−.152), although small and medium-size cities having the administrative status of municipality tended to be fertile ground for PKB support (.145).

Development Unity Party (PPP)

Like Golkar, PPP was a creation of New Order authorities, established as a fusion of four Islamic parties and intended as the sole vehicle for orthodox Muslims' political aspirations. Voting for PPP could be expected, therefore, to have been sensitive to the degree of Islamicness of the community (F3). Since it came into being through a fusion in 1973, we would expect that it drew support from both modernist (Masjumi) and traditionalist (NU) areas in 1955 (see Chapter 6).

As can be seen from Table 7.6, the general Islamicness of the context mattered less than the previous party alignment of the community. The expectation about influence from areas of previous Masjumi support (.409) is confirmed, but not the one about NU. The strongest influence came from areas of PPP support in the 1997 election (.505), indicating that the party in the electorate or party identification was an important influence on voting choices for PPP. The regression results also show that the party tended to be disadvantaged by large metropolitan areas, which is reflected by the negative influence from urbanization (−.297) and by areas having higher levels of illiteracy (−.170). We can infer that, compared to PKB, PPP had less appeal to poor and lower-class voters. Finally, it should be pointed out that this model accounts for only 35 percent of the variation among districts in the PPP vote, making it the least powerful of the six models discussed in this chapter.

Table 7.6
Model of Influences on Development Unity Party, 1999 Election

Independent Variable	b	B (beta)	T	Significance of T
1. PPP–1997	.003	.505	8.769	.000
2. Masjumi–1955	.002	.409	7.493	.000
3. Urbanization (F1)	-.024	-.297	-4.962	.000
4. Illiteracy (F4)	-.013	-.170	-3.077	.000
(Constant)	.004		.426	.670

Note: R^2 = .35, S.E.E. = .0636, F = 36, Significance = .0005.

National Mandate Party (PAN)

Like PKB and PPP, PAN was clearly perceived as an Islamic party and thus expected to win votes in the more devoutly Islamic areas. However, in contrast to PKB, PAN was identified with modernist Islam. So we would expect influence on PAN from the Islamicness factor and from former Masjumi areas. However, in the campaign PAN was the most inclusive of these three Islamic parties. It attempted to attract a "rainbow coalition" and it was the most cerebral of the Islamic parties, symbolized by its professorial leader, Amien Rais. Hence, we would expect that PAN appealed to a more educated and urban-dwelling constituency than either of the other two Islamic parties.

Table 7.7 puts these expectations to the test. Similar to the pattern with the other new Islamic party (PKB), it was not the general Islamicness of the context that influenced the vote. Rather, the influence of Islam came through areas of Masjumi strength in 1955 (.328) and PPP strength in the 1997 election. However, the best predictor of PAN success was a regional variable: Support for PAN tended to be stronger in Sumatra than in Java–Bali and eastern Indonesia. The positive influence of urbanization (.154) and the negative one of illiteracy (–.155) are supportive of the expectations about PAN's more urban-dwelling and educated constituency. Finally, the party's appeal was enhanced in communities of lower inequality (–.287).

SUMMARY AND CONCLUSION

Substantively, the objective of this chapter was to explain the underlying bases of voters' choices in the 1999 Indonesian election. In previous chapters we observed that in 1955 most electors voted on the basis of religion, ethnicity or region, or economic interest (class). But Suharto's New Order government repressed or modified the electoral expression of these cleavages through prohibitions on some parties and the fusion of others. Research on New Order elections indicated that the religion-based voting did not disappear, with orthodox Muslims (*santri*) voting disproportionately for the Development Unity Party and syncretists (*abangan*) and non-Muslims preferring Golkar or PDI. In addition, some evidence was found that voting reflected a new divide between younger voters concentrated in the cities and urbanized areas and older voters in the rural areas. When the New Order controls were lifted in 1998 the question arose as to whether the traditional social cleavages would reappear or whether society and politics had been permanently transformed by the social engineering and economic development of the New Order.

Table 7.7
Model of Influences on National Mandate Party, 1999 Election

Independent Variable	b	B (*beta*)	T	Significance of T
1. Sumatra region	.053	.379	7.818	.000
2. Masjumi–1955	.013	.328	6.820	.035
3. Relative inequality (F5)	-.016	-.287	-6.519	.000
4. PPP–1997	.001	.230	4.825	.000
5. Illiteracy (F4)	-.001	-.155	-3.334	.001
6. Urbanization (F1)	.001	.154	3.264	.001
(Constant)	.013		2.114	.035

Note: R^2 = .60, S.E.E. = .038, F = 67, Significance = .0005.

The analysis in this chapter addressed these issues. Using the powerful statistical technique of multiple regression analysis, the independent effects of a variety of social-based influences on voting choices for the five top parties were measured. Urbanization (F1), which was particularly well measured, influenced the vote for four parties.[15] It enhanced the voting choices for PDI-P and PAN, but was detrimental to PKB and PPP. In other words, we can conclude that the urban–rural divide was a reality in the 1999 election and that it was articulated by these four parties, with urbanites preferring PDI-P or PAN and rural voters tending toward PKB and PPP. Apparently electors choosing Golkar were rather evenly divided between urban and rural areas. Contrary to expectations that urbanization fosters political pluralism, we found a dampening effect on the effective number of parties. Apparently any tendencies toward greater political pluralism in urban areas was overcome by greater exposure to the mass media campaigns of a few wealthy parties, and thus greater concentration of the vote in those parties.

The general Islamicness (F3) of an area had a strong negative impact on the vote for the largest party, PDI-P, attesting to the continued reality of religious-based voting. It had a weak but positive influence on the voting for Golkar and on the number of effective parties. Surprisingly, however, the Islamicness of the context did not help explain voting choices for any one of the three Islamic parties (PPP, PKB, and PAN). Perhaps this finding of no effect is an artifact of the fragmentation of the vote among these three and several smaller Islamic parties in the more orthodox Islamic areas. However, we did discover inheritance from areas supporting Islamic-based parties in the 1955 and 1997 elections on the electoral fortunes of Islamic parties in 1999, which will be discussed later. In other words, more important for the electoral success of PKB, PPP or PAN in the 1999 election than the (general) Islamicness of the community was the level of support for particular parties in previous elections.

In gauging effects of Islam on the direction of the vote, a word of caution is in order. My "seemingly unrelated regressions" can obscure the collective influence of Islam on the outcome of the 1999 election.[16] This can be plausibly measured by simply accumulating the vote for Islamic parties. PKB, PPP, and PAN combined obtained about 30 percent of the vote. If we add the vote for minor Islamic parties, we can infer that Islamic religion likely influenced the voting of approximately one-third of the electorate. If this estimate of one-third of the electorate is compared with the average vote for PPP during the six New Order elections (23 percent), we can conclude that Islamic, religious-based voting increased in the 1999 election. However, if the estimate is compared with the results of the

1955 election, the proportion of voters choosing Islamic parties declined in 1999.

Illiteracy (F4) had a negative impact on the effective number of parties and on the vote for four parties (PDI-P, Golkar, PPP, and PAN), but a positive effect on support for PKB. Since illiteracy and low education are a function of poverty, we can infer that PKB was more successful than any of the other four parties in attracting voters in poorer areas. The negative influence of economic development (F6) on support for PKB is consistent with this inference; these two findings are part of a single pattern.

Areas of higher relative inequality (F5) gave rise to a larger "effective number of parties" (N-index), possibly because in those areas there was a larger proportion of voters whose wealth allowed them some political autonomy. They were thus more able to choose new parties than were poor voters, who were more under the influence of patrons, superiors, and so on. In these areas there was also a higher probability of voting for PDI-P, but a lower probability of votes being cast for PAN or Golkar.

We found a significant regional dimension to the voting for most of the parties, which no doubt encompassed important ethnic factors, such as those bearing on the effective number of parties in Bali and South Sulawesi, discussed earlier. Despite the use of very rough or rudimentary measures (dummy variables), these influences ranked first or second in the models for four out of five parties. Votes for PDI-P and PKB came disproportionately from Java and Bali, those for PAN from Sumatra, and those for Golkar from eastern Indonesia (residual). It is important to note the multiplicity in the findings that arises from the technique of multiple regression. It allows us to isolate and measure the effects of individual variables while simultaneously controlling for the effects of all other variables in the model. Hence, for example, from the model for PDI-P we can infer that its electors came heavily from Java or Bali in addition to those who resided in particular areas of PKI and PNI strength in 1955. In another example, Golkar drew support in areas of eastern Indonesia that were different from the areas where it dominated in the 1997 election, where Masjumi was strong in 1955, where Islamicness was higher, and where relative inequality was lower.

Following up on correlations established in the previous chapter, the legacies of the pattern of voting in 1955 for each of the "big four" (i.e., PNI, Masjumi, NU, and PKI) were subjected to more rigorous empirical testing in this chapter. The regression models, by controlling statistically for the other determinants (independent variables) in the model, enabled us to gauge the independent effects of areas of support for 1955 parties on areas of support for 1999 parties. The overarching finding is that the effects did not disappear (i.e., the statistical associations in Chapter 6 were not spurious). Second, when the variables in each model are ranked according to relative influence (as measured by the size of the *beta* coefficient), the influences from 1955 were stronger on the three new parties.[17] These findings add further evidence of social-based voting in 1999.

The models also illumine how voting choices changed between the 1997 and the 1999 elections. The votes for PDI-P in 1999 came from areas that voted most heavily for Golkar or PDI in 1997. In contrast, electors choosing PKB and PAN resided largely in areas of PPP strength in 1997.[18] In other words, the evidence here indicates that despite PKB's and PAN's attempts to attract voters across the religious divide, they were largely unsuccessful, contributing rather to the fragmentation of orthodox Muslim votes across three parties (PKB, PAN, and PPP). This is further evidence of the salience of religious-based voting in 1999.

The findings of this chapter can be compared and contrasted to those of Liddle and Mujani. On the basis of their sample survey of individual voters, they assessed the relative impact of seven influences on voters' choice of party, including three "sociological factors" of religion, region or ethnicity, and class.[19] Our studies are mutually reinforcing in that both found a substantial relationship between religion and party choice and between regional or ethnic differences and party choice.

My findings differ, however, with regard to class, party identification, and, possibly, the relative importance of social-based voting. They did not find significant influence of class on voting choice and argue that class cleavage was not articulated by the large parties. But I found some influence of class on support for PDI-P, PKB, and PAN.[20] Second, they were unable to establish persuasively whether voters chose their party because of the preference for the party or for the party leader. In contrast, my intertemporal (cross-election) analysis and finding of "inheritance" from particular parties in 1955 to particular parties in 1999 provides a basis for arguing that the causal arrow runs from party to leader and not vice versa.[21] Reinforcing evidence comes as well from the strength of the party in the electorate during New Order elections, as noted in Chapter 2.

Finally, Liddle and Mujani argue that attachment to national leaders is "by far the most important" of the seven influences on partisan choice they studied. Lacking comparable psychological data collected from surveying individuals, I have little basis to assess their claim except to note the magnitude of the coefficients of determination (R^2) on the models reported in this chapter. If coefficients of determination (R^2) are compared across the six models, they can be arrayed between a minimum of .35 for the model on PPP and a maximum of .72 for the model of voting for PKB. This means that the PPP model explains 35 percent of the variation among districts, the model for PKB explains 72 percent of the variation, and so on. The (simple) average of the coefficients in all six models is .57. Explanatory models that on average account for 57 percent of the variation are quite respectable for models in the social sciences. The variance left unexplained by the models, the residual, represents the outside limit that can be attributed to individual (psychological) calculus, the unique characteristics of particular areas, and measurement error. In other words, social- and contextual-based influences on voting choice in the 1999 election were at least as important as individual–psychological ones, and may have been more so.

This chapter also had methodological objectives. I have sought to demonstrate how quantitative data, disaggregated to the district level and covering nearly the entire country, can be utilized to test theories, search for patterns, and generate new questions for in-depth research about Indonesian electoral behavior. Due to the relatively large number of units of data collection and analysis (N = 300+), much of the regional variation is preserved and used as an analytical lever in more powerful multivariate statistical techniques. Because they are collected or generated periodically, often at regular intervals (e.g., censuses, elections), these data facilitate intertemporal analysis. Using them is also very cost-effective, as they are routinely collected or generated and publicly available.

NOTES

1. For example, Liddle and Mujani drew a national probability sample of almost 2,500 respondents "within limitations imposed by geography, level of development, population densities, and cost." They report that the difference between partisan choice in the election (population) and in their sample averaged about 12 percent, which is about four times the margin of error usually achieved in voter surveys in Western democracies (±3 percent). See William R. Liddle and Saiful Mujani, "The Triumph of Leadership: Explaining the 1999 Indonesian Vote," 2000, Table III-1.

2. Because of their special characteristics, quite unique in Indonesia, I excluded from the analysis all the districts in the (primate city) of Jakarta and the provinces of East Timor and Irian Jaya. This resulted in the exclusion of 8 percent of total districts and 6 percent of all voters.

3. This index responds to the need for a measure of the number of parties that takes into account their relative attraction or support. The least arbitrary way is to let the vote shares determine their own weights in the following way: A party with a fractional share of 40 percent also receives a weight of .40 so that its weighted value is .40 × .40 = .16. A party with a 10-

percent share receives a much smaller weighted value of .10 × .10 = .01. The Rae fractionalization index (F-index) is thus $1 - \Sigma$ pi, where pi is the fractional share of the ith component and Σ stands for the summation over all vote shares. This F-index varies from 0 to 1, with 0 fractionalization corresponding to extreme concentration (one party winning all votes) and vice versa. See Rein Taagepera and Matthew Soberg Shugart, *Seats and Votes: The Effects and Determinants of Electoral Systems* (New Haven: Yale University Press, 1989), 77–81.

4. An example of data collected by BPS are financial statistics from regional governments. An example of data they generate is the decennial population census.

5. Factor analysis is a statistical technique for classifying a large number of interrelated variables into a limited number of dimensions or factors. It is a useful method for constructing multiple-item scales, where each scale represents a dimension in a more abstract construct. The procedure involved a principal component analysis rotated to an oblimin solution. The eigenvalue of the sixth or weakest factor was 1.015. The total communality or percentage of variance among all the variables that is accounted for by the six factors is 78 percent. This means that 22 percent of the variation in the original twenty-four variables occurs randomly, rather than according to the shared pattern depicted in the six factors.

6. A factor loading is similar to a correlation coefficient; it varies between 0 and 1 and can be interpreted in the same way.

7. Bivariate analysis suggests that the religious teachers indicator is a more valid measure of Muslim than Christian piety. The bivariate correlation between Christians and religious teachers is weaker and negative (−.38) compared to the correlation between Muslims and religious teachers (.45). In other words, in areas where religious teachers were present in public schools, those teachers tended to be Muslim, regardless of the level of Christians in the district. Apparently Christian youth did not obtain religious instruction in the public schools.

8. $N = 1/(1 - F)$.

9. Because of the collapse of PDI in the 1997 election due to a regime-orchestrated internal schism, the effective number of parties during the New Order was operationalized by averaging the N-index across the last two elections (1992 and 1997). In a few districts the index for a single election was utilized due to missing data.

10. In order to make the analysis at least somewhat sensitive to regional effects, regional differences were very roughly operationalized by creating three dummy variables (eastern Indonesia, Java–Bali, and Sumatra) and entering them, alternately, into the regression equations. For explanation and statistical rationale, see Michael S. Lewis-Beck, "Applied Regression," in *Series: Quantitative Applications in the Social Sciences, No. 22* (Beverly Hills, Calif.: Sage, 1980).

11. The average number of effective parties for Sumatra was 4.88, for Java–Bali 3.83, and for eastern Indonesia 3.64. Note the difference between Java–Bali and Sumatra is 1.05, whereas the difference between Java–Bali and eastern Indonesia is only 0.19.

12. Lance Castles, personal communication, July 2000.

13. Evaluation of regression models is a complex topic on which a large literature exits. Suffice it to mention here that several criteria were utilized, including maximizing the adjusted R^2 and minimizing the standard error of the regression.

14. After PDI won about 15 percent of the national vote in the 1992 election, its highest ever, the New Order government orchestrated a split in PDI and it nearly collapsed in the 1997 election, drawing only about 3 percent of the vote. Because of this stronger showing in 1992, I tested for influence from areas of PDI strength in 1992, but they were insignificant, suggesting that PDI support in 1992 may have been "inflated" by orthodox Muslims who temporarily supported the party as the best way to express opposition or criticism of government policies, but who subsequently abandoned PDI in 1997.

15. Urbanization (F1) accounted for the most variance (36 percent) among the twenty-four indicators of the socioeconomic context during factor analysis.

16. For this point I am indebted to Charles Cappell.

17. In the model for PDI-P, PNI–1955 and PKI–1955 ranked first and second, respectively. In the model for PKB, NU–1955 ranked first. In the model for PAN, Masjumi–1955 ranked second. In contrast, the influence of Masjumi–1955 ranked third in the model for Golkar and second in the model for PPP.

18. When Golkar's vote in 1997 was entered into the equations with PKB or PAN, the *beta* coefficients were statistically insignificant.

19. See Liddle and Mujani, "The Triumph of Leadership," Appendix B. These findings are based on a coefficient of .559 for *santri* in their Religious Voting Model and a coefficient of .686 for Javanese in their Ethnic Voting Model. Although they utilize logistic regression in each model, the dependent variables differ, making it impossible to assess whether religion or ethnicity is the stronger influence. They claim that region or ethnicity is stronger, but the empirical basis appears tenuously based on the difference between r = .22 and r = .31 in bivariate analysis.

20. Class measured as vote for PKI in 1955 influenced the vote for PDI-P, and class measured at illiteracy had positive effects on voting for PKB but negative effects on voting for PKB and PAN.

21. Unfortunately, Liddle and Mujani dropped party identification from their multivariate analysis "because party preference and voting are difficult to disentangle analytically since voters choose party rather than candidate."

CHAPTER 8

Attempts to
Consolidate Democracy

Indonesia's experiences with the electoral reforms of 1999 brought into stark relief the limitations of those reforms and created interest among a large portion of the political elite in further changes to the electoral system prior to the next general election scheduled for 2004. This chapter discusses the changes that were made in the postelection period though the annual session of the Consultative Assembly in August 2002. It thus continues the narrative begun in Chapters 3 and 4. I begin with the problems that emerged in the original design of the General Election Commission (KPU) and how it was radically redesigned. This policy process provides a unique window on the struggle to deepen democracy while simultaneously abolishing vestiges of the old regime. Next I describe recent constitutional amendments and Assembly decisions bearing on electoral reform. Last, I discuss the evolving changes in the three political laws up to the end of 2002 and offer a preliminary assessment.

REFORMING THE GENERAL
ELECTION COMMISSION

The short lifespan of the election commission established in 1999 illustrated well a paradox identified by scholars of democratic transitions. The modes of transition that enhance initial survivability of democracy can preclude future democratic self-transformation of the polity later on during the consolidation phase. To understand how, some background on the function of this institutional reform is useful.

In developing countries undergoing transition to democracy, not only are the stakes in an election higher than in the liberal democracies of wealthy countries, but administrative capacity is weaker.[1] Violence has frequently been the consequence of failure to conduct an election efficiently and impartially. Nascent democracies have sometimes faltered because one political group interprets election irregularities as politically biased. The problem of insulating the election machinery from election contenders, especially from the incumbent government, is compounded by serious technical problems. Administering an election involves a wide range of activities that often need to be undertaken in a short time and in a very tense, politicized environment.[2] If problems occur in any of these activities, people tend to assume that they are politically motivated.

In their effort to insulate elections from politics, most developing countries undergoing democratization have established electoral commissions or electoral management bodies and their struggles for free and fair elections have often pivoted around these commissions. Indonesia is no exception. As the national newspaper of record noted, when the commission was established on March 12, 1999, it was the "star" of the electronic and print mass media.[3] But in the year following the 1999 election, electoral reform became focused on reform of the commission. The following section describes the problems that arose with a multiparty election commission and the process by which it was disbanded and replaced with a nonpartisan, partially independent election commission.

The Failures of the Multiple-Party Electoral Commission

When the new Election Law was formulated and passed into law in early 1999, few people realized that the implementation of provisions about the commission would within a year result in its demise. The law provided for an election commission "which consists of representatives of political parties qualified to contest the election and the government," with the parties and the government having (collectively) equal voting rights.[4] In the debate on the law, two alternatives had been discussed and rejected. The Habibie government, eager to enhance its reformist credentials, had proposed that the commission be composed entirely of political party representatives. But this proposal was rejected by the parties, apparently out of mutual distrust and perceived risk of assuming total responsibility for administration of what was considered the most critical election since 1955. The principle objection to a second alternative for a commission composed entirely of nonpartisan experts appointed by the government was that the selection process would be controlled by the Habibie administration.[5]

When forty-eight parties qualified to contest the election, each party was given a seat and a vote on the commission (in order to give the five government representatives equal voting rights, each of their votes was weighted by a factor of nine). This fifty-three-member commission turned out to be unwieldy, obstructionist, and corrupt, especially after a majority of the parties (twenty-seven) on the commission failed to win any seats in the legislature and forty-two parties failed to qualify for the next election, relegating them to lame duck status on the commission.

The Election Law vested much executive power and authority in the commission. Its members were appointed by and responsible only to the president. They organized themselves and chose their own officers. They had the duty and authority to plan and prepare the election; receive, examine, and approve applications by political parties to contest the election; establish implementing election committees; and coordinate all election-related activities all the way down to nearly 300,000 voting stations.[6] The commission also had the authority to determine how many seats were won by each party in legislatures at three levels (national, twenty-seven provinces, 326 regencies), to approve which candidates filled the seats, and to collect and systematize all data regarding the results of the election. However, adjudicatory authority in these matters was placed with the Supreme Court.

Almost from the beginning, some party representatives on the commission behaved in ways that undermined the high expectations and good will present at its founding. Two party representatives refused to attend the induction ceremony, reportedly because they objected to taking an oath of loyalty to the (Habibie) government. About ten days later, a government representative on the commission revealed that some party representatives were demanding a salary about twice the amount received by members of the House of Representatives at that time. This was followed by the controversial decision prohibiting sitting cabinet ministers from campaigning while allowing themselves, party representatives on the commission, to campaign actively. As election preparations proceeded, frequent allegations of financial irregularities, such as kickbacks in the awarding of contracts for election-related materials, haunted the work of the commission. Many of these allegations were later substantiated by the financial audit agency.

Whatever the political benefits that accrued to the Commission from carrying out what was generally considered a free and fair election, they were soon lost, as the commission was wracked with internal dissension continuously until it was dissolved by government and legislative action in mid-2000. The root of the dissension lay in the election results that indicated forty out of forty-eight parties (83 percent) had combined earned less than 9 percent of the total vote, for an average of 0.23 percent.[7] This meant that within the commission the voice of the PDI-P and the voice of a tiny party were supposed to have equal weight, even though the PDI-P's share of the total vote (34 percent) was 147 times larger than the share of the average tiny party. But there were also contributing factors, especially a lacuna in the Election Law. According to the law, parties falling under a 2-percent threshold were prohibited from competing in the next election.[8] But the law also provided that members of the commission serve five-year terms, ending in 2003, opening the door for the tiny parties to cling to their positions on the commission despite their electoral defeat and consequent lack of legitimacy after the election.[9]

The Election Law required that the commission certify the results of the election.[10] As the pressure mounted on the commission to certify, the tiny parties realized that if about half of them joined together they had enough votes to further delay certification, which required a quorum of two-thirds, and buy more time to maneuver for seats in the legislature. Publicly, however, they took a principled stance, declaring they were holding out until certain election regulation violations were investigated and settled to their satisfaction. Eventually, on August 4, nearly two months after election day, President Habibie intervened and signed a decree validating the results, effectively breaking the stalemate within the commission.

In their attempt to gain legislative seats despite their failure at the polls, the tiny parties on the commission perceived opportunity in the allocation of seats to parties according to "largest remainders" under the proportional representation electoral system. Conflict revolved around the use of *stembus akkord* or the voluntary agreements among parties to combine their remainders in order to improve their chances of obtaining seats. The commission was late in establishing the rules governing these accords, announcing them just weeks before the election. As a result, the parties had little time to form accords, none met the initial deadline for giving notice that they had entered an accord, and the commission extended the deadline. But in the weeks following the election, confusion persisted about which parties had actually formed valid accords, about the validity of local accords for the formation of provincial and district legislatures, and about how to assign the seat(s) won by an accord to the parties within it. The confusion was both caused by and reflected in the actions of the commission, which repeatedly revised the rules.

After weeks of rancorous debate, the commission finally decided on August 30 to retroactively change the rules and abolish vote-sharing agreements.[11]

In light of this background, it is possible to understand that when the new People's Consultative Assembly met in mid-October, the commission was in deep political trouble. The Habibie government therefore had little trouble getting the agreement of the large parties, who were represented in the Assembly, on a key phrase in the decision on basic policies to guide the government over the next five years (GBHN). The phrase that turned out to be the single most important step in reconstituting the commission was a sentence pertaining to domestic politics that read as follows: "conduct a higher quality general election with participation by the people as wide as possible and on the basis of democratic principles, direct, in public, free, secret, honest, just and civilized which is implemented by an *independent and non-partisan* executing body by the year 2004 at the latest" (unofficial translation; emphasis added). Decisions by the Assembly supersede all laws enacted by the House. As we shall see, the phrase "independent and non-partisan" became the legal basis for modifying the Election Law's provisions regarding the commission and for dissolving the commission established in 1999 after only one year.

The Process of Reforming the Electoral Commission

Anyone who thought that the electoral defeat of the tiny parties, the completion of the election (seating of the new House and Assembly and the election of the president and vice president), and the "independent and non-partisan" clause adopted in the broad policies might bring about the resignation of the tiny parties' representatives on the commission was mistaken. The Election Law provided for a five-year term, as mentioned earlier. In addition, the law mandated an evaluation of the electoral system by the commission within three years.[12] Both were cited by the tiny parties as reasons for not changing the commission or for maintaining the status quo.

In late October the commission returned to the news with a new raison d'être. Earlier in the year the Habibie government had submitted bills to the House that proposed the creation of three new provinces and thirty-four new regencies. In the background as well was the cancellation in June of the general election in two regencies of Aceh out of the government's inability to guarantee security in these areas, which were largely under the control of the GAM insurgency. So the commission announced the formation of a local election committee (PPL), consisting of all members of the commission except the chairman, Rudini, and the five government representatives, who boycotted the meeting. The purpose of the PPL was to carry out local follow-up elections for legislatures in the new provinces and districts and repeat elections in Aceh, where they had been canceled. Using questionable procedures, the most vociferous and strident proponent of the tiny parties, Agus Miftach, was elected to lead the PPL. Other leadership positions on the committee went to the tiny parties as well.[13]

About a week later, the committee upped the ante, announcing several controversial decisions. It had scheduled repeat elections in Aceh and follow-up elections in the newly designated administrative areas to be held simultaneously on June 10, 2000. Second, it had decided to summon leaders of the second-largest party, Golkar, for purposes of getting clarification on uses of its funds during the 1999 election. Third, it was sending a letter to newly installed President Abdurrahman Wahid requesting that he review the existence (*keberadaan*) of the five government representatives on the commission. They had boycotted the plenary meeting at which these decisions were taken. Since the meeting was attended by only thirty commission members, these decisions were apparently taken without the presence of a quorum.[14]

Over the next couple of months PPL suffered a series of reversals to its plans for local elections. First, the government postponed indefinitely its plans for splitting Irian Jaya into three provinces after the plans met with strenuous opposition from the Irianese.[15] Then in meetings with the PPL, political parties expressed their reservations about local elections. They questioned the formal legal basis for local elections and the discrepancy they perceived between the PPL's enthusiasm for moving ahead with local elections immediately and the government's silence on the matter.[16]

Meanwhile, objections continued to stream in from the regions. The governor of Aceh asked that local elections be postponed, as security had not improved since they were canceled in June. The deputy governor of Irian Jaya claimed that two of the new regencies being planned lacked office space and housing to accommodate members of a new legislature. The governor of North Maluku said that a huge obstacle to local elections in his area was the tens of thousands of refugees who have fled to Bitung, North Sulawesi, trying to escape the violence that had engulfed his province.[17] He noted further the rough seas during the month the local elections were planned, complicating transportation, and that only ten of the forty-eight parties had opened offices in his new province.

At the end of the year the situation and public discussion stood roughly as follows: The commission had fractured, its meetings boycotted by the government representatives and taken over by the tiny parties. Having lost political legitimacy and support, they clung to formal legal justifications for their existence, including the need to administer local elections. But their plans for local elections were in deep trouble. Neither the parties nor the voters in those places wanted them, and the government had yet to provide any funds for local election preparation. If the failures of the commission had stimulated public discussion and proposals for reform focused narrowly on the commission, the problem of how to manage local elections in certain regions led to awareness that more comprehensive reform of the three political laws was needed.

In early January, the meeting the PPL had sought with the president for at least a month finally took place. The PPL was seeking his support in order to leverage disbursement of the Rp. 240 million they had requested for implementing local elections. But the president told them that he did not want to get involved, as he was concentrating on more serious problems. He observed, however, that the existing legal regulations were insufficient basis for conducting local elections and requested that they consult with the House about the matter. His request was later underscored by an emissary from the Supreme Court, who told the PPL that neither the Election Law nor the laws delineating new administrative areas provided sufficient legal basis. The government would not proceed without a firmer legal basis, which was the responsibility of the House.[18]

The decisive meeting occurred about two weeks later. In a closed-door meeting attended by four leaders of the House from large parties and the minister of home affairs, Surjadi Soedirja, the decision was taken to restructure the commission by changing only three out of eighty-six articles in the Election Law. The minister also told reporters that the government would consider canceling local elections in some regions until the situation there returned to normal: "The local elections will be flexible depending on the province's readiness."[19]

Speaking to the press a few days later, Akbar Tandjung, speaker of the House and chairman of Golkar, gave more details. He said that the government and the House had agreed that a new commission was needed, in line with the mandate in the GBHN ("independent and non-partisan"). First the Election Law would be changed, then the implementation of local elections would be the responsibility of the new commission. He cautioned, however, "because we are facing many domestic problems and without lessening the meaning of democracy, we need to consider whether to hold local elections."[20] Repeating what had been said publicly by a PDI-P legislator a month earlier, he noted that new regency-level legislatures could be selected on the basis of the 1999 election returns.

Why had the government decided to dismiss the commission rather than let it serve out its term? Although publicly Minister Surjadi and Speaker Akbar always referred to the 1999 GBHN mandate, the question persisted because the deadline in the mandate was 2004, a full year after commission terms expired. Additional insight that worsening conflict in the regions played a role came from Andi Mallarangeng, a government representative on the commission and special assistant to the state minister for regional autonomy. He wrote,

Reforming the Commission to become an independent and non-partisan Commission has become urgent when we are faced with holding local elections in newly delineated semi-autonomous regions. . . . The question is, do we want a repetition of the bad dream with the partisan Commission administering those elections? There is no guarantee that the partisan Commission is capable of overcoming its partisanship and objectively concluding the counting of votes. In situations where social conflict has flared up such as in the new regions in Maluku, Papua, Kalimantan, and Aceh, controversy and failure in the counting of votes will exacerbate conflict situations. Local elections intended to transform violent street conflicts into civilized debates in the parliament will instead sharpen and deepen existing conflicts.[21]

Needless to say, the members of the commission who were representatives of tiny parties did not accept these developments. Rudini called the plan to establish a new commission a "conspiracy" by the large parties to destroy the tiny parties. He claimed the plan contradicted the spirit of the 1999 broad policies that gave the commission opportunity until the year 2003 to complete its work. The formation of a new commission, he continued, was intended to stop the previously scheduled and ongoing work of the commission, especially its efforts to expose 1999 election fraud, violations, and crime. He demanded that the government and the House formulate comprehensive reforms, rather than engage in piecemeal change targeted at the commission. He also lambasted the decision-making process that had been used and stated, "Proposed changes to political laws must be conveyed in a transparent manner, socialized in society, and involve political parties."[22] He added, defiantly, that until a new law took effect, the commission had decided to continue carrying out all duties already on its agenda.

The standoff between the PPL on one side and the government (home affairs) and the House leadership on the other continued for about two weeks. Both sides spoke frequently with the press, attempting to build political support. The approximately thirty members of the commission who had reconstituted themselves as the PPL continued to meet regularly and prepare for local elections. A government team of twenty-two persons was drafting revised laws for submission to the House. The government's strategy was to work with the House and use legislation to dismiss the commission as well as to give the new regions more flexibility in selecting members of their legislatures.[23]

On February 8 it became apparent that the government had changed its strategy. Without waiting on the legislative process, Minister Surjadi announced that the president was canceling the plan to hold local elections on June 10 and ordering the commission to cease preparations. Surjadi cited lack of funds and fears that security could not be guaranteed. He sought to convey, however, that the government was not acting unilaterally: "Based on a letter from the House chairman, the government agrees with selecting new members of regional legislatures on the basis of the 1999 Election results. Accordingly, the provisions in Laws No. 45 through 55, 1999 concerning local elections will undergo revision."[24] He also made clear that the government was "temporarily" withholding disbursement of funds for local election preparation.[25]

In early June, ten out of eleven blocs in the House reached agreement on amendments to the Election Law and to ten laws pertaining to the delineation of new semiautonomous areas. The one dissenting bloc, representing only thirteen seats, cited their disagreement with the cancellation of local elections and a commission composed of nonpartisan members.

Outside of the House, Agus Miftach predictably rejected the restructuring of the commission, saying it was illegal because it had not been proposed by the commission. Moreover, he charged, the discussion on the bill had been conducted quietly, illegally, and without a public hearing. Minister Surjadi said that this action spelled the end of the old commission and called on all sides to accept the decision. When asked about stubborn (*ngotot*) members such as Agus Mitfach, he replied, "If there are still those who are stubborn, what kind of a democracy is this? They say they want to uphold the law."[26] A leading national daily newspaper carried the story under the headline, "Polish the Commission, Remove the Tramps" and asked the question, "Why must [electoral reform] be done in stages."[27] The reaction of NGO election monitors was similar. They wondered why the amendments did not address more of the problems in the Election Law.

The Policy Outcome

The legislative process took about four months just to amend three articles of the Election Law, reflecting the tortuous legislative process and indicating that it was not always smooth sailing. The changes are shown in the appendix to this chapter. The most contentious issue, ironically, given the symbolic importance attached to "independent and non-partisan," pertained to the independence of the commission. The 1999 Election Law provided for a secretariat, headed by a general secretary and a deputy general secretary appointed and terminated by the president, to assist the commission in carrying out its work. The law read, "In carrying out its responsibilities, the General Secretary is responsible to the Commission in technical operations and to the government in administrative matters."[28] A coalition of nongovernmental election watchdogs lobbied strenuously for making the general secretary responsible to the commission in all matters: "How can the Commission be truly independent if its structure and budget are directly regulated by the government via the Minister of Home Affairs, since the neutrality of the bureaucracy is still in doubt?"[29] The coalition argued that their monitoring efforts during the 1999 election indicated that the secretariat was a source of ineffectiveness and even corruption, as shown by recent news reports.

While lack of independence from the government was their main concern, they also sought more comprehensive reforms of the commission. They contended that existing law was too general, leaving too many aspects of commission operations open to someone's discretion or handled in an arbitrary fashion. For example, what is the process for soliciting and recruiting commission members? Who has the authority to terminate commission members? On what grounds? Can they be reappointed (multiple terms)? What is the procedure for replacing members who do not serve out their terms? Should the commission decide its own decision rules?

Over the next six months the Wahid administration formulated a list of twenty-two nominees, none of whom were members of the previous commission, and sent them to the House early in 2001. At least one interest group, the Women and Politics Network, complained about the lack of transparency in the nominating process and requested that a quota of positions be reserved for women.[30] Two renowned political commentators publicly urged the House commission with responsibility for screening the nominees to apply clear standards (*tolok ukur*). Representatives of the commission responded by inviting anyone interested to attend its examination of the nominees.[31] Indeed, the commission's interviews with each candidate were open to the press and representatives of interest groups, as was the process of selection that occurred through open voting.

Although partisan politics clearly entered the selection process, evident from slate making and bloc voting along partisan lines, eleven members were chosen for the new electoral commission, all of whom seemed to meet the requirements in the law, including independent and nonpartisan.[32] The process illustrated the greater separation of powers and empowerment of the legislature as compared to the New Order. President Wahid formally appointed the House's eleven nominees in late March 2001.[33]

Conclusions about Reform of the Electoral Commission

Although the election commission presided over what was generally viewed as a competent, free, and fair election by international standards, it suffered a variety of weaknesses that threatened the electoral system with breakdown. The reformers who designed it did not anticipate that forty-eight parties would qualify for representation on the commission. Nor did they have any basis for constructing a rule of weighted decision making, not knowing in advance of the election the parties' respective strength in the electorate. They may have expected that once the election results were known, parties failing to pass the threshold would voluntarily resign. Having had only very limited experience with party politics in the previous thirty-two years of the New Order, they did not anticipate how tiny parties would behave, especially the lengths to which they would go in order to cling to power and access to resources in an economically depressed, fluid, and transitional political environment. Consolidation and certification of the vote proved to be a slow and tortuous process. Administrative problems were partly to blame, but the major cause was tiny-party allegations of voting irregularities, which held up tabulation and certification of the election results at every level. A stalemate within the commission was eventually broken by presidential intervention.

Allocation of seats to political parties based upon the certified results was further delayed because of controversy over vote-sharing arrangements. Major causes were incompetence of the commission and the attempts by some parties that performed poorly in the election to form postelection agreements to share votes. Some even argued they should each be given a seat despite lack of voter support. Again, stalemate occurred in the commission and was eventually resolved by a vote to simply disregard vote-sharing agreements. As a result of the two stalemates, seat allocation for the House could not be finalized until September 1, almost three months after the election. These were probably the main reasons why the commission lost its political support and the newly elected government decided that restructuring the commission was necessary. It became urgent as the government contemplated holding local elections and saw the risk that the commission would exacerbate the conflicts in those regions.

The political elite responded by placing commission reform at the top of the agenda for a second wave of reform. The 1999 multi-party commission was dissolved and replaced with a neutral (non-partisan) one. While the institutional redesign and new personnel looked promising, the process was marred by pseudodemocratic "fragments."

Although the commission may have fomented more frequent conflict, as proportional-type institutions are wont to do, at the same time it may have prevented more intense and violent conflict from erupting. By dispersing authority and victory it may have helped to endear tiny parties representing dissatisfied minorities to the new democratic rules of the game. The tiny parties engaged in a variety of antics (shouting, boycotts, etc.), but within the commission they were socialized enough to prevent them from using more extreme means to vent their grievances.

Observing the policy process, it is interesting to note the symbolic importance of law and concern among players to demonstrate a legal basis for their actions or positions. I say "symbolic" because laws were cited selectively, the spirit of a law was often ignored, the courts were not involved, and in the end due process was truncated or ignored. For example, government officials invoked the "independent and non-partisan" clause of the 1999 GBHN even though the GBHN mandate contained the deadline of 2004, a year after the ending of the commission's term of office. Agus Miftach and the tiny-party company clung to the five-year-term clause, even though the spirit of the law seemed to call for their resignation.

Second, there was little direct public debate among the players, except for an occasional television talk show. Rather, most of the time they debated with one another indirectly through the press. Also, issuing press statements and speaking with reporters was by far the preferred technique in attempting to sway public (i.e., elite) opinion. No efforts were made to educate the political public, for example, by holding public hearings.

Third, the critical decisions were taken by a small group behind closed doors. Perhaps the clearest example was the meeting between four House leaders and two ministers on January 24, where the decision was taken to focus narrowly on replacing the commission rather than more comprehensive reform of the Election Law. We can infer that confronted with more pressing problems, these elites decided to truncate due process and aim for incremental change. Another possibility is that after working with the new House for three months, during which time it produced little legislation, they reduced their expectations about what the House could accomplish.

Observing the antics that went on in the commission, one is struck by the deep mistrust of the government and the political inexperience and naïveté of some of the tiny-party representatives. This makes it difficult to apportion the failure of the commission between agency (inexperience) and structure (too many parties). Insofar as agency was a factor, the failure of the commission can be viewed as a legacy of pseudodemocracy, under which there was little opportunity to gain experience in politics.

Pastor's review of electoral management bodies in developing countries showed that there are four different places to locate electoral management bodies: (1) within the government, (2) within a government ministry but supervised by a judicial body, (3) within an independent election commission manned by experts and directly accountable to the parliament, and (4) within a multiparty commission.[34] Indonesia's experience adds another case in support of his finding that multiparty commissions are unworkable with too many parties. With the amendment to the Election Law, Indonesia has moved in the direction of an independent election commission; however, it is not one that is wholly or continuously accountable to the legislature (recall the criticism of the coalition of election watchdogs). But by giving the House a key screening role in the selection process, Indonesia's revamped election commission nonetheless can be expected to remain sensitive to the political currents emanating from the legislature.

POSTELECTION CONSTITUTIONAL AMENDMENTS AND DECISIONS OF THE ASSEMBLY

The 1945 constitution is a poor foundation for democracy because it lacks specificity and grants a wide range of powers to the executive branch. Many of its articles state that certain powers will be "delineated by law," a phrase that provided wide leeway of interpretation to Presidents Soekarno and Suharto. A related weakness is lack of clarity about a presidential versus a parliamentary system.[35] Under the pseudodemocracy of the New Order, this constitution was deemed sacred by the authorities and any discussion of amending it was considered treasonous. The very fact that amending the constitution was placed on the national political agenda can be viewed as a step in the institutionalization of democracy.

At its October 1999 general session the Assembly made changes to nine articles of the constitution, which collectively became known as the First Amendment. These changes focused on strengthening the legislative and judiciary branches vis-à-vis the executive. In addition, they ratified the GBHN for the coming five-year period, which for the first time the parties played a large role in formulating. Of direct relevance to electoral reform were the provisions on reconstituting the General Election Commission on an independent and non-partisan basis and on abolishing appointed, military seats in the House, restricting them to the Assembly, by the next election in 2004.[36]

The Assembly reconvened for its first yearly session in August 2000 and passed seven changes to the constitution, collectively designated the Second Amendment, and issued several other decrees (*ketetapan*).[37] Many of these changes were intended to further clarify the separation of powers and checks and balances among the three branches of government, thus continuing what had begun in the previous general session. Other changes pertained to civil–military relations, the decentralization of power to the regions, and a bill of rights. They largely left intact, however, the hybrid structure of the government (presidential with parliamentary characteristics) and its attendant ambiguities.

Pertaining to electoral reform was an amendment specifying that the legislatures at all three levels of government (DPR, DPRD, DPRD-II) will become fully elected bodies as a result of the next general election in 2004, thus ending the appointed seats (reserved domain) for the military and police. This should help to separate the executive and legislative branches and facilitate improvement of the House's oversight role. Another step was taken toward subordination of the military and police to civilian authority with a decree requiring House approval of the president's nominees for the positions of military commander and national police chief. However, these positive steps in the direction of democratic consolidation were diminished by another provision that allowed the military and police to maintain their representation in the Assembly at current (thirty-eight seats) or lower levels until 2009. In terms of the concepts introduced in Chapter 1, this was a step backward (deconsolidation or "backsliding"), as some party elites went "knocking at the barracks" for support in the political struggle.[38]

Under the New Order all important decisions were reserved to the central government, which was firmly under President Suharto's control, making it a highly centralized political and economic system. Consequently, one of the major demands of the reform movement has been decentralization of power, and after Suharto resigned many regions began voicing their discontent. Both the (transitional) Habibie administration and the democratically elected Wahid administration responded to these developments with a policy of "wide ranging regional autonomy" within the framework of the unitary state: "Despite these concessions by the center, many regions remained dissatisfied that regional autonomy was based only in laws that were in essence a 'gift' from the center that could be rescinded at any time by a decision of the DPR and the President."[39]

Responding to these pressures to enshrine decentralization in the constitution, the Assembly amended the section pertaining to regional authorities. These changes included providing for the democratic election of heads of regions and devolution of authority over all matters not reserved by law to the central government. A number of additional proposals that had been placed on the Assembly's agenda proved highly controversial and discussion on them stalemated.

However, the Assembly returned to these tough issues during its annual session in November 2001. Once again, agreement on all the reforms that had been placed on the agenda proved elusive, yet agreement was reached on the following points, collectively designated the Third Amendment:

1. The sovereignty of the people will no longer be exercised in full through the highest institution of the state (Assembly), but rather in accordance with the constitution (this is a prerequisite to no. 2).
2. A Constitutional Court will be established that is empowered to undertake constitutional interpretation and judicial review of legislation, resolve disputes between state institutions, rule on motions to dissolve political parties, resolve election-related disputes, and rule on motions to impeach the president.
3. The Assembly's constitutional function of promulgating broad policies (GBHN), within which the government executive is required to operate regardless of the executive's agreement with those policies, will be nullified (President Habibie ran afoul of the 1998 GBHN on corruption, as did President Abdurrahman Wahid of the 1999 GBHN).
4. There will be first-round direct presidential and vice-presidential elections held simultaneously with the general election. Any ticket winning more than 50 percent and also polling more than 20 percent in at least half of the provinces will be elected.
5. The president and vice president will no longer be impeachable on policy grounds, and the Constitutional Court will have the authority to decide the legal issues involved in impeachment.
6. A new Chamber of Regions will be established that is directly elected with equal membership from each province and with legislative powers on issues relating to regional autonomy, center–region relations, and natural resource management.
7. A new independent judicial commission will be created to deal with judicial appointments and judicial ethics issues.
8. All compulsory taxation and levies will be required to have a basis in law.

Constitutional changes again monopolized the agenda of the Assembly at its annual meeting in 2002. Collectively labeled the Fourth Amendment, many of the provisions dealt with specifications (details) of the agreements reached in previous amendments. But one article, however, represented a major redesign in the structure of representative institutions: Beginning with the next general election in 2004, the Assembly will be entirely elected, and will consist of two chambers—the House of Representatives and the Chamber of Regions. Hence, the military's "reserved domain" and other appointive seats will be abolished.

Taken together, the four constitutional amendments since 1999 undergird a fundamental overhaul in the structure of the Indonesian state. The unique hybrid presidential system (with parliamentary characteristics) of the original 1945 constitution, shown capable of being used to underpin authoritarian rule, has been discarded in favor of a conventional presidential system as found, for example, in the Philippines, the United States, and many Latin American countries. Now there are constitutional checks and balances; clearer separation of powers between the legislature, executive, and judiciary; and sovereignty resides with the people who vote directly for leaders and representatives more along the lines of advanced democracies. Although many key decisions remain somewhat vague and a host of laws and regulations must be enacted to put these constitutional provisions into effect, the basic conditions are in place to make the system work.

NORMATIVE AND EMPIRICAL CONSIDERATIONS IN DESIGNING INDONESIA'S ELECTORAL SYSTEM

Continuation of reforms to deepen and institutionalize democracy are necessary. Comparative evidence suggests that systems undertaking transition cannot remain static; they either move toward consolidation or experience backsliding and breakdown (i.e., returning to the pseudodemocracy of the New Order).[40] Reforms of the three 1999 political laws are currently under consideration, including introduction of more majoritarian aspects (e.g., SMDP), which raises concern about the possible negative effects on ethnic and communal conflict management. In this effort, political elites should realize that choices in electoral system design are seldom easy and straightforward; rather, they involve normative trade-offs.[41]

One trade-off is between efficiency and governability on the one hand and representativeness on the other. Historically, election laws in Indonesia have emphasized representativeness and inclusiveness through proportional representation. In 1999 the election of 92 percent of the House and about 85 percent of the Assembly by proportional representation indicated the high value placed on achieving representativeness through the electoral system. But the introduction of a threshold required of parties in order to compete in the next election reflected a concern for efficiency and governability by preventing tiny parties from obtaining seats and excessive fragmentation of power in the House.

A second, related trade-off is between party coherence and voter choice. Indonesia's emphasis was clearly on party coherence, as voters chose among parties, not individual candidates, who were selected by parties (i.e., closed party list). The 1999 electoral law attempted to modify these emphases slightly through a unique and complex "PR plus," which combined proportional representation by province with some elements of a plurality system. Rather than assigning individual seats based solely on the ranking of candidates on party lists, they were assigned "with reference to party results at the district level." But this attempt to let voters help select which candidates represent parties was compromised by party leaders who were unwilling to give up a portion of their power.

Third is the trade-off between ballot simplicity and accessability and the appropriateness of the ballot in theoretical terms. Indonesia can be situated at the simplicity end of this continuum, as voters only need to select one party on each of three ballots (one ballot for the legislature at each of three levels).

The important point is that no one electoral system is better than another. Rather, there are a series of trade-offs, and what electoral system would be best for Indonesia depends on what Indonesians want it to do for them.[42] The experiences with the system designed in 1999 and the subsequent debate indicate that a consensus on goals for the electoral system continues to elude Indonesia's political elite. Among the questions under debate are as follows: How important is it to have a governing majority and to avoid coalitions? How important is it to have representative accountable to constituencies and to avoid a strong role for central party leaders? How important is it to avoid disparities between votes cast and seats won by a party? How important is it to limit the number of parties? Precisely because one cannot maximize both values in each trade-off, "the choice of electoral system should depend on the particular historical patterns of cleavage and conflict in each country and on which threats to democracy are judged to be most severe."[43]

Overall (countrywide) in Indonesia, two patterns of cleavage and conflict have been apparent since the 1950s. The results of the 1999 election indicated the continuing salience of a fundamental cultural–religious cleavage splitting the population into roughly equal halves, between devout Muslims attracted to Islamic-based parties and a diverse (residual) group who prefer religiously inclusive, nationalist-based parties.[44] The half preferring Islamic-based parties are divided between "modernists" and "traditionalists." This means that at least three political parties are likely to be sustained by the broad divisions in Indonesian society. A complicating factor is the sharp increase in (relatively) isolated nationalist, ethnic, and religious conflict in various regions outside Java, most notably in Aceh, West and Central Kalimantan, Central Sulawesi, Maluku, West Papua (Irian Jaya), and Timor, which are reflective of a tendency worldwide for transitions to democratic politics to create fertile conditions for nationalism and ethnic conflict.[45] Current proposals for electoral design need to be evaluated in light of these characteristics of Indonesia's political landscape.

What seems clear is that Indonesia needs an electoral system designed to produce conciliation rather than polarization. A system that results in multipolar fluidity would be preferable to one tending toward bifurcation. It should encourage the formation of multiethnic coalitions and prevent a single majority from achieving permanent domination. Thus, what is at stake is how best to design the institutions of Indonesia's young democracy to manage religious, ethnic, and nationalist political activity. Electoral-system design is increasingly being recognized as one of the key levers of constitutional engineering that can be applied to the interests of political accommodation and stability in ethnically divided societies. "Proportional institutions . . . decrease the stakes of competition, decrease the intensity of competition, and increase direct access to political institutions. . . . Majoritarian institutions, therefore, increase the stakes of competitions, increase the intensity of competitiveness, and decrease direct access to political institutions."[46]

The argument for proportionalism assumes the persistence of religious and ethnonationalist identities (thus, discouraging them from being played out politically is only to suppress the inevitable), respects the integrity of communal boundaries, and seeks to institutionalize these cleavages and make them a visible object of conflict management efforts.[47] Using data on a pool of 830 minorities over a forty-five-year period, Cohen found empirical support for this theoretical argument that proportional institutions are more effective than majoritarian institutions as democratic instruments of ethnic-conflict management.

Other comparativists make similar arguments. Based on his study of five states in southern Africa, Reynolds contends that "PR systems uniformly outperform their plurality counterparts. . . . If inclusive parties are to evolve in a plural society, then they will be best facilitated by the necessity of broad-based party lists rather than the confines of choosing candidates for ethnically homogeneous single-member districts."[48] Diamond writes, "If any generalization about institutional design is sustainable . . . it is that majoritarian systems are ill-advised for countries with deep ethnic, regional, religious, or other emotional and polarizing divisions. . . . The overriding imperative is to avoid broad and indefinite exclusion from power of any significant group."[49] He argues that electoral system designers should attempt to (1) create incentives for groups to form coalitions or to pool votes in national politics, (2) distribute power vertically so that territorially based groups can have some control over their own affairs, and (3) ensure that all ethnic and nationality groups have political equality. Citing Reynolds's comparative study of five electoral systems in southern Africa, he advises, "As a general rule, a moderately multiparty system, produced by a moderate system of proportional representation, makes more sense for most emerging democracies. This can be achieved either by relying on moderately sized multimember districts or by choosing an electoral threshold . . . which will weed out very small parties."[50] One implication for contemporary Indonesia is that proposals to introduce more majoritarian aspects into Indonesia's electoral system should be evaluated very carefully.

APPENDIX:
CHANGES TO LAW NO. 3/1999 PERTAINING TO
THE GENERAL ELECTION COMMISSION

Article 8, Verse 2

From: The General Election is implemented by the General Election Commission which is free and autonomous (*bebas dan mandiri*) consisting of representatives of political parties qualified to contest the election and of the government, and which is responsible to the President.

To: The General Election is implemented by the General Election Commission (Commission) which is independent and non-partisan.

Article 9, Verses 1–3

From: The members of the Commission consist of one representative from each party qualified to contest the election and five representatives of the government.

To: The members of the Commission consist of eleven persons.

From: Government and political party representatives have equal voting rights.

To: Every member of the Commission has the same voting right.

From: Political party representatives are selected by the respective party central executive board and government representatives are designated by the President.

To: Candidates for membership on the Commission are nominated by the President and sent to the House for its approval through its commission having authority in domestic political affairs.

Those who can be nominated are Indonesian citizens who fulfill the following requirements:

a. Physically and mentally healthy;

b. Have the right to vote and be elected;

c. Possess a strong commitment toward upholding democracy and justice;

d. Possess personal integrity which is strong, honest, and fair;

e. Possess adequate knowledge about politics, parties, elections and have leadership ability;

f. Is not a member or officer of a political party;

g. Holds neither a political position nor an administrative position in the civil service.

Members of the Commission who have been approved by the House are installed by a Presidential decision.

Before beginning their service, members of the Commission take an oath in front of the President.

Article 83

From: The term of service for the Commission administering the 1999 General Election ends one year prior to the 2004 General Election.

To: The term of service for the Commission administering the 1999 General Election ends on the date this bill becomes law.

NOTES

1. There tends to be a big contrast in the administrative dimension of elections between advanced and developing countries. In advanced countries where there is a relatively high degree of administrative competence, most people take for granted the administrative dimension of elections. Because they assume that the process will be honest and impartial, few citizens concern themselves with the institutions, rules, and procedures for conducting elections. It is interesting to note that neither Great Britain nor the United States has a central office for conducting national elections. Nor are the local institutions responsible for administering elections independent; they reside in government offices. This pattern is widespread. "Of twenty advanced industrialized democracies, the governments—not inde-

pendent commissions—are responsible for conducting the elections in fifteen, or 75 percent." Robert A. Pastor, "A Brief History of Electoral Commissions," in Andreas Schedler, *The Self-Restraining State* (Boulder, Colo.: Lynne Rienner, 1999), 77.

   2. Ibid., 77–78.

The conduct of elections includes the following: appointing and training registration and election officials; delineating the boundaries of voting areas; designing a voter registration system and establishing voting sites; registering voters on-site or at home and aggregating and publishing a registration list at national and local levels; publishing and distributing the list widely enough to provide voters and parties an opportunity to review and correct the list; establishing and enforcing rules on campaigning, access to the media, and financing; ensuring security of the voters, the candidates, and the polling stations; registering and qualifying political parties and candidates; collecting information on all voters and processing the data onto voter identification cards; distributing voter identification cards and ensuring that they are received by the right people; producing election materials; printing and securing the ballot; delivering the election materials to the appropriate sites; certifying that voters are on the registration list and that they vote privately and in accordance with the procedures (often including dipping one's finger in ink); counting the ballots; ensuring that the results are delivered to the election offices; adding the count and announcing the results; investigating and adjudicating complaints; and certifying the final results.

   3. "KPU, Riwayatmu Kini" (KPU, Your Story Now), *Kompas*, June 2, 2000.
   4. Law no. 3/1999, Chapter III, Articles 8.2 and 9.2.
   5. Blair A. King, private communication, April 23, 2001.
   6. The initial applications by political parties were approved by a transitional committee known as the "Team of Eleven," since party representatives to the commission had to be chosen before the commission could be constituted.
   7. Hereafter I will translate the Indonesian term for these parties (*partai gurem*) as "tiny parties."
   8. Law no. 3/1999, Chapter VII, Article 39, Verse 3.
   9. Ibid., Article 83.
   10. Ibid., Chapter X, Article 65.
   11. National Democratic Institute for International Affairs and the Carter Center, "Post-Election Developments in Indonesia: The Formation of the DPR and the MPR," August 26, 1999; NDI, "The 1999 Presidential Election, MPR General Session, and Post-Election Developments in Indonesia," November 28, 1999.
   12. Law no. 3/1999, Chapter III, Article 11.
   13. "Pemilu Lokal di 34 Daerah, Butuh Biaya Rp. 200 Milyar" (Local Elections in 34 Regions Require 200 Billion Rupiah), *Media Indonesia*, November 2, 1999.
   14. "Pemilu Susulan pada 10 Juni 2000" (Supplementary Elections on 10 June 2000), *Kompas*, November 8, 1999.
   15. "Pemakaran Irja Ditunda" (Division of Irian Jaya Postponed), *Suara Pembaruan*, November 29, 1999.

16. "Partai Politik tak Antusias Ikuti Pemilu Lokal" (Political Parties Unenthusiastic about Participating in Local Elections), *Kompas*, December 24, 1999.

17. "Daerah belum Siap Menyelenggarakan Pemilu Lokal" (Regions Unprepared for Conducting Regional Elections), *Media Indonesia*, December 21, 1999; "Pemilu Lokal Banyak Kendala" (Many Obstacles to Local Elections), *Kompas*, December 21, 1999.

18. "Presiden Minta Pemilu Lokal Dikonsultasikan ke DPR" (President Requests Consultations with House on Local Elections), *Republika*, January 4, 1999.

19. "Govt Plans Amendments to 1999 Law on Election, Commission," *Jakarta Post*, January 18, 2000.

20. "Pemeriintah-Dewan Sepakat Gantikan KPU Pimpinan Rudini" (Government and House Agreed on Replacing KPU Led by Rudini), *Media Indonesia*, January 25, 2000.

21. "Reformasi KPU" (Reform the KPU), *Tempo*, February 6, 2000.

22. "Akbar Tandjung dan Rudini Beda Pendapat" (Akbar Tandjung and Rudini Differ in Opinion), *Kompas*, January 28, 2000.

23. "Depdagri Susun Draf Revisi UU No. 3/99" (Government Drafts Revision to Law no. 3/1999), *Media Indonesia*, February 8, 2000.

24. "Pemilu Lokal Dibatalkan" (Local Elections Cancelled), *Media Indonesia*, February 9, 2000.

25. "Pemerintah Tahan Dana Pemilu Lokal" (Government Withholds Funds for Local Elections), *Republika*, February 9, 2000.

26. "Memoles Komisi Menggusur Petualang," (Polish the Commission, Remove the Tramps), *Republika*, June 7, 2000.

27. Ibid.

28. Law no. 3/1999, Article 9, Verse 11.

29. "KPU Tetap tidak Independen" (KPU Still Not Independent), *Kompas*, June 9, 2000.

30. "Jaringan Perempuan Minta Kuota KPU" (Women's Network Requests Quota on KPU), *Kompas*, March 3, 2001.

31. "Masyarakat Diundang Lihat 'Fit and Proper Test' KPU" (Community Invited to Witness 'Fit and Proper Test'), *Kompas*, March 7, 2001.

32. For a political analysis of the selection process, see "Dapatkah KPU Pilihan DPR Independen dan Nonpartisan?" (Can the KPU Elected by the House Be Independent and Non-Partisan?), *Kompas*, March 14, 2001. For biodata on the successful nominees, see "Profil Singkat 11 Anggota KPU" (Short Profile of KPU Members), *Kompas*, March 14, 2001. Among the eleven members were ten university lecturers or professors, two persons who were involved in designing the three reform political laws in 1998–1999, a cofounder of Indonesia's first election-monitoring organization, two women (giving "gender balance"), and one resident each from South Sulawesi and West Papua (lending "regional balance").

33. One newly selected electoral commission member worried publically that President Wahid's refusal to appoint the House's selection for chief justice of the Supreme Court might also occur with the House's choices for the commission. "Anggota KPU Harapkan UU Politik Secepatnya Dibahas

dan Direvisi" (KPU Members Hope Political Laws Can Be Discussed and Revised Quickly), *Kompas*, March 12, 2001.

34. Robert A. Pastor, "A Brief History of Electoral Commissions," in *The Self-Restraining State*, ed. Andreas Schedler, Larry Diamond, Marc F. Plattner (Boulder, Colo.: Lynne Rienner, 1999).

35. "On the one hand, the position of the Assembly as the sole repository of popular sovereignty, the highest state institution and the body charged with electing the President and Vice President and receiving their 'accountability speech' makes the system look somewhat parliamentary. On the other hand, the position of the President as both head of state and head of government, with a fixed term and the inability to dissolve the DPR makes the system look more presidential." National Democratic Institute for International Affairs (NDIIA), "Indonesia's Bumpy Road to Constitutional Reform: The 2000 MPR Annual Session," September 19, 2000.

36. NDI, "The 1999 Presidential Election."

37. One of these established the hierarchy of laws and regulations as follows (in descending order or authority): the 1945 constitution, Assembly decrees (*ketetapan*), laws passed by the House (*undang-undang*), government regulations in lieu of laws (*Perpu*), government regulations (*peraturan pemerintah*), presidential decrees (*keputusan presiden*), and regional regulations (*peraturan daerah*). See Decision no. 3/2000 of the Assembly (MPR).

38. An interpretation supported by R. William Liddle, "Indonesia in 2000," *Asian Survey* 41, 1 (2001): 208–220.

39. NDIIA, "Indonesia's Bumpy Road," 11.

40. Andreas Schedler, "What Is Democratic Consolidation?" *Journal of Democracy* 9, 2 (1998): 91–107.

41. Larry Diamond, *Developing Democracy* (Baltimore: Johns Hopkins University Press, 1999), 100.

42. Donald Horowitz, private communication, May 11, 2001.

43. Diamond, *Developing Democracy*, 103.

44. The Islamic-based parties include PKB, PPP, PAN, PBB, PK, PIB, PID, PKU, PNU, SUNI, PDR, PUI, PCD, PSII, PSII-1905, PMB, PII-MASYUMI, PP, PUMI, PAY, and KAMI, whereas the other residual category would include PDI-P, Golkar, PDKB, KRISNA, PKD, PNI-Supeni, PNI-MM, MURBA, PRD, PUDI, PBN, PSPSI, PSP, PPI, PNI-FM, PNBI, PND, PADI, PKP, PCI, MKGR, IPKI, PR, PILAR, PKM, PARI, and PBI.

45. Jack Snyder, *From Voting to Violence* (New York: W. W. Norton, 2000).

46. Frank S. Cohen, "Proportional versus Majoritarian Ethnic Conflict Management in Democracies," *Comparative Political Studies* 30, 5 (1997): 612.

47. "Majoritarian attempts to crosscut political ethnic cleavages into irrelevance only suppress them and preserve them as latent sources of tension. Proportional mechanisms prevent such suppression of ethnic cleavages by proliferating, dispersing, and expanding the opportunities for their ventilation." Ibid., 613.

48. Andrew Reynolds, *Electoral Systems and Democratization in Southern Africa* (Oxford: Oxford University Press, 1999), 104.

49. Diamond, *Developing Democracy*, 104.

50. Ibid., 106.

CHAPTER 9

Indonesian Electoral Reform in Comparative Perspective

As the twentieth century drew to a close, Southeast Asia was sharply divided between three countries which had experienced major political changes and were undergoing democratization and those that remained authoritarian or pseudodemocratic. The transition to electoral democracy was most clearly demarcated in the Philippines and Indonesia with the fall of Marcos (1986) and Suharto (1998), respectively. In the case of Thailand, one can point to several signposts, including the move to an elected prime minister in 1988, the collapse of the military interregnum in 1992, and the 1997 financial crisis, which precipitated the new constitution. This overall political commonality among the three countries creates interest in comparing their experiences with electoral reform as an analytical tool to deeper understanding of the choices in design of electoral institutions and their likely effects on the consolidation of democracy. The arguments of this chapter can be found in schematic form in Tables 9.1 and 9.2.

PROCESSES OF CHANGE

Type of Transition

The earliest transition occurred in the Philippines, where the insurrection that ousted Marcos was a predominately urban, middle-class phenomenon. Although the movement that propelled Aquino to power had populist characteristics, the "People Power Revolu-

Table 9.1
Transition to Electoral Democracy in Indonesia, Thailand, and the Philippines

Dimensions	Indonesia	Thailand	Philippines
a. Type of Transition	Pacts between military and civilian political leaders	Pacts between military and civilian political leaders	Collapse of prior regime Middle-class insurrection
b. Economic Context	International and domestic economic crises	International economic crises	No significant domestic economic crisis
c. Sociocultural Context	Weak democratic tradition	Partial practice of democracy	Democratic tradition
d. Instrument of Transition	Piecemeal constitutional engineering	Partial constitutional engineering	Total constitutional engineering; Restorative
e. Process of Transition	Muddle through and noniterative	Iterative	Iterative

Table 9.2
Choice in Institutional Design and Democratic Consolidation in Indonesia, Thailand, and the Philippines

Dimensions	Indonesia	Thailand	Philippines
a. Institutional Context			
- Structure of National Government	Presidential, Unicameral, and Bicameral	Kingdom, Parliamentary, and Bicameral	Presidential and Bicameral
- Party Systems	Multiparties and old cleavages	Multiparties and fluid party system	Multiparties and fluid party system
- Ideology	Not significant	Not significant; Patronage	Relative nonsignificant (families and clans)
- Election Success	Sociocultural cleavages and personalism	Personalism and patronage	Clans and populism
- Executive Election	Superparliamentary (MPR) based on political game	Parliamentary based on coalition (majority party)	Direct (plurality)
- Individual Right	Some disenfranchisement	Participative	Participative
b. Type of Electoral Reform	Mixed (PR Plus)	Mixed (MMD and SMD)	Mixed (MMD and SMD)
c. Election Administration	Muddle through and deadlock	Relative smooth	Smooth
d. Effects on Democratic Consolidation	Piecemeal	Partial	Significant

193

tion" owed relatively little to the left or the rural poor. During her presidency, little headway was made on narrowing economic inequalities. Her principle accomplishment was the reestablishment (restoration) of the institutions of electoral democracy: "She used the considerable political capital available to her in the early months of her presidency to effectuate the drafting and adoption of a new constitution and initiation of local, congressional, and ultimately presidential elections."[1] As noted in Chapter 1, comparativists have delineated four ideal types of democratic transition—pact (or compromise), imposition, reform, and revolution—which provide a set of concepts for comparing transitions.[2] The Philippines experience seems to have been a variation of the reform mode, with the impetus coming from the middle strata more than from ascendant masses. Although it involved the dramatic collapse of the prior regime in the face of massive popular opposition, mass actors largely failed to gain control over the traditional elites.

Transitions in Indonesia and Thailand were triggered and, to a large extent, powered by the financial crisis that hit both countries in 1997, causing severe economic contraction, from which they have yet to recover. These two countries began their "transitions from above" through pacts between military and civilian leaders, which gradually evolved into reform as more elites and mass actors became involved. Regime change based on gradual installment and compromise are expected to bring less transformation of social and economic inequalities but more attention to the institutional arrangements of the successor regime. Indeed, the negotiated transitions in Indonesia and Thailand were associated with specific and critical attention to the institutional arrangements of democracy. Interim President Habibie wanted to go down in history as the father of Indonesian democracy. Unlike Aquino, who took over the helm of a country with a long (pre-1972) democratic tradition and thus could restore democracy, Habibie's task was more formidable, democracy having been absent for three times longer (over forty years). Moreover, he had only about a year to prepare for a free and fair national election that would establish Indonesia as an electoral democracy.[3] In Thailand, attention to the institutional arrangements of democracy was indisputably reflected in the new constitution, 339 articles long.

Methods and Instrumentalities

All three countries adopted new rules of the political game, but they used different methods and instrumentalities. In Indonesia the legacy of the past weighed heaviest, as reformers were unable to replace the 1945 constitution with one more suitable for a democracy. Not surprising in light of its origin as a temporary emergency document during the independence struggle, this constitution lacked specificity and granted a wide range of powers to the executive branch. It was replaced in 1950, when Indonesia switched to a parliamentary system. President Soekarno returned to the 1945 Constitution by executive fiat in 1957, declaring it the legal foundation for his Guided Democracy. During Suharto's thirty-two-year rule, it was elevated to essentially sacred status and proposals to amend it were tantamount to treason. Considering that about 80 percent of the legislators (MPR) in 1998 were holdovers from the old regime, it is no wonder that the 1945 constitution was largely retained with some new rules in the form of constitutional amendments, MPR decrees, and new (organic) political laws. To date the new legislature, elected in 1999, has continued this piecemeal approach to constitutional reform, although a lively debate has erupted between legislators and legal experts who are calling for a constitutional convention to design a new constitution from scratch.[4] They charge that political considerations of the moment rather than long-range and systematic thinking about how best to build Indonesia's new democratic order are driving the deliberations on constitutional change.

In the Philippines, as mentioned, Aquino focused on drafting and adopting a new constitution. Using the executive powers of the presidential office, she appointed all forty-eight members of the constitutional commission, attempting to make it reasonably representative.[5] The commission's draft was subsequently ratified by 78 percent of the voters in a national referendum in 1987.

A quite different process was used to formulate a new constitution in Thailand. A larger, elected constitutional assembly of ninety-nine persons was given drafting responsibility and they were involved in extensive public consultation over eight months, including hearings in various regions.[6] But instead of being submitted to the entire electorate as in the Philippines, it was ratified by the House. Substantively, the new constitution represented a radical departure from its predecessors as well, including increased guarantees of individual rights, mandates, decentralization, an elected Senate, separation of the elected Parliament and the cabinet (MPs or senators are no longer allowed to simultaneously hold a cabinet post and a seat in Parliament), a new electoral system based on a combination of single-member districts and a party-list system and new requirements for candidates, constitutional and administrative courts, the election commission, and the National Countercorruption Commission.

Iterative Process

In all three countries a series of organic laws specifying details and implementation procedures were needed in addition to the general provisions in the constitutions or constitutional amendments (including Assembly decrees in Indonesia). Hence, the Indonesian House passed three political bills in January 1999, revised the articles pertaining to the election commission already in 2000, and is currently considering additional changes in time for the next election in 2004. In the Philippines, the Omnibus Election Code (OEC), the Election Modernization Act (Republic Act [R.A.] 8437), and the Party-List System Act (R.A. 7941) are among the codes that supplement the constitution in regulating the electoral system. Thailand supplemented its new constitution with organic laws on the election commission (1998), on the election of members of the House of Representatives and members of the Senate (1998), and on political parties (1998). Already some of the new institutions and laws have survived legal challenges.

THE STRUCTURE OF THE NATIONAL GOVERNMENT

From 1998 until approximately 2002 Indonesia had a "presidential system with parliamentary characteristics."[7] The position of the president, who is head of state and head of government with a fixed term (five years) and limited number of terms (two) and who is unable to dissolve the legislature, made the system look presidential. At the same time, the system had several attributes usually found in parliamentary systems. The Consultative Assembly was the sole repository of popular sovereignty, the highest state institution, whose decrees were supreme (not subject to judicial review). It had responsibility for electing and terminating the president and vice president, including assessing the president's annual "accountability" speech. Since Suharto left power in 1998, reforms have focused on separating and specifying more clearly the respective powers of each branch of government and on strengthening the position of the legislative and judicial branches vis-à-vis the executive branch. They have also included adoption of a bill of rights and greater decentralization of power to the regions within the overall framework of unitarian government.

Indonesia's legislature during the same period could be characterized as "unicameral with bicameral characteristics." Of the approximately 700-member Assembly, 500 members (71 percent) formed the sitting legislature or House of Representatives. The larger Assembly was uninvolved in the regular legislative process; its roles were amending the constitution, assessing government performance annually, electing the president and vice president on a quinquennial basis, and establishing overall policy guidelines. Both chambers included a "reserved domain" consisting of thirty-eight appointed seats for the military (to be discontinued after 2004). In 1999, 462 representatives were elected in twenty-seven electoral districts, using basically a closed (party list) proportional representation system.

The Philippines has a more straightforward presidential system on the U.S. model. The president, who is limited to one six-year term, and the vice president are directly and independently elected by plurality (first past the post). The legislative branch is segmented (or parallel) bicameral, with the House composed of 208 representatives who are elected by SMD plurality and 52 seats (i.e., 20 percent) that are selected by PR closed party list (but due to a 2-percent threshold, only fourteen PR seats were filled in 1998 and only sixteen in 2001). House members are limited to a maximum of three consecutive terms of three years each. The Senate consists of twenty-four senators elected at large using the plurality principle. Senators are limited to a maximum of two consecutive terms of six years each: "The limitation on tenure is prescribed by the Constitution to discourage the revival of pre-1972 political dynasties and promote a more equal access to representatives of other parties."[8] The Supreme Court has the power of judicial review, and considerable authority has been devolved to subnational governments within the framework of the unitary state.

Thailand combines characteristics of a traditional kingdom and a modern parliamentary system on the Westminster model. Sovereign power belongs to the Thai people. Hence, the (hereditary) monarch exercises power as head of state through the National Assembly, the Council of Ministers, and the courts in accordance with the constitution. The legislative branch is segmented (or parallel) bicameral, with a 200-member nonpartisan Senate elected by either the SMD or MMD plurality formula. Senators serve a six-year nonrenewable term. The House of Representatives consists of 500 members, of whom 400 are elected by SMD plurality and 100 by closed party lists in provincially based, electoral districts. As is customary in a parliamentary system, cabinet members and MPs have a maximum term (four years), but may have to stand for election sooner if the government falls or decides to call an election. The kingdom is indivisible, and hence unitary by definition. Although decentralization has been given a boost by the new constitution, it is not as extensive as in Indonesia and the Philippines.

PARTY SYSTEMS

Regulations Governing Parties and
Their Effect on the Party System

After interim Indonesian President Habibie lifted some of the restrictions on party formation in mid-1998, parties mushroomed, although parties based on ideologies considered by the government to
be antithetical to the loosely defined national ideology (*Pancasila*)
continued to be prohibited. Out of 141 parties that were declared
and officially registered, only 48 qualified to compete in the election and to receive government subsidy, which required having established a party organization in at least nine provinces and half of
the districts in those provinces. These requirements were intended
not only to screen out fly-by-night parties, but especially to discourage narrowly ethnic or regional parties. Second, parties that competed in the 1999 election must have obtained at least 2 percent of
seats in the House or 3 percent in the regional legislatures in order
to qualify for the next election in 2004. Only 6 parties (out of 48) passed
this threshold. All elected representatives belong to parties, owe their
selection to their ranking on party lists, and serve five-year renewable
terms. They can be, and sometimes were, recalled midterm and replaced
by their parties. These regulations, plus government subsidization, have
promoted multiple inclusive parties with mass-based organizational
structures. As we would expect in a proportional, closed-party-list
electoral system, party discipline seems to be stronger than in the
Philippines and Thailand; in the three years following the 1999 election, little party switching occurred.

The new Philippines constitution calls for "a free and open party
system" to replace the previous two-party system. This phrase, in
tandem with the strong protection accorded civil rights in the constitution, probably results in the least regulation of parties among
the three countries. The election of some representatives to the House
using the party-list system beginning in 1998 is another incentive to
multipartyism. Proliferation of parties accelerated in 1998 when the
constitutional provision for electing 20 percent of the House through
party lists began to be implemented. The provision was intended to
ensure representation for poor and marginalized groups, such as labor, the urban poor, farmers, fisherfolk, and women. Parties that
fielded candidates in the SMD races were theoretically prohibited
from participating in the party-list component of the elections.[9] Although only fourteen seats could be filled in 1998, those seats were
distributed to thirteen parties.[10] In the 2001 election, sixteen seats
were distributed among ten parties.[11] Another likely cause of the

recent increase in the number of legislative parties is through the "presidential connection" or the increase in the number of viable presidential candidates, each one of whom adopts or creates a different party to mobilize support.[12]

In Thailand, similar to Indonesia, parties are regulated by a specific law that requires they uphold the national ideology (nation, king, religion). Previous requirements forcing parties to become mass-based parties, fielding candidates nationwide, have been loosened. There are no restrictions on party switching and parties that nominate candidates for parliament but fail to win seats are no longer automatically disbanded.[13] All these provide incentives for multipartyism. Similar to the Philippines, the lack of public funding results in high demand for wealthy candidates able to run strong campaigns, party switching has been common, and voters do not appear to punish candidates who switch parties. As a result, Thailand's party system is also considered weak and unstructured, perhaps epitomized by the unprecedented margin of victory in the 2001 parliamentary election won by a two-year-old party founded by Thailand's richest person, Thaksin Shinawatra.

These incentives for proliferation of parties were theoretically countered since 1997 by the nonpartisan individual contestation for seats in the Senate, election of 80 percent of the House by SMD plurality, and application of a 5-percent threshold to the 20 percent elected from party lists. But as one scholar correctly predicted, "Overall . . . the new Constitution is likely to have a series of rather contradictory effects on parties and on electoral practices."[14] Indeed, the 2001 election of House members seems to have reflected both incentives for multipartyism and a more simplified two-party system. On the one hand, any rich and clever person aspiring to found a new party should be emboldened by the unprecedented achievement of the Thai Rak Thai Party. This "vehicle newly formed for [Thaksin Shinawatra's] political ambitions" within two years almost captured a majority of seats in the House.[15] Moreover, eight parties are represented in the House, five of which met the party-list threshold of 5 percent.[16] On the other hand, the two largest parties combined won 78 percent of the seats, suggesting that use of SMD gave impetus to a two-party system.[17]

Lack of Ideology and Avoidance of Substantive Policy Stands

In Indonesia each of the five top vote-getting parties (PDI-P, Golkar, PKB, PPP, PAN) campaigned on similar broad and inclusive themes, such as combating corruption, collusion, and nepotism, building a people's economy and improving income inequality, reducing the political role of the military, and bringing human rights violators to justice, as they attempted to build broad coalitions across the major sociocultural divide separating adherents of "civil Islam" and those preferring a secular–nationalist civil order. Parties emphasizing exclusive themes or particular ideologies such as Islam, Christianity, or socialism obtained less than 3 percent of the vote combined.[18]

The three main parties in the Philippines, Lakas, LAMMP, and the Liberal Party, are loose coalitions of provincial and regional political clans and families mainly put together to contest elections. Concerned essentially with vote maximizing, their platforms have a catch-all character. As vehicles for seekers of elective offices, they espouse popular principles to please as many voters as possible. There is little programmatic diversity and political differentiation among the main parties. All three subscribe to the ideas of free enterprise, limited government, and civil rights and liberties. A de facto consensus exists on major economic issues, including the importance of economic growth, the leading role of the private sector, and coming to terms with globalization of the economy.[19]

Thai parties also shun substantive policy stands. There are no clear left- or right-wing parties, nor have labor, green, or royalist parties appeared: "The basis of party formation of Thailand is constituted by the political ambitions of individuals or of factions. . . . Party policy content has been essentially local in character."[20] However, the increase in discussion of national policy issues during the 2001 election campaign, stimulated in part by the competition among parties for the new party-list seats, suggests that change may have begun.

Determinants of Election Success

Essentially three factors explain the electoral success of Indonesian parties in the 1999 election. One was the personal attraction of the party leader, with the prime example being Megawati Soekarnoputri and PDI-P. A second factor was identification with the social basis of the party. For example, devout Muslims of the "traditionalist" school voted disproportionately for PKB (and PPP), while those of the "modernist" school voted heavily for PAN. Financial resources were the third factor; Golkar's second-place finish depended heavily on its superior campaign war chest and ability to play the game of "money politics."

The 1998 Philippine election indicated that name recognition from a film career, wealth, and other personal characteristics were the most important determinant of success for a presidential candidate. Joseph Estrada's victory, as Fidel Ramos's before him, illustrated the old adage that "it is the Filipino president who creates his party and not the party which creates the president." Both established a new party to serve as their electoral vehicle, Lakas and LAMMP, respectively, and each party quickly became the majority party as supporters of defeated candidates switched to the new president's party.[21] Important as well was Estrada's populist message, promising to narrow the substantial gap between rich and poor. His victory may also have reflected a shift in voting patterns: "Historically, candidates for national office tended to be elected in large part on the basis of their ethno-linguistic and regional ties. . . . Estrada targeted the lower classes rather than build an agglomeration of regional support bases. And for the first time in Philippine history, a large part of the lower classes voted along socioeconomic rather than ethno-linguistic or regional lines."[22]

In Thailand, candidates' election success depended mostly on their patrons, factions, and own efforts and achievements, rather than on their party affiliation. Traditionally money was used to buy votes, but signs of change were evident in 2001, when large amounts were spent on media, U.S. style. According to Nelson, "Parliamentary elections are often competitions for supremacy among various *phuaks* [factions or local political groups]. Parliamentarians thus can switch political parties and still get elected."[23] This raises the question of whether the linkages between Thai parties and their supporters are long-lasting, exclusive, and significant in terms of electoral success. "Any linkages which exist are clearly not exclusive. . . . Major business groups are known to make contributions to a variety of leading parties and to develop reciprocal relationships that outlast particular governments or coalitions. . . . This does not mean that Thai parties have no linkages with society, but that the linkages are overlapping, conditional."[24] An important reason for the dearth of mass-based parties is that representative interest groups (e.g., labor unions) are prohibited by law from organizational links with or contributing to political parties. Surveys indicate that the role parties play in a democracy is widely appreciated, but their history of fractiousness and of electoral spending violations has resulted in parties having a bad reputation.

RELATIONSHIPS BETWEEN EXECUTIVE AND THE INSTITUTIONS OF DEMOCRATIC REPRESENTATION

Leader of Largest Party Becomes Head of Government

In both Indonesia and Thailand it is widely accepted that the head of the largest party, based on the number of representatives in the House, should be the head of government. Postelection public-opinion polling in Indonesia in 1999 indicated that most Indonesians expected Megawati Soekarnoputri, the leader of the party that got the most votes (PDI-P), to be elected president by the Assembly. When Abdurrahman Wahid was elected instead by a narrow majority of Assembly representatives, riots broke out in Jakarta and several provincial capitals throughout Indonesia. After more than a year in office and the breakup of the coalition that elected him, his narrow base of support in the PKB, which placed third in the election (winning 12.6 percent of the total vote), is widely considered among Indonesians to have been a major reason for his weak performance. Wahid himself acknowledged, "By rights, she [Megawati] should have become President."[25] Less than two years after he ascended the presidency, Wahid was impeached and Megawati installed.

From 1992 through early 2001 in Thailand, the leaders of parties winning a plurality of seats in parliament ascended to the prime ministership after having built a coalition that controlled a majority of seats. These were Chuan Leekpai and the Democrat Party, Banharn Silpa-archa and the Chart Thai party, Chavalit Yongchaiyudh and the New Aspirations party, and (for a second time) Chuan Leekpai and the Democrat Party. Most recently, Thaksin Shinawatra's Thai Rak Thai Party won an unprecedented 248 seats and a majority of 262 after the postelection merger with Seritham Party, making choice of executive even more automatic.

In the case of the Philippines, the chief executive is chosen through direct election by a simple plurality of votes and serves a single six-year term. Hence, Fidel Ramos was elected to the presidency in 1992 with only 24 percent of the total vote and Joseph Estrada with 38 percent in 1998. After ascending to office, each president proceeded to create a majority party, as mentioned earlier.

Elected versus Appointed Representatives and Rules on Concurrent Positions

Indonesia is unique (until 2004) among the three countries in having reserved thirty-eight appointed seats for the military (and police) in the House, and another sixty-five appointed seats for (nonmilitary) group representatives in the Assembly. Only the thirty-eight military appointees are allowed to hold concurrent positions in the executive branch of the state; all other representatives are prohibited from serving concurrently as another type of civil servant.

All members of both legislative chambers in the Philippines and Thailand are elected and all are prohibited from holding concurrently any other office or employment in government. Under the 1997 constitution, Thailand switched to a fully elected Senate with six-year terms. Senators are prohibited from canvassing for votes and from belonging to a political party. New also is the separation of the Parliament and the cabinet. If a senator or MP accepts a cabinet post, he or she must resign from Parliament.

INDIVIDUAL RIGHTS

Indonesia added a new constitutional amendment on human rights in 2000. Twenty-five rights are recognized in it, including the right of every person to citizenship status, to associate, to assemble, and to express opinions. The state and the government are charged with responsibility for the "protection, advancement, upholding and fulfillment of human rights" (Article 28 I [4]). One clause, taken from Article 11(2) of the Universal Declaration on Human Rights, prohibits prosecutions under retrospective legislation. This has created a dilemma for human rights activists, because it juxtaposes international human rights standards and the calls for justice for past human rights violations.[26] Indonesian citizens who are at least seventeen years of age or who are (or have ever been) married have the right to vote. Voting in the 1999 election was voluntary and universal (no groups were systematically disenfranchised except in a few areas of Aceh, where the election was canceled out of security considerations, resulting in the disenfranchisement of at most 100,000 eligible voters), and voter turnout was around 93 percent.[27] There are no provisions for popular initiatives and referenda.

The 1987 Philippine constitution recognizes an extensive list of individual human rights. It guarantees universal adult suffrage, which begins at age eighteen, a year later than in Indonesia. However, "overseas Filipinos, of whom there are an estimated four million, remain disenfranchised due to congressional failure to pass the absentee voter legislation required by the Constitution. The Philippine Congress similarly has failed to pass implementing legislation for popular initiative and referendum."[28] Voting is voluntary. In 1992 voter turnout was 75 percent, and apparently increased to 81 percent in 1998.[29]

Similarly, Thailand's 1997 constitution provides increased guarantees for individual rights, including freedom of speech and association and a provision mandating the establishment of a human-rights commission. As in the Philippines, universal adult suffrage begins at age eighteen. During the prior decade, voter turnout ran about 60 percent.[30] Under the new constitution voting is compulsory and voter turnout increased to 72 percent in the 2000 senatorial elections and to 70 percent in the 2001 parliamentary elections. Other possible reasons for improved voter turnout included excitement over the new constitution, the novelty of SMD, and the first opportunity to elect a senator. Although voting is compulsory, voters had the option of casting a vote for "none of the above." In the 2000 and the 2001 elections, 3.5 and 3.4 percent of the voters, respectively, exercised this option. For the first time citizens were given the right to initiate a recall procedure against an elected MP.[31]

TYPE OF ELECTORAL SYSTEM

Mixed Systems in All Three Countries

Indonesia adopted a unique and complex "PR plus" electoral system that combined proportional representation by province with some elements of a plurality system. That is, seats were allocated to parties in proportion to the parties' overall vote in each province, but rather than assigning individual seats based on the ranking of candidates on party lists, they were assigned with reference to party results at the district level.

In the Philippines senators were elected in a single nationwide constituency, and each voter has twelve nontransferable votes to cast.[32] The top twelve vote getters are winning candidates. In contrast, the members of the Thai Senate were elected by plurality from seventy-six electoral districts based on provinces using both MMD and SMD, depending on the population of the province. The important point here is that Philippine senators, much fewer in number and with a national constituency, have a more distant relationship to the electorate than Thai senators, who represent (and are accountable to) much smaller constituencies. Minority groups are thus more likely to be represented in the Thai Senate. As mentioned earlier, the lower houses of both the Philippines and Thailand are segmented, with 80 percent of the representatives chosen by plurality in SMDs and 20 percent by proportionality from party lists. Beyond this similarity, there were several differences. First, the Philippine House is about half the size of the Thai House. The population–representative ratios are about 150,000 to 1 in Thailand and about 300,000 to 1 in the Philippines (and about four times higher, 600,000 to 1, in Indonesia).

Second, the regulations governing party-list seats were quite different.[33] In the Philippines a party must receive at least 2 percent of the votes cast in the party-list component in order to win a seat, and "traditional parties are barred from contesting these seats and participating parties are limited to a maximum of three seats."[34] No such prohibition exists in Thailand, but the threshold is higher, at 5 percent. Thus, in the party-list segment minorities are more likely to be represented in the Philippines than they are in Thailand, somewhat balancing the antiminority bias of the Philippine Senate, noted earlier. These expectations were borne out in the election results. Parties or sectors represented in the thirteen party-list seats chosen in the Philippines included urban poor, women, workers, peasants, veterans, and one professional group, the Association of Philippine Electrical Cooperatives.[35] In Thailand the 100 party-list seats were divided among the five largest parties in nearly identical proportion to their share of SMD seats.[36]

Intended and Unintended Effects of the Electoral Systems

One important question concerns the degree of bias in favor of larger parties. "All electoral systems give an advantage to stronger parties but that bias is much less pronounced in PR systems."[37] Whether degree of bias is a problem is a normative issue and depends upon one's preference between two ideal types of democratic competition, proportionalism and majoritarianism. "Proportional institutions . . . decrease the stakes of competition, decrease the intensity of competition, and increase direct access to political institutions. . . . Majoritarian institutions . . . increase the stakes of competition, increase the intensity of competitiveness, and decrease direct access to political institutions."[38]

Table 9.3 shows the discrepancy between votes and seats resulting from the 1999 Indonesian election and the 2001 Thailand election for the House of Representatives. The columns labeled "deviation" are the (simple) difference in percentage points between proportion of votes and the proportion of seats received by the main parties. The closer those proportions are to one another, the closer the deviation will be to zero. Thus, looking down the deviation column for Indonesia, notice that the party getting the most votes (PDI-P) had a very small deviation from proportionality of –0.6, but if we look down the deviation column for Thailand, notice that the party getting the most votes (TRT) had a very large deviation of +12.9.

These data support several inferences. As would be expected with an SMDP system, Thailand's electoral system is more biased in favor of stronger parties than Indonesia's system, which is based on proportional representation. In other words, the majoritarian tendencies in Thailand's system are much stronger. Indeed, without the SMD design included in the new constitution, the unprecedented majority position achieved by the Thai Rak Thai Party in the House in the 2001 election would have been virtually impossible. The segmented design (i.e., 100 party-list seats) moderates the majoritarian bias, but only slightly.[39] A similar analysis of the 1998 Philippine election could not be carried out due to unavailability of data.

Table 9.3
Overall Deviation from Proportionality, Indonesia, and Thailand

	INDONESIA				THAILAND			
Party	% Votes	% Seats	Deviation		Party	% Votes	% Seats	Deviation
PDI-P	33.7	33.1	-0.6		TRT	37.1	50.0	+12.9
Golkar	22.4	26.0	+3.6		Dem	25.9	24.3	-1.6
PKB	12.6	11.0	-1.6		NAP	9.4	7.0	-2.4
PPP	10.7	12.6	+1.9		CPP	8.9	5.5	-3.4
PAN	7.1	7.4	+0.3		CTP	8.6	8.8	+0.2
PBB	1.9	2.8	+0.9		Serith.	4.0	3.5	-0.5
					Rassad.	3.3	0.5	-2.8
Average[a]			1.5					3.4

Sources: Indonesia, General Election Commission, 1999 election. Thailand, Michael H. Nelson, mimeograph, 2001 Election of House of Representatives, constituency votes only.

[a]Simple, unweighted average; sign/direction disregarded, since deviation can be either plus or minus.

Another important issue is the effects of an electoral system on the party system. A convenient metric on which the three systems can be compared is the "index of effective number of parties."[40] This index was 4.7 for Indonesia, 3.7 for the Philippines, and 4.3 for Thailand.[41] Although the electoral system in each country produced a pattern of multipartyism, it was highest in Indonesia, which is not surprising given its use of proportional representation. This adds more evidence to the well-established positive relationship between PR and multipartyism found in the literature on comparative electoral systems. More surprising are the relatively high values of the indices for the Philippines and Thailand, where use of SMDP would be expected on theoretical grounds to produce values closer to 2, reflecting a pattern of two-party competition.

Indonesia's negotiated transition raises the question of how much it broke with the previous regime. One measure is the extent of continuity (incumbency) in the members of the House. A recent study found that 252 members (50 percent) had served there during the previous regime.[42] There was institutional inheritance as well in the form of the PR closed-party-list system. During Suharto's New Order period, policy intervened to prevent PR from promoting multipartyism, since the number of parties was limited by law. With the lifting of that restriction and forty-eight parties qualifying to contest the 1999 election, a concern understandably arose about excessive proliferation of parties and fragmentation of power in the House. As it turned out, although twenty-one parties won seats, the top five vote getters shared 90 percent of the seats in the House, and all of them were inclusive parties.

Indonesian reformers' attempts to combine PR with an element of a plurality system was intended not to weaken the incentive toward multipartyism, but rather to strengthen vertical accountability (i.e., ties between particular constituencies and House members). It met with mixed success, as party leaders wanted to maintain as much control as possible over which candidates were elected. Ninety-seven (21 percent) of the elected House members ended up representing districts other than those to which they were originally assigned. Selection of the sixty-five group representatives by methods other than direct election was difficult and highly controversial as well.

A major objective of the Philippine electoral reform since 1987 has been to make politics more inclusionary, accountable, and competitive. Progress has been modest, at best:

The single-member districts for the House of Representatives advantage local socioeconomic elites, who are better financed and better able to mobilize local clientelist networks, and prevent the mobilization of opposition. By putting a premium on the fund-raising capabilities of would-be candidates, the at-large (i.e. nationwide) elections for the Philippine Senate similarly limit entry to members of wealthy families or their agents and to established film and media personalities.[43]

However, a recent study found that the three-term limit and the first election of party-list representatives in 1998 have "dented the stranglehold of political families" in the current House: "The 220 members of the current House represent a wider range of families, groups, social classes and political leanings than the previous two-post Marcos legislatures."[44] The rules governing the election of party-list representatives, as noted earlier, give a boost in the direction of inclusiveness and proportionality as well as an incentive for the excessive proliferation of small parties; the fourteen seats elected in the first round were divided among thirteen parties. Perhaps the biggest challenge to realizing the promise of the party-list system is low elector participation. In 2001, polls indicated that only 15 percent of the electorate knew about the election for party-list representatives and only 30 percent voted for party-list candidates.[45] Thailand presented a marked contrast, where the same parties were allowed to compete for both constituency and party-list seats but required to pass a higher threshold, resulting in only five parties qualifying for party-list seats.

Several policies can be identified in the Philippine case that have had the (perhaps unintended) effect of weakening political parties. These include the elimination of party representatives in the board of election canvassers, the limited public funding of parties and candidates, and the prohibition on political advertising, which increase party dependence on incumbents, media personalities, and wealthy individuals.[46] The lack of regulation of party switching has also contributed to the generally unstructured and weak party system.

Use of the SMDP (first past the post) and nontransferable vote rules have had some unexpected effects. Electing the president and vice president by plurality in the context of an increasing number of viable candidates has resulted in winning with small margins. Fidel Ramos in 1992 and Joseph Estrada in 1998 were elected by small minorities, with 24 and 38 percent of the vote, respectively, which gave them less legitimacy than desired in a presidential system.[47] Second, many seats in local government and congressional districts have gone uncontested. Apparently this phenomenon was due to pragmatic agreements among political parties and groups to temporarily join forces in order to field a single candidate: "Such a practice raised concern in various sectors for its likely negative effect on the consolidation of democracy, as genuine political choice was not available to the voters where this practice occurred."[48]

One of the intentions of Thailand's constitution writers was to promote a stronger Senate. However, their ideal of a powerful and nonpartisan Senate based on territorial representation apparently has not materialized. In the 2000 election campaign a number of candidates affiliated themselves with various political parties, many others received patronage support from political parties in the constituencies they were contesting, and still others were relatives of already sitting national and local politicians.[49]

Several changes in Thailand's rules were intended to reduce vote buying and combat other corrupt election practices. Forcing all eligible voters to cast their votes (mandatory voting) and increasing the number of constituencies while reducing the number of House positions to one per constituency (SMD) were intended to discourage money politics (mandatory voting was expected to lower the price of a vote and SMD to raise the cost of buying enough votes to win). Counting all ballots cast in the district at one location made it more difficult for candidates to verify that their canvassers had delivered the votes. Requiring elected MPs who took cabinet positions to resign from the House was designed to discourage MPs from buying their way into office in the House and then attempting to recoup their investment through corrupt practices while serving in a ministerial position. It was also hoped that electing some MPs from party lists would be less vulnerable to money politics than voting for specific individuals. Anecdotal evidence from the 2001 election suggests that these measures were a partial success; although money politics did not disappear and large amounts were spent, it was widely believed to have been less effective because election outcomes were often more unpredictable.[50]

Although the design of the electoral system has enormous influence on a democratic political system, limitations are apparent in all three countries. Just two years after its freest and fairest election in forty-four years and the first peaceful transfer of executive power in Indonesia's fifty years of independence, the Wahid government floundered and the state grew steadily weaker, unable to manage the multidimensional crises facing the country. In both the Philippines and Thailand some electoral institutions appear to have generated incentives that weaken parties and encourage politicians to enrich themselves or to concentrate on delivering pork-barrel programs to narrow groups of constituents and political benefactors. Writing about the Philippines, Montinola argues,

Despite the presence of the new party-list generation of representatives in Congress, political dynamics in the body have not changed. Members of Congress have already made clear that they will delay passage of legislation unless they receive their traditional perquisites of office, including the "pork barrel funds" that legislators spend at their discretion, much of which in the past has ended up simply lining the pockets rather than benefiting poor constituents.[51]

Suchitra Punyaratabandhu is equally pessimistic about the party list as a deterrent to corruption in Thailand. The party list, rather than deterring money politics, may have only changed its locus: "Lists of the larger political parties obviously provide greater attraction and it becomes all-important for candidates to be ranked high on the lists, preferably among the top ten. . . . One may anticipate contributions to party coffers in exchange for a desirable place on the party's list."[52]

ELECTION ADMINISTRATION

Independent Election Commissions

All three countries chose to establish special commissions and vest them with the responsibility for administration of elections as the centerpiece of their efforts to keep elections insulated from the incumbent government and the political process. However, commissions in all three have been lightening rods for controversy, nonetheless. Compliance or noncompliance with election laws and regulations has been largely dependent on these commissions.

Indonesia's 1999 election law called for a commission consisting of five representatives from the government and one from each of the parties qualifying to contest the election, having equal voice and serving five-year terms. The commission was constituted when forty-eight parties qualified, but with fifty-three members it did not function well. When the results of the election plunged forty-two of the parties into lame-duck status because they failed to pass the threshold for the next election, the commission broke down into factions and a deadlock ensued over certification of the election results, necessitating presidential intervention. There were other problems of design as well. The commission's implementing unit (secretariat) remained part of the government, so lines of authority and responsibility were blurred. Neither the commission nor a separate network of monitoring and supervisory committees had adjudicatory authority, so prosecuting Election Law violators was cumbersome and virtually never occurred. Several party members on the commission were indicted for corruption. Hence, commission reform was high on the agenda of the new Wahid government. Within the first year the House revised the law, dismissing the initial commission members and mandating a new nonpartisan and independent body consisting of eleven experts appointed by the president with the consent of the House.

The Philippines Commission on Elections (COMELEC) is a constitutional body. Its seven members are (political) appointees of the incumbent president with the consent of the House, but have security of tenure (terms concurrent with the president). Most of the commissioners are lawyers by training, with some having been circuit judges in local courts. According to Velasco, "There were problems at both the 1987 and 1992 elections but these were overlooked because of the authority of the COMELEC leadership. Fraud at the 1995 elections and repeated administrative lapses subsequently have eroded that authority, and COMELEC has been criticized as inefficient and subservient to the power wielders."[53]

Similarly in Thailand, the election commission (ECT) is constitutionally based. Its five members are appointed by the king on the advice of the Senate and serve single seven-year terms. Commissioners may not have been members of political parties for the five years preceding their appointment and may not be permanent civil servants or employees of state agencies or local government units. In addition to wide-ranging administrative authority, the commission has adjudicatory authority, making it more powerful than the commissions in Indonesia and the Philippines. In the 2000 senatorial election the commission's ability to suspend electoral results in eight provinces gave unprecedented credibility to the power of electoral reform. That power allowed the commission to send some provinces back to the polls to elect senators four more times. In preparation for the 2001 House elections, an election law amendment was passed that granted the ECT the power to "red card" or disqualify candidates involved in vote buying or other forms of fraud at any stage of the election. However, disqualification requires a consensus of all five commissioners and is subject to scrutiny by the Council of State, the government's legal advisory body. In the 2001 election for the House, the commission disqualified the initial results in sixty-two districts (16 percent) and ordered repeat elections in those areas. Following the election, a commissioner alleged that 100 members of the victorious Thai Rak Thai Party were involved in poll fraud, yet no red cards were issued, suggesting internal dissension in the ECT.[54]

Restrictions on Campaigning

Indonesia placed more restrictions on campaigning than either the Philippines or Thailand. First, the campaign period was shorter (seventeen days compared to forty-five days in the Philippines and

Thailand).[55] Second, the campaign was divided into rounds, with each party assigned particular days and all parties taking turns on a rotating basis. These restrictions, initiated under the previous regime, were justified by the authorities as useful for conflict management, but the effect was curtailment of civil rights of expression and assembly nonetheless.

All three countries placed restrictions on campaign finance and spending in their efforts to combat "money politics." In this regard, Thailand's election authorities have been the most activist, which was reflected in the high number of disqualifications and repeat elections mentioned earlier.

Voting and Counting

In Indonesian elections voters received three identical ballots, one for the legislature at each of three levels. Party names and symbols were listed on the ballot and voters indicated their preference by punching a hole in the party symbol of their choice. Ballots were manually counted at each of over 300,000 polling stations.

Philippine and Thailand elections had more similarities in voting and counting than either did with the Indonesian methods. In the elections for the House, voters indicated two preferences, one for district (constituency) candidate and one for party (from whose list individual representatives were selected). Both countries moved the manual counting of ballots to a single location within each electoral district and no longer at each polling station, an arrangement designed to reduce vote buying.[56]

Comparing the three countries, the Philippine electoral system placed the heaviest demands on voters. Due to the MMD system used in electing senators and the holding of national and local elections simultaneously, a voter was expected to write the names of twenty or more candidates on the ballot.

CONCLUSION

Larry Diamond has observed that the choice of electoral system involves trade-offs between competing values, so one size does not fit all. Rather, "the choice of electoral system should depend on the particular historical patterns of cleavage and conflict in each country and on which threats to democracy are judged to be most severe: the possible exclusion, alienation, apathy, and illegitimacy of majoritarian outcomes or the potential fragmentation, low governability, and even paralysis of proportional ones."[57]

One of the normative trade-offs he mentions is between efficiency and governability on the one hand and representativeness on the other. If the three countries are compared in terms of this continuum, taking into consideration the cumulative effects of the electoral systems at the national level, the Philippines and Thailand are located toward efficiency and governability, whereas the emphasis in the Indonesian system is clearly on representativeness. The contrast is perhaps most clearly seen in the outcomes of the recent elections. In Thailand, where contests for the constituency seats are decided by the plurality rule, the Thai Rak Thai Party won 50 percent of the seats with only 37 percent of the votes, illustrating efficiency (more seats than votes) and governability (control of a majority of seats taking into account party-list seats and merger with the Seritham party). Estrada became president of the Philippines with only 38 percent of the vote in a crowded field, perhaps illustrating efficiency (no run-off election), but definitely leaving a majority (62 percent) of the electorate feeling unrepresented in the presidency. Another exclusionary aspect was electing senators at-large, which advantaged members of wealthy families and established film and media personalities. In marked contrast to both the Philippines and Thailand, Indonesia's election of 92 percent of the House by proportional representation with twenty-one parties gaining seats—over twice as many as in the other two countries—indicates the high value placed on achieving representativeness through the electoral system. This difference is mirrored also in the index of "effective number of parties" mentioned earlier, on which Indonesia scored 4.7, compared to 4.3 for Thailand and 3.7 for the Philippines.

A second trade-off is between party coherence and voter choice. Indonesia's electoral system clearly emphasized the former. Voters chose among parties that qualified to compete in the election. The attempt to let voters help select which candidates represent parties (i.e., "PR plus") was compromised by party leaders who were unwilling to give up a portion of their power. The clout of party leaders was further revealed by their selection of the president from the party that finished in third place with only 13 percent of the popular vote (11 percent of the seats).

Last is the trade-off between ballot simplicity (accessability) and appropriateness of the ballot in theoretical terms. Indonesia can be placed on the simplicity end of this continuum, the Philippines at the opposite end, and Thailand somewhere in between. Because the Philippines has many more elected positions, much more is expected of a Filipino voter, not to mention the burdensome procedure of writing the names of twenty or more candidates on the ballot.[58]

It is fair to conclude that the Philippines electoral system is the most institutionalized by virtue of number of elections (1987, 1992, 1995, and 1998) judged free and fair by international standards and the number of peaceful and constitutional transitions in power (e.g., Aquino–Ramos–Estrada–Arroyo). Increasingly, former insurgents, separatists, and rebels have abandoned armed struggle and are contesting in the electoral area. However, it does not necessarily follow that democracy is most consolidated there as well:

Philippine democracy continues to be marked by electoral fraud, violence, and the domination of traditional elites, and characterized by weak parties and factionalism based primarily on personalities and regional and linguistic identities rather than on ideology. Democratic consolidation is stymied further by continuing human rights abuses committed by corrupt police, a politicized military, and the various insurgent movements. Continuing debates over the fundamental constitutional arrangement also call Philippine democratic consolidation into question.[59]

What implications can be drawn from the foregoing comparative analysis for consolidation of democracy in Indonesia? One is the importance of distinguishing between a mixed structure of national government and a mixed electoral system. The structure of Indonesia's national government has been described as "presidential with parliamentary characteristics" and "unicameral with bicameral characteristics." This mixed character was a source of problems and even paralysis during the Wahid administration. In light of Indonesia's negotiated transition, perhaps the political elite's piecemeal approach to constitutional reform can be understood, but it perpetuated the ambiguities and contradictions as much as clarified them. Moreover, there is nothing inherently wrong with mixed systems, as France's semipresidential system demonstrates. Rather, the problem in Indonesia is that the mixed system established by the 1945 constitution, together with the First and Second Amendments, resulted in "a high probability of divided government, temporal inflexibility, a less inclusive executive, greater executive instability, and less democracy."[60] Consequently, not until the Third and Fourth Amendments (2002) did the structure of national government inspire optimism about the prospects for democratic consolidation. Both the Philippines and Thailand (unexpectedly, given its negotiated transition) took a more comprehensive and systematic approach to constitutional reform that focused on designing and then socializing a new constitution. The admirable result is systems that are more consistently presidential (the Philippines) or parliamentary (Thailand).

The mixed character of the electoral systems is another matter entirely. These days systems that combine elements of proportional representation and SMD and MMD plurality have a certain cachet around the world. As we have seen, both the Philippines and Thailand have attempted to moderate the strong majoritarian tendencies of their electoral systems by electing 20 percent of the members in the lower chamber through proportional representation. Since these party-list provisions have just begun to be implemented, any attempt at assessing them would be premature. The implication for Indonesia is that setting aside an allotment of seats that are filled using SMD would likely be a more successful way of introducing more direct accountability between representatives and voters into its (predominantly) proportional system than the current "PR-plus" system.

At the same time, the experiences of the Philippines and Thailand suggest caution, and that electoral reform has limitations as a lever on persistent, deep-rooted obstacles to democratic consolidation. In the normative trade-offs mentioned here, some Indonesian reformers would like to shift the balance in their political system toward greater efficiency and governability, more direct vertical accountability of representatives to the electorate, and more voter choice. They propose to accomplish such rebalancing, in part, through switching from proportional to more majoritarian institutions such as SMDP in electing representatives. But the experiences of the Philippines and Thailand under their new constitutions and election rules suggest that majoritarian institutions may have less effect that expected. Recall the Philippine experience with dealmaking among parties in advance of the election, resulting in many uncontested seats and voters being denied genuine choice. Thailand found out that building a clean and nonpartisan Senate by making senators responsive and accountable to particular constituencies was insufficient; it had to be accompanied by rigorous law enforcement (i.e., raising the costs of election fraud). Nor did the switch to SMDs for electing most House members noticeably decrease the importance of money in the campaign, although the form and type of spending may have changed.

A related issue is that the needs of transitional versus consolidated democracies may be quite different. Insofar as Indonesia is more accurately classified as undergoing transition, its electoral institutions should maximize inclusiveness; they need to be perceived as clearly fair to all parties and as presenting minimal areas for potential preelection conflicts (such as drawing electoral-district boundaries). These goals would seem to be best achieved by regional or national PR lists. Less deeply divided transitional democracies and/

or more consolidated democracies, on the other hand, may be more able to withstand the pressures of majoritarian institutions that they adopt in order to increase efficiency, governability, and voter choice.[61]

Finally, the three-nation comparison raises some interesting questions about political parties and the consolidation of democracy. Why was party switching endemic in the Philippines and Thailand, but not in Indonesia? This analysis suggested party switching was both a symptom and a cause of weak parties, and that the party system was stronger in Indonesia for two reasons: (1) the deeper rootedness of the major Indonesian parties in the sociocultural cleavages of their society and (2) the use of the proportional representation electoral rule creates party coherence. If, as Blondel and Velasco argue, strong parties may not be necessary to establish democratic regimes but are necessary for the long-term consolidation of these regimes, the relatively stronger party system in Indonesia bodes well for the consolidation of democracy there.[62]

NOTES

1. Jeffrey M. Riedinger, "Caciques and Coups: The Challenges of Democratic Consolidation in the Philippines," in *Democracy and Its Limits*, ed. Howard Handelman and Mark Tessler (South Bend, Ind.: Notre Dame University Press, 1999), 181.

2. Guillermo O'Donnell and Philippe Schmitter, *Transitions from Authoritarian Rule: Tentative Conclusions about Uncertain Democracies* (Baltimore: Johns Hopkins University Press, 1986), 37–47.

3. For an apologetic study of Habibie's presidency, see Bilveer Singh, *Habibie and the Democratisation of Indonesia* (Singapore: Crescent Design Associates, 2000).

4. See "PAH I BP MPR Tolak Adanya Konstitusi Baru" (Assembly Committee Rejects Idea of New Constitution), *Kompas*, April 11, 2001: "Proses dan Hasil Perubahan Konstitusi Masih Berantakan" (Process and Outcome of Constitutional Change Still in Disarray), *Kompas*, April 16, 2001; "UUD 1945 dan Perubahannya Perlu Ditata Kembali" (1945 Constitution and Changes Need Reorganization), *Kompas*, April 18, 2001; "Waktunya Membuat Konstitusi Baru" (It Is Time to Make a New Constitution), *Kompas*, April 19, 2001.

5. Riedinger, "Caciques and Coups," 182.

6. Suchitra Punyaratabandhu, "Thailand in 1997: Financial Crisis and Constitutional Reform," *Asian Survey* 38, 2 (1998): 165.

7. This phrase is taken from National Democratic Institute for International Affairs (NDIIA), "Indonesia's Bumpy Road to Constitutional Reform: The 2000 MPR Annual Session," September 19, 2000.

8. Renato. S. Velasco, "The Philippines," in *Democracy, Governance, and Economic Performance*, ed. Ian Marsh, Jean Blondel, and Takashi Inoguchi (Tokyo: United Nations University Press, 1999), 172.

9. In 2001 a number of mainstream political parties competed for party-list seats, including one of the three main parties, Lakas-NUCD, the party of President Joseph Estrada. Incumbent party-list representatives charged that COMELEC failed to properly implement the rules of the party-list system. Four of the seven COMELEC commissioners were appointed by Estrada. Apparently 162 organizations, parties, and coalitions were allowed to participate in the polls. See <http://www.philstar.com/philstar/archive.asp?archive=true&category_id=4&content_id=42992>.

10. Gabriella R. Montinola, "The Philippines in 1998: Opportunity amid Crisis," *Asian Survey* 39, 1 (1999): 67. She explains that the other thirty-eight seats remained vacant for three reasons: (1) a 2-percent threshold of all votes cast in the party-list component, (2) too little voter education on this component of the election resulting in wasted, unrecorded, or misrecorded votes, and (3) incomplete specification in the law, leaving it up to the discretion of COMELEC, the implementing agency, which had not yet decided by the time of Montinola's writing how to allocate the vacant seats.

11. See <http://www.inq7.net/opi/2001/jun/09/opi_bocunanan-1.htm>.

12. Yuko Kasuya, "Presidential Connection: Parties and Party Systems in the Philippines," paper presented at the meeting of the Association of Asian Studies, Chicago, March 2001.

13. Dan King, "Thailand," in Marsh, Blondel, and Inoguchi, *Democracy, Governance, and Economic Performance*, 218.

14. Ibid.

15. Seth Mydans, "Corruption Case against Thailand's Leader Tests Rule of Law," *New York Times*, April 10, 2001, p. A7.

16. These are the figures after the merger of the Seritham party with the Thai Rak Thai, with the former contributing fourteen SMD seats but no party-list seats.

17. Election results are taken from Michael H. Nelson, "Thailand," unpublished manuscript.

18. The eleven Islamic parties were KAMI, PUI, PKU, MASYUMI BARU, PSII, PSII-1905, PPIIM, PBB, PNU PID, and PUMI. The three Christian parties were PDKB, Krisna, and PKD. The four socialist parties were PBN, PRD, Murba, and PNI-MM.

19. Velasco, "The Philippines," 176.

20. King, "Thailand," 211.

21. Velasco, "The Philippines," 178–180.

22. Montinola, "The Philippines in 1998," 67.

23. Nelson, "Thailand."

24. King, "Thailand," 214.

25. Seth Mydans, "Parliament in Indonesia Votes Censure of President," *New York Times*, May 1, 2001, p. A8.

26. NDIIA, "Indonesia's Bumpy Road to Constitutional Reform."

27. *Jakarta Post*, July 16, 1999.

28. Riedinger, "Caciques and Coups," 183.

29. For 1992, see "Report of the Commission on Elections to the President and Congress of the Republic of the Philippines on the Conduct of the Synchronized National and Local Elections," Government of the Philip-

pines, May 11, 1992, Vol. 1, p. 2. For 1998, see <http://(www.codewan.com. ph/peoplespower/statistics>.

30. King, "Thailand," 210.

31. These statistics are taken from Nelson, "Thailand."

32. Twenty-four senators serve staggered terms of six years and senatorial elections are held every three years. Thus, in any single election twelve senators are elected.

33. Implementation of the constitutional provision for party-list seats began in the Philippines in the 1998 election and in Thailand in 2001.

34. Riedinger, "Caciques and Coups," 188.

35. See <http://www.codewan.com.ph/peoplespower/statistics/ partylist2.htm>.

36. Nelson, "Thailand."

37. Andre Blais and Louis Massicotte, "Electoral Systems," in *Comparing Democracies*, ed. Lawrence LeDuc, Richard G. Niemi, and Pippa Norris (Thousand Oaks, Calif.: Sage, 1996), 69–70.

38. Frank S. Cohen, "Proportional versus Majoritarian Ethnic Conflict Management in Democracies," *Comparative Political Studies* 30, 5 (1997): 612.

39. If only data on party-list votes and seats enters the calculation, the deviations are as follows: TRT +7.3, Democrat +4.6, NAP +1.0, CPP +0.8, and CTP +0.7. Thus, the party-list segment advantaged these five parties, which obtained the most votes and passed the 5-percent threshold, whereas the constituency segment advantaged the strongest party (TRT), with the CTP being a slight exception (+0.2).

40. Marku Laakso and Rein Taagepera, "Effective Number of Parties: A Measure with Application to West Europe," *Comparative Political Studies* 12 (1979): 3–27.

41. For the Philippines, see Yuko Kasuya, "Presidential Connection: Parties and Party Systems in the Philippines," paper presented at the meeting of the Association of Asian Studies, Chicago, March 2001. Thailand data are based on vote share in SMDs at the aggregate (national) level. The index drops to 4.0 using vote shares for party lists. See Nelson, "Thailand."

42. "50 Persen Anggota DPR Mantan Politisi Orde Baru," *Kompas*, April 10, 2001.

43. Riedinger, "Caciques and Coups," 184.

44. Philippine Center for Investigative Journalism, "Families Remain Strong in Congress, but Their influence Is Waning," March 29–30, 2001. See <http://www.pcij.org/stories/2001/ties.html>.

45. See <http://www.inq7.net/opi/2001/jun/09/opi_bocunanan-1.htm>.

46. Velasco, "The Philippines," 172–173.

47. Ibid., 174.

48. Carolina G. Hernandez, "The Philippines in 1995: The Growth amid Challenges," *Asian Survey* 36, 2 (1996): 143.

49. Bidhya Bowornwathana, "Thailand in 1999," *Asian Survey* 40, 1 (2000): 94–95. This assessment is supported by the election commission's unwillingness to certify the election results in seventy-eight districts and requirement of repeat elections in those places.

50. Daniel Unger, personal communication, June 2001.

51. Montinola, "The Philippines in 1998," 69–70.

52. Suchitra Punyaratabandhu, "Thailand in 1997," 165–166.

53. Velasco, "The Philippines," 173.

54. Shawn W. Crispin and Rodney Tasker, "Thailand Incorporated," *Far Eastern Economic Review*, January 18, 2001.

55. In years that include a campaign for president in the Philippines, the period is sixty days.

56. In Thailand, "counting the ballots at each polling station (there were over 62,000 polling stations used in the last election, or approximately one polling station for every 250 votes cast) allowed candidates to check whether their network of canvassers down to the sub-village level had been effective. By removing the opportunity to do such checking, the constitution drafters hoped to make vote buying less attractive; it will be more difficult to check not only that votes bought were actually cast, but also which canvassers were effective and which might have simply kept the money for themselves." King, "Thailand," 217.

57. Larry Diamond, *Developing Democracy* (Baltimore: Johns Hopkins University Press, 1999), 100.

58. In the 1995 midyear elections some 60,311 candidates contested approximately 17,342 seats, including 12 for the Senate, 204 for the House, 76 each for governors and vice governors, 672 for the provincial boards, 1,605 for mayors, and 13,092 for municipal and city councillors. Hernandez, "The Philippines in 1995," 142.

59. Riedinger, "Caciques and Coups," 176.

60. Blair A. King, "The Retention of a Paper Constitution and the Prospects for Democratic Consolidation in Indonesia," May 2001.

61. Ben Reilly and Andrew Reynolds, "Electoral Systems for Divided Societies," in *Democracy and Deep-Rooted Conflict: Options for Negotiators*, ed. Peter Harris and Ben Reilly (Stockholm: IDEA, 1998).

62. Jean Blondel, "The Role of Parties and Party Systems in the Democratization Process," in Marsh, Blondel, and Inoguchi, *Democracy, Governance, and Economic Performance*; Velasco, "The Philippines."

Chapter 10

Conclusion

This study had two overarching objectives. The first was to determine how and why Indonesia succeeded in installing democracy after forty years of authoritarian and pseudodemocratic rule. In order to understand the impetus and extent of reform, I began historically, noting how the six elections conducted by Suharto's New Order regime were managed in ways that served regime purposes. But the controls were never complete nor the domination total. The elections acquired a degree of autonomy, exposing inconsistencies between official rhetoric and actual practice, raising questions about transparency and accountability, and representing as well as controlling and, to some extent, reflecting the underlying divisions in Indonesian society (see Chapter 2). Suharto was compelled to resign suddenly and unexpectedly on May 21, 1998, only two months after having been reelected for a seventh presidential term. The details of his fall and what actually brought it about at that particular point in time were outside the scope of this study and are discussed elsewhere.[1] My concern, rather, was with the success of democratic installation in the following seventeen months and attempts to consolidate electoral democracy during the Wahid administration.

That success depended heavily on the mode of transition, which began as a "pact" from above and evolved into "reform" involving election-validated representatives of the masses. This path during the transitional phase left its mark on the form and substance of the new democracy. Most of the incumbents remained in place, the policy processes involved intense bargaining and protracted negotiation, and the outcomes reflected compromise and half-hearted reform. Yet only small segments of society, some elements of the student movement on the left and New Order hardliners on the right, opposed the new rules and institutions inaugurated in January 1999.

Electoral reform, which begin in mid-1998 under interim President Habibie, spearheaded the transition to democracy. His replacement of about 20 percent of the legislators who were closest to Suharto greatly facilitated passage of reform legislation in late 1998 and early 1999, a factor that has been insufficiently appreciated in previous reporting and analysis, which typically views the legislative bodies as obstructionist "Suharto appointees." Chapter 3 highlighted the reformers' initial proposals and traced the policy debate and the compromises reached. These included continued adherence to the electoral principle of proportional representation, regulations biased in favor of political parties with broad geographical organization and support, and legislatures malapportioned in favor of the military and regions other than Java. Restrictions on the political rights of civil servants was the most intractable and difficult issue in the entire package of laws, and for good reason. It probably contributed more than any other single factor to the subsequent electoral defeat of the reigning Golkar party by the Indonesian Democratic Party of Struggle. It well illustrated a more general principle that a relatively small change in the design of an electoral system can have major consequences on who governs.

These policies were then juxtaposed with actual practices during the 1999 election and their effects on the election outcomes were weighed (see Chapters 4 and 5). As the election approached, for the first time in over three decades there was genuine uncertainty at all levels of society about political outcomes. Yet the campaign and election were surprisingly peaceful, in marked contrast to the previous one in 1997 and to the violence that punctuated the intervening period. Virtually all the opinion polls taken after the reforms were enacted in January 1999 indicated high levels of acceptance for the new rules and institutions of democratic representation. The election outcomes were also accorded a high level of legitimacy, at least until mid-2000, when the Wahid administration became embroiled in allegations of corruption and conflict with the House.

Despite some continuities with previous election administration, including a short and highly controlled campaign and the lack of prosecution of Election Law violators, the differences were more consequential. For example, executive authority over the election was vested largely in a more independent agency, the General Election Commission, which was widely credited with having presided over the freest and fairest election since 1955. However, flaws in its design, together with an underspecified and occasionally ambiguous corpus of laws governing the election, caused the commission to overreach its authority and made it vulnerable to immobilizing conflict, with both tending to undercut the legitimacy of the election. The citizenry was more involved in election administration than in any election during the New Order, reflecting a collective realization of the importance of this election for political reform and democratization in Indonesia. The requirement that a nominee for the legislature be scrutinized by a particular constituency instead of government security agencies, although unevenly implemented, resulted occasionally in the rejection of nominations.

The democratizing changes brought about by the electoral reform can be summarized under the following six headings:[2]

1. Entry and exit controls on the electoral arena. The government control over whether a party may contest an election, who may stand for election as the representative of a party, and who may serve as leader of a party has been substantially decreased. Evidence includes the shift from three to forty-eight election contestants (but likely to decrease in 2004), the relocation of power to dissolve parties from the executive to the judiciary, abolishment of discretionary screening (*litsus*) of candidates, and the cessation of "special operations" toward party leaders.

2. Public-sector support. Formal pressure on employees in the public sector to support Golkar has ended. Now, employees and military personnel are expected to maintain strict neutrality in the workplace and they must choose between continued employment or party membership.

3. Controls on party policy platforms. Parties have much greater leeway to organize around any ideals or principles and to advocate any policies of their choosing, provided they do not conflict with *Pancasila* (e.g., Marxism/Leninism) and do not threaten national unity. Several parties and party leaders banned during the New Order returned to the electoral arena.

4. Restrictions on organizational and campaign activities. Some of these continued for reasons of conflict management and maintenance of public order, but they were also applied to Golkar and its supporters, as authorities were under pressure to enforce the regulations equally (i.e., act neutrally).

5. Unequal resourcing and media access. Control of resources was still biased toward the former state party, Golkar. However, this problem was modified somewhat by the flow of resources to a major competitor of Golkar, PDI-P, and popular pressure on media executives to provide equal access.

6. Partisan electoral umpire. Election administration was moved out from under direct control of the executive branch. A new electoral commission was established as an independent statutory agency (*bebas dan*

mandiri). Originally composed of government and political party representatives (thus a semipartisan agency), it became an arena of partisan politics resulting in stalemate and paralysis part of the time. It was
reconstituted in 2000 on a nonpartisan basis. Regional election committees were dominated by party representatives. Election committees
at the critical village and polling-station levels were no longer under
the control of the government. The casting and counting of ballots was
monitored by hundreds of thousands of domestic and international poll
watchers, who used several parallel vote counts.

   In sum, the 1999 election was judged to have been "free and fair"
by international standards, a verdict powerfully supported by the
defeat of Golkar, which had swept the previous six elections by
margins of 3 or 4 to 1. This event and the peaceful succession of
legislative and executive power were critical events signaling that
Indonesia had evolved from a pseudodemocracy to an electoral democracy. Continuation of reform efforts after November 1999 both
led and reflected in amendments to the constitution can be viewed
as democratic consolidation; that is, as strengthening and deepening democracy while simultaneously removing vestiges of the previous regime.
   The second major objective of this study was to explain the direction of the vote (influences on voting choice) in 1999 and to search
for clues about underlying social change and continuity in the electorate. In this effort I also had the methodological objective of demonstrating the insights to be gained from statistical analyses of
quantitative election returns and data taken from periodic censuses,
which are publicly available at low cost.
   Intrigued by the popularity of the "broad continuity" thesis (i.e.,
the assumption that the 1999 election had more in common with
Indonesia's first election in 1955 than with any of the intervening
six elections conducted by the Suharto government), I generated
hypotheses about common ideological, social, and religious bases
of party support in the two elections. After overcoming certain logical and empirical obstacles, they were subsequently tested empirically by measuring association between areas of support for parties
in the two elections, largely confirming the thesis of broad continuity in election outcomes.
   This continuity had two dimensions, one being the continued reality of the basic cleavage in the electorate between areas supporting nationalist, religiously inclusive parties and areas supporting
Islamic parties. The other dimension was the reemergence of a division within the Islamic community between traditional and modernist orientations, with the modernists much more divided than in
1955. These findings support the inference that attempts by Suharto's

New Order government for over thirty years and across six elections to blunt or modify the electoral expression of divisions in the electorate based on religion, ethnicity or region, or economic interest (class) through fusion of parties, enforcement of a sole ideological basis (*Pancasila*) for every political organization, and attempts to build a predominate party system with Golkar and its platform of developmentalism in the lead largely failed. At the same time, it should be recognized that the divisions in the electorate as reflected in the pattern of voting in 1999 are not as deep or as pronounced as they were in 1955 (see Chapter 6).

The second approach to explaining the direction of the vote in 1999 involved building models of the underlying bases of voters' choices for the top five parties based on total votes. Using the powerful statistical technique of multiple regression analysis, the independent effects of a variety of social-based influences on voting choices for the five top parties were measured. Urbanization had a positive influence on votes for PDI-P and PAN, but a negative effect on support for PKB and PPP. The Islamicness of an area enhanced voting for Golkar but restrained voting for PDI-P. Ironically, no effect was found on the fortunes of the three largest Islamic parties unless the area was a previous source of PPP votes, in which case there was a tendency for fragmentation of the vote among the Islamic parties. In other words, the evidence of fragmentation of the Islamic vote in 1999 is stronger than the evidence that the new Islamic-based parties (PKB and PAN) made inroads into areas of previous Golkar strength. The three large parties that were most identified with Islam obtained about 30 percent of the vote combined. If we add the vote for minor Islamic parties, we can infer that the Islamic religion likely influenced the voting of approximately one-third of the electorate. If this estimate of one-third of the electorate is compared with the average vote for PPP during the six New Order elections (23 percent), we can conclude that Islamic, religious-based voting increased slightly in the 1999 election.

Illiteracy, which tends to be a function of rural poverty, had a negative impact on the number of effective parties (N-index) and on voting for three parties (PDI-P, PAN, and PPP). They were less successful than PKB in attracting voters in poorer rural areas. However, PDI-P had strong appeal in areas of higher (economic) inequality. Support for four of the five largest parties had a distinct regional dimension. PDI-P and PKB drew support disproportionately on Java and Bali, PAN on Sumatra, and Golkar in eastern Indonesia (everywhere else but Java–Bali and Sumatra) (see Chapter 7).

As far as is known, the only other empirical study of influences on voting choices in the 1999 election with which these findings can be compared is the one by Liddle and Mujani. Our studies are mutually reinforcing, in that both found voting choices were affected by religion and by ethnic (or regional) differences.[3] Our findings differ, however, with regard to class, party identification, and, possibly, the relative importance of social-based voting. They did not find a significant influence of class on voting choice and argue that class cleavage was not articulated by the large parties. But I found some influence of class on support for PDI-P and PKB. Second, they were unable to establish persuasively whether voters chose a party out of their preference for the party or rather for the party leader. In contrast, my (cross-election) analysis and finding of "inheritance" from particular parties in 1955 to particular parties in 1999 provides strong evidence that the causal arrow runs from party to leader and not vice versa.[4] Reinforcing evidence comes as well from the strength of "the party in the electorate" during New Order elections as noted in Chapter 2.

Finally, Liddle and Mujani argue that psychological attachment to national leaders is "by far the most important" of the seven influences on partisan choice that they studied. Lacking comparable psychological data collected from surveying individuals, I have no direct contrary evidence. However, if the coefficients of determination (R^2) are compared across all the regression models, they range from .35 to .80, with an average of .57. This means that (on average) a quite respectable 57 percent of the variation among districts is explained by the contextual and social-based variables in my models. The variance left unexplained by the models, the residual, represents the outside limit that can be attributed to individual (psychological) calculus, the unique characteristics of particular areas, and measurement error. In other words, this study has shown that social- and contextual-based influences on voting choice in the 1999 election were at least as important as individual and psychological ones.

What is the relation between explaining the influences on voting choices (second major question) and the successful installation of democracy (first major question)? Understanding the determinants of partisan choice is fundamental to understanding the national political process and to designing institutions that will sustain and help consolidate Indonesian's young democracy. For example, the continued importance of social-based voting, as demonstrated in Chapters 6 and 7, helps explain the relative stability of party identification, as compared with the Philippines and Thailand (see Chapter 9), and caution against any wholesale switch to majoritarian electoral institutions (see Chapter 8).

At the turn of the century three countries in Southeast Asia were undergoing democratization: Indonesia, the Philippines, and Thailand. This overall commonality creates interest in comparing their experiences with electoral reform as a means of better understanding the choices in design of electoral institutions and the likely effects on the consolidation of democracy. Choices involve trade-offs between competing values. The Philippines and Thailand emphasize efficiency and governability, whereas Indonesia has given preference to representativeness. Indonesia's electoral system values party coherence over voter choice, which gets priority in the other two countries.

Both the Philippines and Thailand have attempted to moderate the strong majoritarian tendencies of their electoral systems by electing 20 percent of the members in the lower chamber through the party-list system (proportional representation). An implication for Indonesia is that a similarly mixed electoral system, setting aside a portion of seats to be filled using the district-plurality system, would likely be a more successful way of introducing more direct accountability between representatives and voters than either its current "PR-plus" system or switching to a district-plurality system in the election of all seats. Some Indonesian reformers have advocated majoritarian institutions as a check on fragmented, multiparty systems and on the practice of money politics. But the experiences of the other two countries suggest that these maladies may be more vulnerable to other antidotes, such as thresholds and law enforcement (i.e., raising the costs of election fraud) (see Chapter 9).

The heightened social conflict and political instability that marked the twenty-one months of the Wahid administration raise the question of whether Indonesia is in the throes of a protracted political transition, a long labor with a high risk of stillborn birth. Or, alternatively, do they reflect a second struggle to consolidate and deepen democracy while simultaneously identifying and removing the nondemocratic elements from the previous regime, an unruly toddler forging identity amidst the pressures of socialization? The argument for a protracted transition would appear to rest heavily on a particular definition of "pact," the characteristics of which seem to be too small or missing in the Indonesian experience.[5] However, if "pact" is defined as inclusive of all significantly threatening interests, as often consisting of a series of agreements that are interlocking and dependent on each other, and, although inclusionary, as simultaneously aimed at restricting the scope of contestation, representation, and policy agenda in order to reassure traditional elites that their vital interests will be respected, it becomes plausible to argue that a pact was achieved, beginning with the agreement that brought about the resignation of Suharto and continuing in the compromises forged on procedural issues (i.e., about the rules of the game) under Habibie's watch.[6] The pact was honored, by and large, in the implementation of the 1999 election. The seating of new, mostly elected legislative bodies and the swearing in of the Wahid administration demarcated the successful installation of electoral democracy.

What appears to have happened since then illustrates well the fundamental paradox identified by scholars who study democratic transitions and consolidations comparatively. The modes of transition that enhance the initial survivability of democracy by limiting unpredictability preclude democratic self-transformation of the economy and policy later on. For example, we have earlier noted that, relative to the Philippines and Thailand, the Indonesian electoral system tends to maximize the value of representativeness (e.g., proportional representation), which was reflected in twenty-one parties obtaining seats in the House with none holding a majority, making compromise and coalition-building essential. In addition, there was broad agreement among the political elite, both hardliners (supporters of Suharto's New Order) and reformers (opponents), that executive power had become excessive and arbitrary and needed to be reigned in. As a result, both the 1998 and 1999 Assemblies amended the constitution in ways that empowered the legislature and the judiciary while weakening the executive branch. In other words, the parliamentary characteristics in what is formally a presidential structure of national government were strengthened. The combined effect of all these factors has been "divided government, temporal inflexibility, a less inclusive executive, greater executive instability, and less democracy."[7] In short, the modes that facilitated democratic transition and installation became obstacles to consolidation, at least until a major overhaul of the constitution was effected (Third and Fourth Amendments).

Another example is the election commission. The experiences with election fraud and manipulation during the New Order made the need for transparent and neutral election administration critical to a successful transition. To win support from most factions of the political elite and build legitimacy for the new institution, the initial design for the commission reflected high valuation on accommodation and compromise (e.g., all parties were represented, decision making by consensus [until it broke down], and ambiguous lines of authority). Unanticipatedly, too many parties emerged and qualified for representation on the commission, and tiny parties that failed in the polls attempted to gain seats, nonetheless, by blackmail. The integrity and legitimacy of the election was threatened and it became clear that institutional redesign was required prior to the next election. If history and the initial pact among the political elite required a multiparty commission in the transition phase, the new commission established in early 2001 reflected a realization and agreement by the elite that a very different type of institution was needed for the next consolidation phase. Hence, the new appointees to the commission are nonpartisan, independent professionals who have publicly eschewed an expansive interpretation of their responsibilities.

In the latter part of the 1990s a debate broke out among some comparativists about the role of elections in new democracies.[8] In an article titled "The Rise of Illiberal Democracy," Fareed Zakaria argued that advanced democracies have erred in their approach to countries in transition which has "overemphasized multiparty elections and neglected the basic tenets of liberal governance."[9] Other "antielectoralists" asserted that the holding of elections was itself the facade that impedes the building of genuine democracy.

On the other side of the debate were those who contended that "the emergence of electoral democracies has been the best indicator of subsequent progress in the areas of civil liberties and human rights."[10] The Indonesian experience lends support to the "electoralist" camp. After the demise of Suharto's thirty-two-year rule, Indonesians found themselves with weak government, fragmented opposition, and a divided military. The 1999 transitional election in Indonesia was not an artificial experiment in social–political engineering. On the contrary, it was "demand driven," and viewed by the vast majority of Indonesians as an important part of the solution to their internal problems. Their commitment to the electoral process and the political changes set in motion by that election will likely sustain their struggle for democracy for the foreseeable future.

NOTES

1. Geoff Forrester and R. J. May, eds., *The Fall of Soeharto* (Singapore: Select Books, 1999); Donald K. Emmerson, "Exit and Aftermath: The Crisis of 1997–98," in *Indonesia beyond Suharto*, ed. Donald K. Emmerson (Armonk, N.Y.: M. E. Sharpe, 1999); R. William Liddle, "Indonesia's Democratic Opening," *Government and Opposition* 34, 1 (1999): 94–116.

2. This analytical framework is borrowed from Andrew MacIntyre, "Indonesia," in *Democracy, Governance, and Economic Performance*, ed. Ian Marsh (Tokyo: United Nations University Press, 1999), 261–286.

3. See R. William Liddle and Saiful Mujani, "The Triumph of Leadership: Explaining the 1999 Indonesian Vote," 2000, Appendix B. This conclusion is based on a coefficient of .559 for Santri in their Religious Voting Model and a coefficient of .686 for Javanese in their Ethnic Voting Model. Although they utilize logistic regression in each model, the dependent variables differ, making it impossible to assess whether religion or ethnicity is the stronger influence. They claim that region or ethnicity is stronger, but the empirical basis appears tenuously based on the difference between r = .22 and r = .31 in bivariate analysis.

4. Unfortunately, Liddle and Mujani, "The Triumph of Leadership," dropped party identification from their multivariate analysis "because party preference and voting are difficult to disentangle analytically since voters choose party rather than candidate."

5. Michael Malley, "Beyond Democratic Elections: Indonesia Embarks on a Protracted Transition," *Democratization* 7, 3 (2000): 153–180. For Malley, pacts are possible when two factors are present: (1) the political opportunity to negotiate a pact and (2) a consensus about fundamental aspects of the existing and ideal political systems. While the political opportunity has been present in Indonesia, consensus has not. Hence, "Under these conditions, pacts are likely to be limited, at best, and regime change is likely to be accomplished only by prolonged and repeated struggles to reform specific institutions" (p. 155).

6. Terry Lynn Karl, "Dilemmas of Democratization in Latin America," *Comparative Politics* 23, 1 (1990): 11–12.

7. Blair A. King, "The Retention of a Paper Constitution and the Prospects for Democratic Consolidation in Indonesia," paper presented at the Conference on Consolidating Indonesian Democracy, Ohio State University, Columbus, May 2001.

8. The debate is described and joined in Elizabeth Spiro Clark, "Why Elections Matter," *Washington Quarterly* 23, 3 (2000): 27–40.

9. Fareed Zakaria, "The Rise of Illiberal Democracy," *Foreign Affairs* 76, 6 (1997): 22–43.

10. Adrian Karatnycky, "The Decline of Illiberal Democracy," *Journal of Democracy* 10, 1 (1999): 112–125.

Bibliography

BOOKS AND ARTICLES

Alfian. *Hasil Pemilihan Umum 1955.* Jakarta: LEKNAS, 1971.

Alfian, and Nazaruddin, S., eds. *Masa Depan Kehidupan Politik Indonesia.* Jakarta: Rajawali, 1988.

Aloysius Arena Ariwibowo, Andi Jauhari, Budi Setiawanto, Hermanus Prihatna, Rudy Moechtar, Sapto Heru Purnomojoyo, and Sri Muryono. *Pemilu 1997.* Jakarta: PT. Panakencana, 1997.

Ariwibowo, Ariel Heryanto, Arief Budiman, Ifdhal Kasim, Mohammad Zaidun, and Riswanda Imawan. *Mendemokratiskan Pemilu.* Jakarta: Lembaga Studi dan Advokasi Masyarakat (ELSAM), 1996.

Blackburn, Susan, ed. *Pemilu: The 1999 Indonesian Election.* Clayton, Australia: Monash University, Monash Asian Institute, 1999.

Bourchier, David, and Legge, John, eds. *Democracy in Indonesia, 1950s and 1990s.* Clayton, Australia: Monash University, Centre of Southeast Asian Studies, 1994.

Bowornwathana, Bidhya. "Thailand in 1999." *Asian Survey* 40, 1 (2000): 87–97.

BPHPR. "White Book on the 1992 General Election in Indonesia." Cornell University publication no. 23, Cornell Modern Indonesia Project, Ithaca, N.Y., 1994.

Budiman, Arief, ed. *State and Civil Society in Indonesia.* Clayton, Australia: Monash University, 1990.

Clark, Elizabeth Spiro. "Why Elections Matter." *Washington Quarterly* 23, 3 (2000): 27–40.

Cohen, Frank S., "Proportional versus Majoritarian Ethnic Conflict Management in Democracies." *Comparative Political Studies* 30, 5 (1997): 607–630.

Collier, David, and Levitsky, Steven. "Democracy with Adjectives." *World Politics* 49 (1997): 430–451.

Dahl, Robert A. *Polyarchy: Participation and Opposition.* New Haven: Yale University Press, 1971.

Department of Information, Republic of Indonesia. *Indonesia 1990: An Official Handbook.* Jakarta: Department of Information, 1990.

Diamond, Larry. *Developing Democracy.* Baltimore: Johns Hopkins University Press, 1999.

Diamond, Larry, Linz, Juan J., and Lipset, Seymour Martin, eds. *Politics in Developing Countries: Comparing Experiences with Democracy.* Boulder, Colo.: Lynne Rienner, 1995.

Eklof, Stefan. "The 1997 General Election in Indonesia." *Asian Survey* 37, 12 (1997): 1181–1196.

Emmerson, Donald K., ed. *Indonesia beyond Suharto.* Armonk, N.Y.: M. E. Sharpe, 1999.

Feith, Herbert. *The Indonesian Elections of 1955.* Ithaca, N.Y.: Cornell Modern Indonesia Project, 1957.

———. *The Decline of Constitutional Democracy.* Ithaca, N.Y.: Cornell University Press, 1962.

Forrester, Geoff, and May, R. J., eds. *The Fall of Soeharto.* Singapore: Select Books, 1999.

Gaffar, Afan. *Javanese Voters.* Yogyakarta: Gadjah Mada University Press, 1992.

Handelman, Howard, and Tessler, Mark, eds. *Democracy and Its Limits.* South Bend, Ind.: Notre Dame University Press, 1999.

Haris, Syamsuddin, Sanit, Arbi, AS Hikam, Muhammad, Salamm, Alfitra, and Cahyono, Heru. *Pemilian Umum di Indonesia.* Jakarta: LIPI, 1997.

Harris, Peter, and Reilly, Ben, eds. *Democracy and Deep-Rooted Conflict: Options for Negotiators.* Stockholm: IDEA, 1998.

Hefner, Robert W. "Islamizing Java? Religion and Politics in Rural East Java." *Journal of Asian Studies* 45, 3 (1987): 533–554.

Hein, Gordon R. "Indonesia in 1982: Electoral Victory and Economic Adjustment for the New Order." *Asian Survey* 23, 2 (1983): 178–190.

Hernandez, Carolina G. "The Philippines in 1995: The Growth amid Challenges." *Asian Survey* 36, 2 (1996): 142–151.

Hill, Hal. *The Indonesian Economy since 1966.* Rev. ed. Cambridge: Cambridge University Press, 2000.

Hsien, John Fuh-sheng, and Newman, David, eds. *How Asia Votes.* New York: Seven Bridges Press, 2001.

Irwan, Alexander, and Edriana. *Pemilu: Pelanggaran Asas LUBER.* Jakarta: Pustaka Sinar Harapan, 1995.

Karatnycky, Adrian. "The Decline of Illiberal Democracy." *Journal of Democracy* 10, 1 (1999): 112–125.

Karl, Terry Lynn. "Dilemmas of Democratization in Latin America." *Comparative Politics* 23, 1 (1990): 1–21.

Kasuya, Yuko. "Presidential Connection: Parties and Party Systems in the Philippines." Paper presented at the meeting of the Association of Asian Studies, Chicago, March 2001.

King, Blair A. "The 1992 General Election and Indonesia's Political Landscape." *Contemporary Southeast Asia* 14, 2 (1992): 154–173.

————. "The Retention of a Paper Constitution and the Prospects for Democratic Consolidation in Indonesia." Paper presented at the Conference on Consolidating Indonesian Democracy, Ohio State University, Columbus, May 2001.

Komisi Pemilihan Umum (KPU). *Buku Evaluasi Pelanggaran dan Kecurangan Pemilihan Umum Tahun 1999.* Jakarta: KPU, 2000.

Komite Independen Pemantauan Pemilu (KIPP). *Laporan Hasil Pemantauan Pemilu 1997.* Jakarta: KIPP, 1997.

————. *Kekerasan Politik Dalam Pemilu 1999.* Jakarta: KIPP, 2000.

————. *Menata Reformasi Paska Pemilu 1999.* Jakarta: KIPP, 2000.

Laakso, Marku, and Taagepera, Rein. "Effective Number of Parties: A Measure with Application to West Europe." *Comparative Political Studies* 12 (1979): 3–27.

LeDuc, Lawrence, Niemi, Richard G., and Norris, Pippa, eds. *Comparing Democracies.* Thousand Oaks, Calif.: Sage, 1996.

Lee, Oey Hong, ed. *Indonesia after the 1971 Elections.* London: Oxford University Press, 1974.

Lewis-Beck, Michael S. *Series: Quantitative Applications in the Social Sciences.* No. 22. Beverly Hills, Calif.: Sage, 1980.

Liddle, R. William. "Evolution from Above: National Development and Local Leadership." *Journal of Asian Studies* 32 (1973): 287–309.

————. "The 1977 Indonesian Election and New Order Legitimacy." In *Southeast Asian Affairs.* Singapore: Institute for Southeast Asian Studies, 1978.

————. "Indonesia in 1987: The New Order at the Height of Its Power." *Asian Survey* 28, 2 (1988): 180–191.

————. "Indonesia's Democratic Opening." *Government and Opposition* 34, 1 (1999): 94–116.

————. "Indonesia in 1999: Democracy Restored." *Asian Survey* 40, 1 (2000): 32–42.

————. "Indonesia in 2000." *Asian Survey* 41, 1 (2001): 208–220.

Liddle, R. William, and Mujani, Saiful. "The Triumph of Leadership: Explaining the 1999 Indonesian Vote." 2000.

Lipset, Seymour Martin, ed. *The Encyclopedia of Democracy.* Washington, D.C.: Congressional Quarterly Press, 1995.

Lipset, Seymour Martin, and Rokkan, Stein, eds. *Party System and Voter Alignments.* New York: Free Press, 1967.

MacIntyre, Andrew. "Indonesia in 1992: Coming to Terms with the Outside World." *Asian Survey* 33, 2 (1993): 204–210.

Mallarangeng, Andi Alfian. "Contextual Analysis on Indonesians' Electoral Behavior." Ph.D. diss., Northern Illinois University, 1997.

Malley, Michael. "Beyond Democratic Elections: Indonesia Embarks on a Protracted Transition." *Democratization* 7, 3 (2000): 153–180.

Manning, Chris, and Van Dierman, Peter, eds. *Indonesia in Transition.* Singapore: Institute of Southeast Asian Studies, 2000.

Marsh, Ian, Blondel, Jean, and Inoguchi, Takashi, eds. *Democracy, Governance, and Economic Performance.* Tokyo: United Nations University Press, 1999.

Montinola, Gabriella R. "The Philippines in 1998: Opportunity amid Crisis." *Asian Survey* 39, 1 (1999): 64–71.

National Democratic Institute for International Affairs (NDIIA). "The 1999 Presidential Election, MPR General Session and Post-Election Developments in Indonesia." November 28, 1999.

———. "Indonesia's Bumpy Road to Constitutional Reform: The 2000 MPR Annual Session." September 19, 2000.

National Democratic Institute for International Affairs and the Carter Center. "Post-Election Developments in Indonesia: The Formation of the DPR and the MPR." August 26, 1999.

Nelson, Michael H. "Thailand." manuscript. n.d.

Nishihara, Masashi. *Golkar and the Indonesian Elections of 1971.* Ithaca, N.Y.: Cornell University, Modern Indonesian Project Monograph Series, 1972.

O'Donnell, Guillermo, Schmitter, Philippe, and Whitehead, Laurence, eds. *Transition from Authoritarian Rule: Comparative Perspectives.* Baltimore: Johns Hopkins University Press, 1986.

O'Donnell, Guillermo, and Schmitter, Philippe. *Transitions from Authoritarian Rule: Tentative Conclusions about Uncertain Democracies.* Baltimore: Johns Hopkins University Press, 1986.

Panitia Pengawas Pemilihan Umum Tahun. *Pengawasan Pemilihan Umum 1999.* Jakarta: Panwas Pusat, 1999.

Punyaratabandhu, Suchitra. "Thailand in 1997: Financial Crisis and Constitutional Reform." *Asian Survey* 38, 2 (1998): 161–167.

Rae, Douglas W. *The Political Consequences of Electoral Law.* New Haven: Yale University Press, 1967.

Rawski, Fredrick. "Draft Report on Panwaslu." Unpublished manuscript, July 23, 1999.

Reynolds, Andrew, ed. *Electoral Systems and Democratization in Southern Africa.* Oxford: Oxford University Press, 1999.

———. *The Architecture of Democracy.* Oxford: Oxford University Press, 2001.

Schedler, Andreas, Diamond, Larry, and Plattner, Marc F., eds. *The Self-Restraining State.* Boulder, Colo.: Lynne Rienner, 1999.

Schiller, Jim. "The 1997 Indonesian Elections: 'Festival of Democracy' or Costly 'Fiction'?" Occasional paper no. 22, Centre for Asian-Pacific Initiatives, University of Victoria, Canada, 1999.

Schmitter, Philippe C., "Recent Developments in the Academic Study of Democratization." Paper presented at the Inauguration and Colloquium of the Habibie Center, Jakarta, May 1999.

Schwarz, Adam, and Paris, Jonathan, eds. *The Politics of Post-Suharto Indonesia.* New York: Council on Foreign Relations, 1999.

Singh, Bilveer. *Habibie and the Democratisation of Indonesia.* Singapore: Crescent Design Associates, 2000.

Snyder, Jack. *From Voting to Violence.* New York: W. W. Norton, 2000.

Sonata, Thamrin, ed. *UU Politik Buah Reformasi Setengah Hati.* Jakarta: Yayasan Pariba, 1999.

Surbakti, Ramlan, "Pemilihan Pada Pemilu 1992: Antara Kendala dan Peluang." Paper delivered at the Seminar Nasional IX Asosiasi Ilmu Politik Indonesia, Surabaya, August 6–8, 1992.

Suryadinata, Leo. *Political Parties and the 1982 General Election in Indonesia.* Singapore: Institute of Southeast Asian Studies, 1982.

———. *Elections and Politics in Indonesia.* Singapore: Institute of Southeast Asian Studies, 2001.

Taagepera, Rein, and Shugart, Matthew Soberg. *Seats and Votes: The Effects and Determinants of Electoral Systems.* New Haven: Yale University Press, 1989.

Taylor, R. H. "Delusion and Necessity: Elections and Politics in Southeast Asia." *Items* (Social Science Research Council) 48, 4 (1994): 85.

———. *The Politics of Elections in Southeast Asia.* New York: Woodrow Wilson Center Press, 1996.

United States–Indonesia Society. "Parliamentary Election in Indonesia." Workshop Proceedings, Washington, D.C., June 22, 1999.

Utrecht, Ernst. "The Military and the 1977 Election." Occasional paper no. 3, James Cook University, Queensland, 1980.

Wagner, Steven. "Preliminary Summary of Public Opinion Preceding the Parliamentary Election in Indonesia—1999." (Processed for International Foundation for Election System, n.d.)

———. "Survey of the Indonesian Electorate Following the June 1999 Elections." (Processed for IFES, n.d.)

Ward, Ken. *The 1971 Election in Indonesia: An East Java Case Study.* Cheltenham: Monash University Papers on Southeast Asia, 1974.

Zakaria, Fareed. "The Rise of Illiberal Democracy." *Foreign Affairs* 76, 6 (1997): 22–43.

NEWSPAPERS, MAGAZINES, AND INTERNET

Far Eastern Economic Review

Forum Keadilan

Jakarta Post

Kompas

Kompas On-Line

Media Indonesia

New York Times

Republika

Suara Pembaruan

Tempo

The Straits Times

Index

Indonesian National Party (Partai
Nasional Indonesia, PNI), 34,
124–134, 161
Industrialization, 40
Inequality, 144, 161
International Foundation for Elec-
tion Systems, 102 nn.10, 11, 27
Islamicness, 40, 146, 160

Java and Javanese, 40, 131–133
Judiciary, 84–85, 89, 108

Karatnycky, Adrian, 229
Karl, Terry, 6–7, 9–11
King, Blair, 36, 228
King, Dan, 219 n.56
Korupsi, kolusi, nepotisme (KKN),
48

Laws and statutes, 19, 23, 66–69,
189 n.37
LeDuc, Lawrence, 7
Leekpai, Chuan, 202
Liddle, R. William, 5, 8, 162–163,
225–226
Lijphart, Arend, 7
Lipset, Seymour Martin, 8

MacIntyre, Andrew, 223
Majid, Nurcholish, 83
Makassarese, 149
Mallarengang, Andi Alfian, 33, 39–
40, 45 n.66, 69, 174
Malley, Michael, 227
Masyumi (Majelis Syuro Muslimin
Indonesia, Consultative Assem-
bly of Indonesian Muslims), 34,
125–134, 161
Methodology, 9, 17, 128–129, 135–
138, 142–146, 163–165
Miftach, Agus, 172–175
Military (ABRI): Dual function
doctrine, 59; representation in
legis-latures, 56–60, 72 n.26, 102
n.7
Money politics, 52, 102 n.11
Montinola, Gabriella, 209, 217 n.10

Moon and Star Party (Partai
Bintang Bulan, PBB), 125–127
Mujani, Saiful, 162–163, 225–226
Multipartyism, 30, 51, 82–83, 107,
168–171

Nasution, Adnan Buyung, 86
National Awakening Party (Partai
Kebangkitan Bangsa, PKB), 125–
134, 139 n.10, 154–156, 158–163
National Democratic Institute for
International Affairs (NDIIA), 71
n.19, 189 n.35
National Mandate Party (Partai
Amanat Nasional, PAN), 125–
134, 158–162
National Unity Cabinet, 82
Nelson, Michael, 201
NU or Nahdlatul Ulama (Awakening of Islamic Teachers' Party),
34–35, 125, 161
New Order (Suharto regime): electoral system of, 17–41, 42 n.12;
floating mass doctrine, 70 n.13;
patterns and trends, 24–27, 38–
40; simplification of political
life, 35; special investigation of
candidates (*litsus*), 26

Pancasila ideology, 2, 25, 36, 42
n.20, 51
PAN Party. *See* National Mandate
Party
Pastor, Robert, 179, 186 n.1, 187 n.2
PBB Party. *See* Moon and Star Party
PDI Party. *See* Indonesian Democ-
racy Party
PDI-P Party. *See* Indonesian
Democracy Party of Struggle
People's Consultative Assembly
(Majelis Perwakilan Rakyat,
MPR), 49–50, 55–58 179–182
Philippines: constitutional change,
195; democratic transition, 191–
194; election administration, 211;
election success, reasons for,
200; electoral system, 204–210;

ABOUT THE AUTHOR

Dwight Y. King is Professor of Political Science and Associate, Center for Southeast Asian Studies, Northern Illinois University, DeKalb. He is the author of *Interest Groups and Political Linkage in Indonesia, 1800–1965*.